"Nolo's home page is worth bookmarking."
—WALL STREET JOURNAL

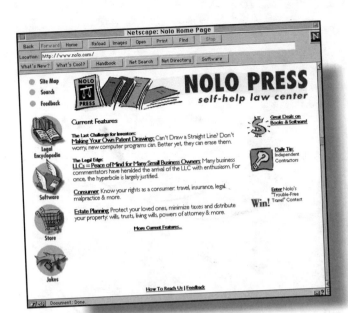

LEGAL INFORMATION ONLINE
www.nolo.com

24 HOURS A DAY

AT THE NOLO PRESS SELF-HELP LAW CENTER ON THE WEB, YOU'LL FIND:

- Nolo's comprehensive **Legal Encyclopedia**, with links to other online resources
- **Downloadable demos** of Nolo software and sample chapters of many Nolo books
- An **online law store** with a secure online ordering system
- Our ever-popular **lawyer jokes**
- **Discounts** and other good deals, our hilarious SHARK TALK game

THE NOLO NEWS

Stay on top of important legal changes with Nolo's quarterly magazine, *The Nolo News*. Start your free one-year subscription by filling out and mailing the response card in the back of this book. With each issue, you'll get legal news about topics that affect you every day, reviews of legal books by other publishers, the latest Nolo catalog, scintillating advice from Auntie Nolo and a fresh batch of our famous lawyer jokes.

First Edition

DO YOUR OWN DIVORCE IN OREGON

By Robin Smith

YOUR RESPONSIBILITY WHEN USING A SELF-HELP LAW BOOK

We've done our best to give you useful and accurate information in this book. But laws and procedures change frequently and are subject to differing interpretations. If you want legal advice backed by a guarantee, see a lawyer. If you use this book, it's your responsibility to make sure that the facts and general advice contained in it are applicable to your situation.

KEEPING UP TO DATE

To keep its books up to date, Nolo Press issues new printings and new editions periodically. New printings reflect minor legal changes and technical corrections. New editions contain major legal changes, major text additions or major reorganizations. To find out if a later printing or edition of any Nolo book is available, call Nolo Press at 510-549-1976 or check the catalog in the *Nolo News,* our quarterly newspaper.

To stay current, follow the "Update" service in the *Nolo News.* You can get a free one-year subscription by sending us the registration card in the back of the book. In another effort to help you use Nolo's latest materials, we offer a 25% discount off the purchase of the new edition of your Nolo book when you turn in the cover of an earlier edition. (See the "Recycle Offer" in the back of the book.)

This book was last revised in: August 1997.

1ST EDITION	August 1997
EDITOR	PERI H. PAKROO
BOOK DESIGN	JACKIE MANCUSO
	SUSAN PUTNEY
COVER DESIGN	TONI IHARA
PRODUCTION	SUSAN PUTNEY
ILLUSTRATION	MARI STEIN
INDEX	SAYRE VAN YOUNG
PROOFREADER	BOB WELLS
PRINTING	VERSA PRESS, INC.

Smith, Robin, 1958–
    Do your own divorce in Oregon / by Robin Smith. -- 1st ed.
        p. cm.
    Includes index.
    ISBN 0-87337-382-0
       1. Divorce--Law and legislation--Oregon—Popular works.
    I. Title
    KF02500.Z9S63 1997
    346.79501'66--dc21   97-14097
                                                                         CIP

ALL RIGHTS RESERVED. Printed in the U.S.A.

Copyright © 1997 by Robin Smith

No part of this publication may be reproduced, stored in a retrieval system, or transmitted in any form or by any means, electronic, mechanical, photocopying, recording or otherwise without the prior written permission of the publisher and the author. Reproduction prohibitions do not apply to the forms contained in this product when reproduced for personal use.

For information on bulk purchases or corporate premium sales, please contact the Special Sales department.
For academic sales or textbook adoptions, ask for Academic Sales. 800-955-4775, Nolo Press, Inc., 950 Parker Street, Berkeley, CA 94710.

ACKNOWLEDGMENTS

Jake Warner and Steve Elias for giving me the opportunity to write this book, for their insight, enthusiasm and good humor.

Peri Pakroo for jumping in midstream and leading the project to completion.

Mark Garretson, "Mr. Comma Man" for his love and support.

My kids for letting mommy have some time to work on the book.

Ingrid Slezak for information on the Family Law Task Force.

The Oregon Mediation Association and Gloria Bryen for information on mediation from a professional mediator's point of view.

Attorney and friend Stuart (Stu) Sugarman for bouncing ideas off as we pedal along.

David and Marta Dahlen for their ongoing commitment to the self-help law movement and to me.

Mike Kennedy at Rush Process Service for an insider's point of view on service.

"Never doubt that a small group of thoughtful,
committed citizens can change the world;
it is the only thing that ever has."
—Margaret Mead

ICONS USED IN THIS BOOK

Throughout the book, these icons alert you to certain information.

Fast Track

We use this icon to let you know when you can skip information that may not be relevant to your situation.

Warning

This icon alerts you to potential problems.

Recommended Reading

When you see this icon, a list of additional resources that can assist you follows.

Cross-Reference

This icon refers you to a further discussion of the topic elsewhere in this book.

See an Expert

Lets you know when you need the advice of an attorney or other expert. ■

Contents

1 You Can Do Your Own Divorce

A. Most Divorces Do Not Need an Attorney 1/2

B. Even Bitter Fights Can Be Resolved 1/2

C. Getting Help Doesn't Always Mean Hiring an Attorney 1/2

2 Should You Use This Book?

A. Your Divorce Must Be Uncontested 2/2

B. When to Get Additional Help 2/3

C. Other Books 2/3

D. Chart: Should I Use This Book? 2/4

3 An Overview of an Uncontested Divorce

A. Co-Petitioner Divorces 3/2

B. Petitioner/Respondent Divorces 3/3

4 Commonly Asked Questions and Answers

A. Can I file in Oregon? 4/3

B. Can I still get a divorce if my spouse does not live in Oregon? 4/3

C. Where do I file? 4/3

D. How long does a divorce take? 4/4

E. What are the filing fees for a divorce? 4/4

F. What if I cannot afford the filing fee? 4/4

G. What are the issues my spouse and I will need to agree on to obtain an uncontested divorce? 4/4

H. My spouse and I don't agree on some important issues. Does that mean we'll need attorneys? 4/5

I. What should I do if my spouse contests (files a response with the court) the divorce? 4/5

J. If my spouse and I reach an agreement after the divorce has already become contested, how do we make the divorce uncontested again? 4/6

K. To get a divorce do I have to prove that my spouse did something wrong, like cheating on me? 4/6

L. Will there be a court hearing? 4/6

M. Can I get temporary custody or child support while the divorce is pending? 4/6

N. What is alimony or spousal support and when is it awarded? 4/7

O. What if I want to move after I file the divorce but before it's final? 4/7

P. What if I decide I don't really want to go through with the divorce after I've already filed the petition? 4/7

Q. What's the difference between an annulment and a divorce? 4/8

R. What's the difference between a legal separation and a divorce? 4/8

S. What happens to retirement funds in a divorce? 4/8

T. What happens to a family business in a divorce? 4/9

U. Can I change my name? 4/9

5 Important Things to Do Immediately

A. Close All Joint Accounts 5/2

B. Obtain Restraining Orders If Necessary 5/3

C. Obtain Temporary Orders If Necessary 5/3

6 Understanding Mediation

A. You Can Mediate Even If You've Already Hired a Lawyer 6/2

B. You Can't "Lose" in Mediation 6/2

C. Who Are Divorce Mediators? 6/2

D. The Difference Between Private Mediation and Court-Ordered Mediation 6/3

E. The Difference Between Mediators and Mediation Services 6/3
F. How to Find a Mediator or Mediation Service 6/4
G. How Mediation Works—An Example 6/5
H. Translating the Mediation Results Into Court Papers 6/7

7 Property and Debt Division

A. Determining Which Property Is Marital Property 7/2
B. Dividing Marital Property 7/4
C. Dividing Debts of the Marriage 7/7

8 Child Custody and Visitation

A. Do Your Best to Reach Agreement 8/2
B. Identifying Marital Children 8/4
C. Making Custody and Visitation Arrangements 8/5
D. Putting Your Agreement in Writing 8/8

9 Child Support—What It Is, How It's Computed

A. Requesting Child Support 9/2
B. Determining Who Will Pay Child Support 9/2
C. Deviating From the Statutory Guidelines 9/3
D. Expenses Included in Child Support Calculations 9/3
E. Encountering Problems With Child Support Arrangements 9/4
F. Before You Fill Out the Child Support Worksheets 9/6
G. Instructions for Completing the Child Support Worksheets 9/7

10 The Forms

    A. Which Forms to Use 10/2
    B. Tips for Filling In the Forms 10/4
    C. Signing and Notarizing the Forms 10/5

11 Filling Out Co-Petitioner Forms

    A. Form-by-Form Instructions 11/2
    B. After You've Completed the Forms 11/15

12 Filling Out Petitioner/Respondent Forms

    A. Form-by-Form Instructions 12/2
    B. After You've Completed the Forms 12/17

13 Filing the Forms

    A. Filing Instructions for Co-Petitioners 13/2
    B. Filing Instructions for Solo Petitioners 13/5
    C. Deadlines 13/12
    D. Dealing With Problems With Your Papers 13/13
    E. Documents Issued by the Court 13/13
    F. Filing Fees by County 13/14

14 After the Divorce

A. Like Divorces, Modifications Can Be Contested or Uncontested 14/2
B. Arrangements That Commonly Need Modification 14/2

15 Beyond the Book: Attorneys, Independent Paralegals and Books

A. Attorneys 15/2
B. Independent Paralegals 15/4
C. Books 15/4
D. Legal Research 15/6

Glossary of Legal Terms

Appendix A—Co-Petitioner Forms

Appendix B—Petitioner/Respondent Forms

Appendix C—Child Support

Appendix D—Miscellaneous Forms

You Can Do Your Own Divorce

A. Most Divorces Do Not Need an Attorney 1/2
B. Even Bitter Fights Can Be Resolved 1/2
C. Getting Help Doesn't Always Mean Hiring an Attorney 1/2

You're probably thinking, "I'm not Perry Mason, so how can I do my own divorce?" Simple. Unless you and your spouse need the judge to decide an issue for you—child custody, for instance, or who gets what property items—your divorce will be a straightforward process involving nothing more than the filing of specific documents in a specific order. This book walks you through that process and provides all the forms needed. There is no need for a court appearance.

A. Most Divorces Do Not Need an Attorney

In the past, divorcing couples hired lawyers and whichever side's lawyer could beat up the other side's lawyer won. As times have changed, so have divorces. Standard forms, plain English and economic necessity have all contributed to a broadening of the choices available for couples who want to do their own divorces.

It may boost your confidence to know that approximately 70% of all Oregon divorces are handled without an attorney. Could that many Oregonians be wrong?

B. Even Bitter Fights Can Be Resolved

Still, you may be thinking that you and your spouse can't even agree on the time of day, let alone the often thorny issues that arise in a divorce. You may also feel too emotionally overwrought to consider handling your own divorce case. These are real concerns faced by many divorcing couples. Fortunately there are ways to deal with these concerns that don't require a courtroom. More and more people who want to keep their children out of the crossfire of an ugly custody battle—and to prevent their life savings from ending up in their lawyers' pockets—are taking control of their own legal situations, hammering out agreements on the crucial issues facing them and finalizing their own divorce paperwork without any costly legal battles. This book shows you how you can do it, too.

Don't put yourself at risk. If your best judgment tells you that you or your children risk physical harm from your spouse, you should consider asking the court for protection. We explain how to do this in Chapter 5, Section B.

C. Getting Help Doesn't Always Mean Hiring an Attorney

When we talk about doing your own divorce, it doesn't necessarily mean that you must proceed without any outside help whatsoever. Not only will this book enable you to do a divorce on your own, it will tell you when outside assistance may be necessary, and how to obtain it. There are many different ways that you can work through a divorce without turning the whole matter over to an attorney. Besides going it completely alone, you can:

- get help from an independent paralegal
- get help from a mediator
- get limited help from an attorney in the role of coach.

Which of these options you choose will depend on the complexity of your case, your ability to pay for assistance and other aspects of your case such as any power imbalance or the level of anger between you and your spouse.

Although this book is written in plain English as much as possible, some jargon is unavoidable. If you get stumped by a word or phrase, check the glossary at the end of the book for a concise definition. ■

Should You Use This Book?

A. Your Divorce Must Be Uncontested 2/2
B. When to Get Additional Help 2/3
C. Other Books 2/3
D. Chart: Should I Use This Book? 2/4

This book should be of value to:

- anyone who wants to handle his or her own uncontested divorce, and

- anyone who wants to understand the Oregon divorce process, even if he or she plans to hire or has already hired a lawyer.

A. Your Divorce Must Be Uncontested

To proceed with your own divorce with the help of this book, your divorce must be uncontested.

Most Oregon divorces are uncontested, meaning that neither spouse formally challenges any aspect of the divorce such as property distribution, child custody or child support. Technically speaking, to contest a divorce means to file an answer (also called a response) to a divorce petition after the petition has been served (delivered) on the spouse.

Just because your spouse doesn't join in the paperwork with you as a co-petitioner doesn't mean that your divorce is a contested one. You can file the petition yourself, have your spouse served, and as long as he or she does not file a response, the divorce is uncontested. So even if you and your spouse are not in total agreement about every aspect of the divorce, your divorce will proceed uncontested unless the spouse who is served with a divorce petition files a response with the court, outlining specifically what he or she objects to in the divorce petition.

When a divorce is contested, the issues in dispute are battled out in court. In uncontested divorces, no hearing is required. And when no hearing is required, no representation by a lawyer is needed to get the divorce through the court process. (However, a lawyer can be very helpful in helping an embattled spouse understand his or her legal rights and negotiate a fair settlement.)

The most common causes of disagreement between divorcing spouses have to do with child custody, visitation and support and property division. Your divorce is most likely to be uncontested if you don't have any children, and you and your spouse haven't acquired any valuable property such as a house or a shared retirement pension during the marriage. However, even if you have children or own valuable property as a married couple, you still can pursue an uncontested divorce, as long as you are able to reach agreement out of court about *everything* pertaining to the divorce including child custody, support, visitation and property division.

If your divorce is contested, but you and your spouse are then able to resolve your differences, your divorce may become uncontested again and you may proceed with the help of this book. Converting a contested divorce back into an uncontested divorce requires you to show the court that you have reached agreement. You can do this by filing a form called a Stipulated Decree. See Chapter 12, Section A, for more information on stipulated decrees. Instructions for filling out and filing a stipulated decree are included in Chapter 12.

We strongly encourage you to try to resolve any disputes outside of the courtroom, either on your own or with outside assistance. You can use a mediator, a lawyer/coach or a book like this one to resolve an issue (such as who gets to keep the house)—then that issue will not need to be resolved by the court and your divorce can proceed uncontested. See Chapter 6 for a detailed discussion of mediation, and Chapter 15 for how to find a lawyer who will coach you rather than fully take over your case and represent you in court.

If your divorce becomes contested and you cannot resolve the dispute on your own or with outside help, you will need either to handle your own contested case (a very difficult task) or to find an attorney to represent you. (See Chapter 15 for more on finding an attorney.)

A checklist of the issues you and your spouse will need to agree on (or at least will not challenge) is included at the end of this chapter.

B. When to Get Additional Help

This book provides detailed information on the laws and issues faced by divorcing Oregon couples, but it doesn't cover everything. Topics not specifically addressed in this book are:

- how to divide retirement plans and pension plans (including IRAs and Keoghs);

- how to assess the appropriate level and duration of spousal support (alimony);

- how to handle situations where the divorcing spouses jointly own two or more pieces of real estate; and

- how to divide and evaluate the value of a business.

If any of these issues affects you, you will need to consult with an attorney to get accurate information about your rights and for assistance in drafting appropriate court forms.

However, the fact that you need some outside help doesn't mean you have to turn the whole matter over to an attorney. You can use attorneys and other professionals such as mediators, tax specialists and accountants to help you with any complex issues that may arise in your divorce. Remember, as long as you and your spouse don't need a judge to decide an issue, there is no reason you can't use this book to do your own divorce paperwork.

Another situation that may make it necessary for you to get outside help is if you do not know how to locate your spouse. A missing spouse is a problem because you'll need them either to sign the divorce paperwork or to be served with the petition. A legal coach or an independent paralegal can help you with the additional forms and procedures necessary for dealing with a missing spouse. Once you have taken care of that, you can still do most of your own divorce using the forms in this book.

See Chapter 15 for information on hiring an attorney and other resources for help with your divorce.

C. Other Books

Although this book gives you the tools necessary to move your uncontested divorce through the necessary court procedures, your individual circumstances may require other tools to help you resolve issues associated with your divorce. Here we list a few books on divorce-related issues that are published by Nolo Press. Other resources are described in Chapter 15.

- *Divorce and Money: How to Make the Best Financial Decisions During Divorce*, by Violet Woodhouse and Victoria Felton-Collins. This book gives step-by-step instructions on how to evaluate and divide such large-ticket property items as houses, pensions, family businesses or investment portfolios. It discusses financial realities as well as the legal rules generally associated with dividing these types of assets. It will help you negotiate these issues with the other spouse. Even if you have to hire an attorney to help you draw up any agreement you reach on these issues, using this book can save you a lot of money in legal fees.

- *Child Custody: Building Parenting Agreements That Work*, by Mimi Lyster. This book helps you design detailed custody and visitation arrangements to best suit your and your children's needs. It covers all the important topics to include in a complete agreement, and provides worksheets to help you work through each of them. It also explains how to use a mediator to help you solve issues that you can't negotiate on your own.

- *How to Mediate Your Dispute*, by Peter Lovenheim. Mediation is an increasingly popular—and effective—alternative to resolving disputes in the courtroom and is used by many divorcing couples. This book provides an in-depth and thorough explanation of how mediation works, and offers instructions for participants to prepare for and participate in the mediation process. A special chapter is devoted to divorce mediation. (See Chapter 6 of this book for more information about mediation in Oregon.)

D. Should I Use This Book?

IF	THEN
You want a divorce	Read this book and see an attorney
You want spousal support	Read this book, read **Divorce and Money**, and see an attorney
There is a retirement plan involved	Read this book, read **Divorce and Money**, and see an attorney
There is more than one piece of real estate	Read this book, read **Divorce and Money**, and see an attorney
You have children, and are in disagreement on custody, visitation and child support. Or, you know what you want and know that your spouse will not contest it	Read this book, and read **Mediate Your Dispute**. If issues are still not resolved, see an attorney
You are in disagreement on how to divide property and debts	Read this book, read **Divorce and Money**, and read **Mediate Your Dispute**. If issues are still not resolved, see an attorney

You can do your own divorce with this book!

If you see an attorney about certain issues in your divorce, that does not mean that you need to hire that attorney to handle your whole divorce for you. You may, after obtaining information from the attorney, still decide to handle some or all of the divorce on your own. It may seem difficult for you to determine which situations or conflicts are appropriate to try to deal with on your own, and which ones really cry out for professional help. This book will provide information on the most common issues that cause problems in a divorce—child custody and visitation, child support and property and debt division—and will help you figure out when and how to tackle problems without hiring an attorney. ■

An Overview of an Uncontested Divorce

A. Co-Petitioner Divorces 3/2

B. Petitioner/Respondent Divorces 3/3

Now that you've decided to use this book to proceed with your divorce—either on your own or with some degree of outside help—let's take a brief look at what to expect over the next few months. As long as neither you nor your spouse challenges any aspect of the divorce, your divorce will proceed through smooth, predictable stages, and should be final within about four months. In some cases you may be able to shorten the process to approximately one month by obtaining a 90-day waiver, a process that is discussed below. If disputes arise, you'll have to resolve them—which may prolong the process.

Once you decide you want a divorce, you must decide whether to try to include your spouse in the process or whether to go it alone. You can file for divorce in one of two ways: as co-petitioners, or as petitioner/respondent. If you file together, you will each be a co-petitioner. If you file alone and have your spouse served, you will be the petitioner and he or she will be the respondent.

A. Co-Petitioner Divorces

If you think you and your spouse can agree on all terms of the divorce, you can proceed as co-petitioners, meaning that both of you will jointly fill out, sign and file the divorce paperwork with the court. A co-petitioner divorce obviously depends on you and your spouse agreeing on all issues, including those relating to any children or property you may have.

After you file with the court the petition and all other documents such as child support worksheets or property settlements, there will be a 90-day waiting period. In some cases, a waiver of the 90-day waiting period may be granted. (See Sidebar on 90-day waivers.) After the 90 days, the judge will sign a divorce decree. After another 30 days, the decree will become final and you and your spouse will be officially divorced.

90-Day Waivers

It is sometimes possible to obtain a waiver of the 90-day waiting period involved in a co-petitioner or petitioner/respondent divorce. To request a waiver, you must submit a form and state the reason that you want the waiting period waived. Most judges will waive the 90-day period only if there is a true emergency affecting a third person. Here are some situations that may justify waiving the 90 days:
- the need for child support to be ordered by the court,
- the need to marry someone with whom you are about to have a child,
- the need to hasten the divorce to alleviate severe emotional distress (courts often do not accept this reason, only in extreme circumstances),
- the need to provide a bank with a final judgment of divorce in order to refinance a house, or to obtain a home or car loan.

Example: *Janell is trying to buy a house to move into after the divorce. Her mortgage company is requiring a divorce decree before they will finalize the mortgage papers. Janell will probably be granted a 90-day waiver for this reason.*

Example: *Suzanne needs the $400-per-month child support that will be ordered by the court. She knows that without a court order Floyd will not pay the child support. She will probably be granted a 90-day waiver.*

Example: *Zola is pregnant with Herb's baby and wants to marry him, but her divorce from Tom is not yet final. She requests a 90-day waiver so that the divorce will be granted earlier and she can marry Herb before the baby is born. The judge will probably grant the waiver.*

Example: *Karla wants her divorce from Dan to become final as fast as possible because she finds the waiting stressful. She requests a 90-day waiver to reduce her stress level. Unless she can prove that her situation is extraordinary—*

such as by providing a therapist's statement that her emotional condition is causing serious health or psychological problems—she will probably not be granted a 90-day waiver.

Chapters 11 and 12 explain how to fill out and file the forms for requesting a 90-day waiver.

B. Petitioner/Respondent Divorces

If you suspect or know that your spouse does not want a divorce or will not agree with you on certain issues in the divorce, you can file the divorce petition yourself (as the petitioner) and have your spouse (the respondent) served with copies of the papers. At that point, if your spouse decides to challenge the divorce he or she must file an answer within 90 days of being served with the petition. (See Sidebar on 90-day waivers.)

Serving Your Spouse

Anyone who files for a petitioner/respondent divorce—that is, if he or she fills out and files the divorce papers alone—must have the divorce papers delivered to the other spouse. This delivery is called service and it must be done according to very specific instructions outlined by law. The reason your spouse must be served is that he or she has the right to know that you have filed for divorce. In addition, the other spouse has the right to file a response to your divorce petition, answering whatever claims or statements were made in it. See Chapter 13, Section B, for more information and instructions on serving your spouse.

If no answer is filed in the 90-day period (meaning that the divorce remained uncontested), the judge will sign a divorce decree. The divorce will then be final 30 days after the decree was signed.

If your spouse files an answer, your divorce will have become contested and you must resolve the disputed issues before proceeding with this book, since contested divorces are outside its scope. If you are able to resolve the issues raised in the answer, however, you may turn your divorce into an uncontested one and use this book to help you through the process. Many divorcing couples, although they disagree at first, are able to resolve their differences through negotiation or with the help of a mediator. Then they file the necessary paperwork to show that they have reached agreement, and proceed on an uncontested basis. See Chapter 4, Section J, on how to turn a contested divorce into an uncontested divorce; and Chapter 6, Section G, on mediating disputes. ■

Commonly Asked Questions and Answers

A. Can I file in Oregon? 4/3

B. Can I still get a divorce if my spouse does not live in Oregon? 4/3

C. Where do I file? 4/3

D. How long does a divorce take? 4/4

E. What are the filing fees for a divorce? 4/4

F. What if I cannot afford the filing fee? 4/4

G. What are the issues my spouse and I will need to agree on to obtain an uncontested divorce? 4/4

H. My spouse and I don't agree on some important issues. Does that mean we'll need attorneys? 4/5

I. What should I do if my spouse contests (files a response with the court) the divorce? 4/5

J. If my spouse and I reach an agreement after the divorce has already become contested, how do we make the divorce uncontested again? 4/6

K. To get a divorce do I have to prove that my spouse did something wrong, like cheating on me? 4/6

L. Will there be a court hearing? 4/6

M. Can I get temporary custody or child support while the divorce is pending? 4/6

N. What is alimony or spousal support and when is it awarded? 4/7

O. What if I want to move after I file the divorce but before it's final? 4/7
P. What if I decide I don't really want to go through with the divorce after I've already filed the petition? 4/7
Q. What's the difference between an annulment and a divorce? 4/8
R. What's the difference between a legal separation and a divorce? 4/8
S. What happens to retirement funds in a divorce? 4/8
T. What happens to a family business in a divorce? 4/9
U. Can I change my name? 4/9

Even though the divorce process itself is actually quite simple and straightforward, the answers to many questions are not always obvious. In this chapter we will address the questions that most often arise during divorces in Oregon.

A. Can I file in Oregon?

You can file for a divorce in Oregon if you or your spouse have lived in Oregon for six months or more. This is called the residency requirement. However, if custody of children will be disputed and the children have not been living in Oregon for the past six months, you should see an attorney. Filing for a legal separation may be an acceptable solution if you and your spouse do not meet the residency requirement but need to establish separate lives and settle issues related to the children and their support. But again, if you have children and they do not meet the residency requirement, see an attorney before proceeding.

Example: *When Stan and Susan separated eight months ago, Susan moved from Washington to Oregon, and has been living there ever since. They have no children. Susan may file her divorce in Oregon.*

Example: *When Lupe and Franco separated eight months ago, Franco moved from Idaho to Oregon. Their children stayed in Idaho with Lupe. Franco and Lupe do not agree on who will have custody of the children. Franco needs to see an attorney. He may or may not be able to file in Oregon. If, however, Franco and Lupe agree on all issues related to the children, they can file in Oregon.*

B. Can I still get a divorce if my spouse does not live in Oregon?

As long as you meet the residency requirement for filing for divorce in Oregon (you have lived there for at least six months), you can file for divorce in Oregon even if your spouse does not. It does not matter whether you are signing and filing the paperwork with your spouse as co-petitioners, or if you are filing alone and having your spouse served. Although you may face some special issues such as having your spouse served in a different state, an out-of-state spouse does not prevent you from filing in Oregon as long as you are a resident. Specific procedures are covered in the forms section.

If you have children who have lived in another state during the past six months and your spouse may fight your divorce, see an attorney. The Oregon courts may not have the power to decide issues in your divorce related to the children.

C. Where do I file?

Divorces are filed by county. You may file in one of two counties, either the county in which you live or the one in which your spouse lives. People sometimes base this decision on which county has the less expensive filing fees.

Example: *James and Jennifer, who are separated, plan to file for divorce as co-petitioners (both filling out, signing and filing the paperwork). James lives in Hood River County and Jennifer lives in Washington County. James and Jennifer may file for divorce in either Hood River or Washington County. Because the Hood River filing fees are lower than in Washington County, James and Jennifer decide to file in Hood River.*

D. How long does a divorce take?

From filing a divorce petition to having it finalized in court usually takes 120 days for an uncontested divorce. From the date you file as co-petitioners or the date you have your spouse served if you are filing as a sole petitioner, there is a 90-day waiting period; after the judge signs the decree there is another 30-day waiting period before the divorce is final.

Under certain circumstances it is possible to waive the 90-day portion of the waiting period. When a 90-day waiver is granted, the judge will sign the divorce decree within approximately two weeks, and the divorce will be final after the 30-day post-decree waiting period (which cannot be waived). Chapter 3 discusses 90-day waivers, and Chapters 11 and 12 explain how to fill out and file the forms to request a 90-day waiver.

Example: *Wes and Janice file a co-petitioner divorce along with a request for a waiver of the 90-day waiting period. If the judge grants their 90-day waiver, their divorce will be signed by the judge in approximately two weeks and become final 30 days after that.*

E. What are the filing fees for a divorce?

The court filing fees range from $113 to $251.50 from county to county. A chart of filing fees by county is included in Chapter 13. As mentioned above, you are required to file in a county where one spouse lives. Therefore, you cannot shop around and file in the least expensive county in the state. But you can file in the less expensive county of the two in which you and your spouse currently live, assuming you live in different counties.

Example: *Susan and her husband Dave both live in Multnomah County. They must file in Multnomah County, even though Multnomah County filing fees are among the highest in the state.*

F. What if I cannot afford the filing fee?

If you meet certain income and property guidelines and are filing the papers alone, you may qualify for a fee deferral. This does not get you off the hook for the fee, however. You, your spouse or both of you will eventually be required to pay the fee in full. In the meantime, your divorce will be granted. You cannot get a fee deferral if you and your spouse file together as co-petitioners. The court figures that two people can come up with the funds to pay the filing fee. See note in Chapter 13, Section B2, for more information about fee deferral judgments.

Example: *Jill and Robert are co-petitioners: they are both signing and filing their divorce petition. Robert has been laid off from his job and Jill is working as a convenience store checker part-time. Even though they have a very low income, Jill and Robert will not be granted a fee deferral if they file together. If, however, Jill files alone and has Robert served, she would probably qualify for a filing fee deferral. Or if Robert files alone and has Jill served, he would also likely qualify for a deferral.*

G. What are the issues my spouse and I will need to agree on to obtain an uncontested divorce?

To obtain an uncontested divorce, a divorcing couple must come to an agreement on how to divide their marital property, real estate and debts. If there are children of the marriage, then custody, visitation and child support must also be resolved. If you cannot come to an agreement on your own, you may use a mediator or other professional to resolve any disputes.

H. My spouse and I don't agree on some important issues. Does that mean we'll need attorneys?

Not necessarily. There is nothing to prevent you from resolving your differences on your own, or with outside help. You can try to settle disputes with your spouse at any time: before filing divorce papers, after filing or even after your spouse has filed papers to make the divorce a contested one. As discussed in detail in Chapter 6, even profound disagreements are often resolved with the help of a neutral professional called a mediator.

Although settlement may seem unlikely even with outside help, the fact is that almost all contested court actions are ultimately settled by agreement rather than by a judge's decision. Sadly, this settlement usually comes after huge attorney's fees have accumulated and unresolved conflicts have hardened into lasting bitterness. It's easy to understand the emotional and financial benefits of keeping your divorce uncontested if at all possible.

The Danger of a Power Imbalance

In some marriages, one spouse thoroughly dominates the other spouse. This situation, known as a power imbalance, creates a substantial risk that the dominant spouse will be able to force a settlement on the other spouse that is both unfair and in conflict with what the law would provide if a judge decided the case. If, on the basis of your marriage, you believe you'll have trouble standing up for your own rights, you will definitely want to work with an attorney, either to assist you in doing your own divorce or to represent you if that becomes necessary. See Chapter 15 on hiring an attorney.

I. What should I do if my spouse contests (files a response with the court) the divorce?

If there is no restraining order between you and your spouse, you may be able to resolve the dispute by talking to one another without any assistance from a third party (such as a friend, a mediator or an attorney). If your spouse has hired an attorney to represent him or her, you are supposed to communicate with that attorney rather than directly with your spouse.

If resolving the dispute on your own is not possible or does not work, you and your spouse can hire a professional such as a mediator to help you. Attempting to mediate the dispute rather than fighting it out in court may well save you thousands of dollars in attorney's fees. Of course this means that your spouse will at least have to agree to participate in the mediation unless the dispute involves custody, visitation or parenting time with the children. In that event, you and your spouse will be ordered by the court to attend mediation (in most counties). See Chapter 6 for specifics on mediation.

Example: *Janice filed for divorce from Miguel. In her petition and decree she asked for custody of their three children. Miguel, who wanted custody of the kids, hired an attorney and filed a response. Janice called the attorney and found out that Miguel wanted custody of the children. Janice and Miguel were ordered to attend mediation. During mediation, they discovered that they both would rather have joint custody of the children, so they negotiated a shared parenting plan. Miguel then told his attorney that her services were no longer needed and asked her to file notice with the court that she was no longer representing Miguel. Janice and Miguel then filed a Stipulated Decree and accompanying forms to make the divorce uncontested (see Chapter 12) and proceeded on their own.*

J. If my spouse and I reach an agreement after the divorce has already become contested, how do we make the divorce uncontested again?

To show the court that your divorce is no longer contested, you must jointly fill out and file a Stipulated Decree and an Affidavit Supporting Decree of Dissolution Without a Hearing. You must wait until the 90-day waiting period has passed—counted from the date of filing or of having your spouse served—before filing the Stipulated Decree and Affidavit. Instructions for these forms are included in Chapter 12, in the section for petitioner/respondent divorce papers.

K. To get a divorce do I have to prove that my spouse did something wrong, like cheating on me?

Oregon is a no-fault state. This means that you do not have to prove that your spouse was unfaithful or did some other nasty act. The only time the court will consider nasty behavior is when considering child custody issues, if the behavior is relevant to that person's custody of a child.

L. Will there be a court hearing?

You will have to attend a court hearing only if your case is contested and you haven't been able to resolve all the issues in your divorce. Only 1% of all divorce cases reach the stage of a court hearing, which means that 99% of all divorces are ultimately settled by the parties themselves.

Example: *Vanessa filed her divorce petition and had Brian served. He got an attorney and filed a response, contesting the property division she asked for in the petition. Rather than using a courtroom to resolve the dispute, Vanessa and Brian decided to try mediation which resulted in a successful compromise. They were then able to proceed with and finalize their divorce without any court hearings.*

M. Can I get temporary custody or child support while the divorce is pending?

Especially when there are children of the marriage, the court may be willing to temporarily place them in one parent's custody and temporarily order the other parent to pay support pending further proceedings. Temporary orders are advised when there is a serious disagreement as to which parent the kids should live with while the divorce is pending, or when the parent who will have the children has no means of supporting them during the divorce.

Since it can take up to several months to get a temporary support order, it is usually only appropriate in a contested divorce where the case can be expected to drag on past the 120 days that it normally takes to get an uncontested divorce. Temporary custody, on the other hand, can be granted more quickly.

If you need a temporary order see an attorney (see Chapter 15 on how to find an attorney).

Temporary custody orders should not be relied on if you fear for your child's safety. If the children are in jeopardy, it may be possible to get a restraining order which would immediately place the children in the custody of the parent seeking the order. (See Chapter 5 for more information about restraining orders.)

N. What is alimony or spousal support and when is it awarded?

Courts will sometimes order one divorcing spouse to make regular payments of a certain amount to the other divorcing spouse for a specified length of time. These payments are alternatively called alimony or spousal support. The court's goal in awarding spousal support is to allow a spouse that worked primarily as a homemaker to get some financial support until he or she can get a foothold in the job market and become self-supporting. Spousal support is not awarded automatically; a court will award it only if it is requested in the divorce paperwork.

The amount of spousal support and the length of time it lasts are usually based on the length of the marriage, the income-earning potential of the spouses and the health and education of the spouse who would receive the support. The right to receive spousal support often ends upon remarriage, but not always. If at the time of the divorce the spouse to be supported is older than 50 (which may make him or her less employable) or has health problems and will likely be unable to find gainful employment, spousal support can be permanent.

The procedures and techniques for requesting spousal support are not included in this book. If you wish to request spousal support or want to know more about the subject, see an attorney or other legal service provider. See Chapter 15 for information on hiring an attorney.

O. What if I want to move after I file the divorce but before it's final?

After the filing of the divorce petition in the correct county, there is no reason that you cannot move. But, if your spouse contests the divorce by filing an answer, you will need to make yourself available for possible court hearings and, if there are children, you may be required to attend mediation and a parenting class depending on which county you file in.

P. What if I decide I don't really want to go through with the divorce after I've already filed the petition?

If you've completed just the first step—filing the petition—but take no further action, the court will eventually send you a notice that your case has been dismissed.

If you have completed the final step—finalization of the divorce decree—you will need to have the decree vacated, which means to have it dismissed. Special forms and procedures are involved in asking the court to vacate a decree, which are not covered in this book. See Chapter 15 on finding an attorney or paralegal.

Q. What's the difference between an annulment and a divorce?

Annulment differs from divorce in that an annulment means there never was a valid marriage. A common reason to annul a marriage is if the marriage was based on fraud. If, for example, your spouse lied to you about something that was an important basis of your marriage (such as a desire to have children or the person's religious beliefs or lack of them) your marriage could be annulled because it was based on fraud (ORS 107.005 and 107.015).

Another fraud that would justify annulment is if either spouse is already married to someone else. Knowingly marrying more than one person at the same time is considered a crime called bigamy. If, however, you marry more than one person by mistake—such as if you thought your previous divorce was final, but it actually was not—you would not be guilty of bigamy (though your second marriage would still be fraudulent).

A marriage can also be annulled if either spouse was not old enough to marry at the time of the marriage (in Oregon, age 18) and did not have parental permission.

The forms for annulment are not included in this book. See Chapter 15 for how to hire an attorney.

R. What's the difference between a legal separation and a divorce?

The important distinction between a legal separation and a divorce is that after a legal separation you are not free to remarry. And unlike a divorce, a legal separation allows you to preserve your spousal inheritance rights, pension rights, and sometimes maintain health insurance coverage.

Despite these differences, in a legal separation you still need to settle all of the same issues as in a divorce. You must divide all property and debts and settle all issues relating to your children.

There are several reasons why you may want to file for legal separation instead of divorce. Some of them are:

- You have not lived in Oregon for six months to meet the residency requirement to file for divorce in Oregon.

- You are not emotionally ready for a divorce but need court-ordered child support or medical insurance.

- You have religious or personal reasons for not wanting a divorce.

Legal separation forms are not included in this book. See Chapter 15 for information on hiring an attorney.

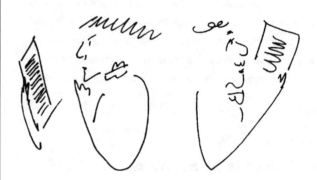

S. What happens to retirement funds in a divorce?

You and your spouse's retirement funds and pension rights that accumulate during your marriage are assets that may be divided in your divorce. Division of retirement funds is not covered in this book. If either of you have retirement savings or pension rights, first read *Divorce and Money* by Violet Woodhouse and Victoria F. Collins (Nolo Press). That book will help you understand any pensions you have and figure out what they're worth. Then, assuming you can reach an agreement about how they should be divided, you'll need to see an attorney to help you complete the necessary forms that you'll have to attach to your divorce papers. Hiring attorneys is covered in Chapter 15.

T. What happens to a family business in a divorce?

A family business must be divided at divorce like any other asset. The first step is to decide whether the business is owned solely by one spouse or jointly by both spouses. Even when one spouse owns the business on paper, if the activity of the other spouse substantially contributed to building the business's value and good will, that other spouse will be entitled to at least part of the business upon divorce.

After ownership issues are sorted out—and assuming there is at least some joint ownership—it will be necessary to determine the value of the business. Whether one spouse will continue to operate the business or if the business is sold, its value will be important in figuring out an equitable division. If one spouse will continue to operate the business, he or she will have to pay the other spouse the value of his or her share in cash or its equivalent in other marital property. If neither spouse wants to continue running the business, the business can be sold and the proceeds divided.

The options available to a divorcing couple regarding a family business are discussed in detail in *Divorce and Money* (Nolo Press). While that book may not provide all the answers, it will go far in helping you deal with a family business in your Oregon divorce. Like pensions, you will probably have to work with an attorney to hammer out the details.

U. Can I change my name?

As part of your divorce, you can change your name back to your maiden name, a prior married name or a name of your choosing. In your divorce petition, include a request to change your name and indicate what name you have chosen. After the judge has signed the divorce decree which will include your name change request, you can use the decree to change your identification and credit cards. Instructions and forms for completing a name change are included in the forms section. ■

Important Things to Do Immediately

A. Close All Joint Accounts 5/2
    1. Bank accounts, stocks and other investments 5/2
    2. Credit accounts 5/2

B. Obtain Restraining Orders If Necessary 5/3

C. Obtain Temporary Orders If Necessary 5/3

If you have just separated from your spouse or plan to separate soon, there are several important things to do right away, such as closing any joint bank accounts or obtaining a restraining order. Although it may be difficult to summon the energy to take care of these tasks during the highly emotional divorce process, the consequences of ignoring them can be catastrophic. Failing to remove your name from joint checking, savings or credit accounts leaves you financially at risk, since as a joint owner you will be liable for any debts your soon-to-be ex-spouse incurs. And an abusive spouse may turn even more violent as a divorce progresses, putting you and maybe your children at risk.

To protect yourself, you should divide your finances and, if necessary, ask for court protection from a violent spouse as soon as possible. Not only will you be safer physically and financially, you may well find it therapeutic and reassuring to be taking back some control of your life.

The following sections discuss the most important tasks for you to complete when you are separating from your spouse. For a full discussion of property and debt division, see Chapter 7 below.

A. Close All Joint Accounts

To limit your liability for any further debt incurred by the other spouse, you should immediately close joint bank accounts, and cancel any credit cards, lines of credit, department store cards or any other open accounts that are in both of your names.

1. Bank accounts, stocks and other investments

All joint accounts belong to both you and your spouse. As joint owners, either one of you can withdraw all funds from a bank account, the contents of a safe deposit box, stocks or other investments without having to notify or obtain permission from the other co-owner. To protect yourself and your share of the accounts, you might take half the funds from joint checking and savings accounts and use them to open individual accounts. Another option is to request your bank, stock broker or other investment professional to freeze an account until contacted in writing by both spouses, or by further court order. A request to freeze an account can often be done by telephone. Before closing joint accounts, be sure that all outstanding checks have cleared.

2. Credit accounts

Allowing joint credit accounts to remain open leaves you vulnerable to debts incurred by your spouse. If your name is on an account, you are responsible for it until you notify the creditor in writing. Even after notification you will still be responsible for the balance due at the time of your notification, but not for debts incurred after that date.

Included in the book in Appendix D is a sample letter for you to notify your creditors. Send a completed form to each one, and be sure each letter is dated. If you send the letter by registered mail, the post office will give you a dated receipt that proves when you sent the letter. Keep a copy of each letter in case you need to prove when you notified a particular creditor. Keeping a copy for yourself is also important in case misinformation later appears on your credit report. You may need to show a credit reporting agency that you closed an account on a certain date in order to clear any mistakes on your credit record.

> **The Value of Playing Fair**
>
> When acting to protect your interests, you ideally should communicate to your spouse what you are doing so that he or she doesn't feel the need to hire a lawyer and jeopardize your ability to have an uncontested divorce. Once your spouse hires a lawyer, you will feel like you need a lawyer too. And once two lawyers are in the case, your chances of having a sane divorce go way down. In addition to sending your spouse copies of letters you mail to banks, etc., you should be willing to give your spouse his or her share of whatever assets you withdraw from a bank or other institution. The more you demonstrate your willingness to play fair, the more likely it is your divorce can be uncontested.

B. Obtain Restraining Orders If Necessary

A restraining order is a court order which prohibits someone who may hurt you—such as an abusive spouse—from going near you or places where you're likely to be, such as your home, office, school or the homes of your friends. To obtain a restraining order against your spouse you must file a request and meet a few court requirements, such as showing the court that he or she recently abused you. If your spouse violates the restraining order he or she can be arrested and possibly fined or jailed. A restraining order also allows you to have temporary custody of your children if they are also in danger.

You are entitled to get a restraining order quickly and at no cost if you have been abused or are in fear of being abused. There is no fee for filing the papers or having them served on your spouse by the sheriff.

To get a restraining order, go to your local county courthouse, request the packet of forms and follow the steps required. Your part of the process basically consists of filling out, signing and filing a request for the restraining order. In most cases you can file the request and have a judge sign it the same day. After the judge signs it, the restraining order is served on your spouse and entered into police records. If you do need a restraining order you may want to file your request along with your divorce papers. That way you can arrange to have all the papers served together, which will save you money if you use a professional process server.

In the Portland area, the Women's Crisis Line number is 503-235-5333. The National Domestic Violence Hotline is 800-799-SAFE.

If you are filing for a restraining order and you are living in a safe place that your spouse does not know, do not use your safe address on your papers. Some people use a friend or family member's address (with permission of course) that the spouse already knows.

Obtaining a restraining order will not prevent you from doing your own divorce (as long as your spouse doesn't contest it).

C. Obtain Temporary Orders If Necessary

If you need immediate court action on issues that wouldn't normally be resolved until the end of the divorce, you can ask the court for a temporary order. For example, if you were separated and your children were living with you, you might need child support payments from your spouse while you waited for the divorce to become final. In that situation you could ask the court for a temporary order for child support rather than wait for the final support order to be issued.

There are a number of situations that might create a need for a temporary order. If you feel your children need protection from your spouse but you can't or don't want to get a restraining order, you may be able to get temporary custody of your children. Another version of this is a status quo order, which is a court order for the children to keep living where they are (with you, presumably), following their current schedule.

If you need temporary financial help until your divorce is final you may be able to get temporary child support or spousal support (alimony).

If you are concerned that your spouse might sell or take more than his or her fair share of your joint assets before the divorce is granted, you can get a court order to freeze those assets. Remember, however, that this type of order will also freeze your access to those assets.

If you need any of the above temporary orders you will need the help of an attorney. See Chapter 15 on finding an attorney. Once you have resolved the issues that required a temporary order, you should be able to pursue your own divorce as long as it hasn't become contested. ■

Understanding Mediation

A.	You Can Mediate Even If You've Already Hired a Lawyer	6/2
B.	You Can't "Lose" in Mediation	6/2
C.	Who Are Divorce Mediators?	6/2
D.	The Difference Between Private Mediation and Court-Ordered Mediation	6/3
E.	The Difference Between Mediators and Mediation Services	6/3
F.	How to Find a Mediator or Mediation Service	6/4
	1. Sources of Information	6/4
	2. Interviewing a Mediator	6/4
G.	How Mediation Works—An Example	6/5
	1. The Introduction	6/5
	2. Sharing Information	6/6
	3. Defining Issues and Clarifying Individual Interests	6/6
	4. Finding Options and Moving Toward a Solution	6/6
	5. Reaching an Agreement and Putting It in Writing	6/7
H.	Translating the Mediation Results Into Court Papers	6/7

Mediation is a marvelous way to resolve differences so that your divorce can proceed uncontested. It provides you and your spouse an opportunity to discuss and deal with your disagreements in a safe, non-threatening environment with the assistance of a neutral person—the mediator. The mediator's role is to help each of you evaluate your goals and options while exploring solutions that are likely to work for both you and your spouse, and for your children if you have any. The mediator will not take sides or make decisions for you. If you can't agree, there is no penalty.

There can be no mediation without both spouses participating. Ideally this participation should be voluntary, and mediators are frequently able to secure the cooperation of both spouses, even if one spouse initially balks at the idea. However, if the court sees that you haven't reached agreement on custody and visitation issues, you and your spouse will be required to participate in at least one mediation session. See Section D below for more on the types of mediation available in Oregon.

Although this chapter provides an overview of how mediation works and how you can use it in your divorce, you may want to learn even more about this subject. If so, get a copy of *How to Mediate Your Dispute*, by Peter Lovenheim (Nolo Press). In addition to explaining the ins and outs of mediation as a dispute resolution process, it has a chapter on the special issues involved in divorce mediation.

A. You Can Mediate Even If You've Already Hired a Lawyer

Mediation can help you even if you and/or your spouse are represented by lawyers. In fact, more and more lawyers are steering their clients towards mediation because it is a cheaper and more efficient way to resolve most types of divorce-related differences than is litigation. Because you and your spouse will be dealing directly with each other, there is no need for either of you to use your lawyers other than for an independent assessment of and advice about what you work out in the mediation, and for getting your case through the court (if you choose to pay the lawyers for that rather than use this book).

B. You Can't "Lose" in Mediation

Well over 80% of all divorce mediations are successful and by all accounts the parties to a mediated divorce are much more satisfied than is true when disputes are left to a judge to decide. However, if the mediation doesn't work for you, you may be out a little money but your legal position will not have changed at all. An unsuccessful mediation simply means that you did not reach a satisfactory agreement—it does *not* mean that any negative legal consequences have happened to you. In fact, you will undoubtedly have learned a lot more about the nature of your disagreement, which will save you time and money if you try a different mediator or end up in court.

C. Who Are Divorce Mediators?

At present, the state of Oregon doesn't regulate mediators, and there is therefore no specific training or educational background that a person must have to be a mediator. Divorce mediators typically come from many backgrounds, including law, family therapy or counselling, social work, childhood development and teaching. Regardless of their professional backgrounds, most divorce mediators have undertaken rigorous training in mediation techniques offered by national and local mediator organizations. In Section F below we provide some tips for finding a mediator who is right for you.

D. The Difference Between Private Mediation and Court-Ordered Mediation

To keep your divorce uncontested, there are several basic types of disagreements you may need to resolve:

- disagreements about who gets what property
- disagreements about whether and/or how much alimony should be paid, and
- disagreements over custody and visitation.

You can always voluntarily use a private mediator to help you resolve any and all of these types of disagreements before you file your divorce and then proceed on an uncontested basis with the help of this book. You also can use a private mediator to resolve your differences even after you have filed for divorce and the other spouse has filed a response—thereby making it a contested divorce. If your post-filing mediation is successful in resolving all issues, you can file a form setting out how you've resolved your differences and then proceed on an uncontested basis. (See Chapter 12, Section A, on filing a stipulated decree.)

For many divorcing couples, the only disagreement is about custody and visitation. If this disagreement finds its way into court—because the other spouse contests the divorce—the court will order you and your spouse to attend court-sponsored mediation. While the court cannot order you to agree, you will be expected to make an honest effort to resolve your differences. If you do, as with private mediation, you can file a stipulated decree and continue the rest of your case on an uncontested basis.

> **When You Might Choose to Use Court-Ordered Mediation**
>
> If child custody/visitation is your only issue, it may be to your advantage to start your divorce off on a contested basis (the other spouse files a response to your petition setting out your differences) and then to use the court-ordered mediation. The reason is that court-ordered mediation is free, whereas you will need to pay the private mediator. On the other hand, you can shop around for a private mediator, but you are pretty much stuck with a mediator assigned by a court.

E. The Difference Between Mediators and Mediation Services

Often, mediators work solo. This is especially true of divorce lawyers who may still practice law but who also offer mediation as an additional service. But it is also common for mediators to work for a private or nonprofit mediation service, an organization that sets up the mediation, pays the mediator and collects the fees from the parties.

If both spouses are willing to mediate their differences, then it may make little difference whether they use a solo mediator or sign on with a service. The important thing will be for them to find a mediator they are comfortable with. However, in this regard, a mediation service will tend to offer a choice of mediators with varied backgrounds and thus make the selection process a little easier. It's a little like the difference between chasing down individual ads when renting a house and working through a centralized listing service.

You generally can tell the difference between a mediation service and a solo mediator by the name. For instance, one mediation service in Oregon is called United States Arbitration & Mediation of Oregon. Solo mediators often go by their own names, such as John L. Briggs, Mediator.

> **Getting a Reluctant Spouse to Mediation**
>
> If your spouse is reluctant to mediate, then you may be forced to use a mediation service rather than a solo mediator. This is because mediation services usually have staff specially trained to convince a recalcitrant spouse to participate in the process, whereas solo mediators—especially those who are lawyers—don't like to "sell" their services.

F. How to Find a Mediator or Mediation Service

If you opt for a private mediator or your disagreement doesn't involve child custody or visitation (in which case you have no choice but to use a private mediator) you must start the process yourselves.

1. Sources of Information

One easy way to find a mediator or mediation service is to consult a mediation directory. There are two that are specific to Oregon:

- The Oregon Mediation Association's Annual Resource Directory and Consumer Guide lists individual mediators and mediation services from around the state. It includes information about fees, training and/or experience. For information, write to OMA, PO Box 2952, Portland, OR 97208, or call 503-294-1017.

- The Oregon Lawyers Alternative Dispute Resolution Directory. For information, write to the Multnomah Bar Association, 630 SW 5th, Ste. 200, Portland, OR 97204, or call 503-222-3275.

Another resource is the National Academy of Family Mediators, 4 Militia Dr., Lexington, MA 02173, 617-674-2663. In addition to providing referrals to individual mediators, this organization also has many books on various aspects of divorce.

If you have joined the online world, check out the Web site at http://www.mediate.com. You will find lots of helpful information on how to find a mediator as well as local referrals.

Another approach to finding a mediator is to ask your friends who have been divorced. If any of them used private mediators, find out whether they were satisfied with the help they received. Recommendations from friends can be very valuable.

The phone directory Yellow Pages also has listings of mediators. Look under Mediation to locate one in your area.

2. Interviewing a Mediator

As mentioned, mediators come from varied backgrounds but they all go through pretty much the same type of training. They learn the basic principles that mediators have found facilitate agreement and they tend to get lots of supervised experience before striking out on their own. Since there is no state certification process to guarantee any of this, however, you should always ask about training and experience. Most mediators will be only too happy to tell you.

Additional questions may cover:

- the mediator's specific experience with the type of dispute you need resolved,

- the mediator's success rate in resolving that type of dispute,

- the mediator's fees,

- how long the mediator expects the mediation in your particular case to last, and

- the probable expense given the nature of your dispute.

Finally, you should try to match the mediator's background with your specific situation. Here are some suggestions:

- If your dispute involves the division of marital property, you may be better off with a lawyer/mediator, since you'll want someone with a firm grasp on the Oregon rules for property division. Non-lawyers, on the other hand, are prohibited by law from providing provide legal information such as property division rules.

- If your dispute is primarily about the children, then you may be better off with a mediator who has a child welfare, social work or counselling background. Disputes over the children usually have less to do with the child custody and visitation laws of Oregon, and more to do with the special needs of children. A mediator who understands children and their needs can be an incredibly valuable resource.

- If the emotional content of your divorce is running high and you think that your disagreements are more psychological than legal, you may want to find a mediator who has a strong background in marital counselling or therapy.

Again, these are only suggestions that you might consider in your selection process. As a general rule, it is far more important for a mediator to be well-versed in the skills of mediation itself than in any particular discipline.

G. How Mediation Works—An Example

Now that we've explained the role that mediation can play in your divorce and how to get the process started, it may help to have an idea of what actually happens in a mediation. Every divorce mediator works a little differently, but there are roughly five stages to every successful mediation. Using Susan and Fred as an example, here is how it works. Susan and Fred have already interviewed a number of mediators and chosen Inez.

1. The Introduction

At the first session Inez greets Susan and Fred, makes them comfortable and goes over the ground rules and the process. Inez goes through a number of introductory issues, explaining that:

- Participation in mediation is voluntary and that either spouse can leave at any time (although most mediators are skilled in keeping the parties at the table).

- The object of mediation is to set aside hostility and to help the parties make some decisions.

- Each person must speak in their turn—no interrupting, no shouting.

- The sessions are confidential and statements made by either spouse can't be used against them if the mediation fails and court becomes necessary.

- Her role as the mediator is to help Susan and Fred reach agreements about highly charged emotional issues. She will remain neutral so that Susan and Fred may control the decisions made. She will help Susan and Fred approach their issues from different angles and fresh perspectives, so as to help them avoid falling into old patterns and finding fault with each other.

- She will use her skills to help Susan and Fred find common ground so they can create options to resolve their differences.

- Part of the mediation will involve Susan and Fred talking face-to-face in the presence of the mediator, and part of it will involve each spouse talking with Inez separately, as needed.

2. Sharing Information

Also at the first session, Inez helps Susan and Fred identify which issues have already been resolved and which issues are still in dispute. Susan and Fred have already agreed that the house has to be sold, but they cannot agree on when and how to sell it. They agree that they both want joint custody but do not agree about how to handle holidays or which days should be spent with each parent. Susan and Fred provide Inez with information on the value of the house, the house payments, their current work schedules and household expenses.

3. Defining Issues and Clarifying Individual Interests

Concerned about disrupting the lives of their young children, Susan wants to sell the house in a few years, when the youngest child starts high school. Fred wants to put the house on the market right away. Fred feels that, with the expenses of two households, they cannot afford to keep making the house payments and that Susan can and should find a less expensive place to live. Susan agrees it will be difficult to make the house payments, but thinks it can be managed once her yearly employment bonus is figured into her income. She also points out that the house is increasing in value—in one year its value rose 16%—and they should wait as long as possible to sell it.

Fred's main concern is over the possibility of only seeing his children every other weekend. Since the two kids are fairly mature, ages ten and 13, he feels that switching households every four days can work. He plans to live in an apartment nearby to make it easier for the children to switch back and forth. Susan, however, worries that maintaining that sort of schedule may be too disruptive to the children.

4. Finding Options and Moving Toward a Solution

After the first session, which lasts for two hours, Susan, Fred and Inez have another one in which they again all participate together. After a while, Fred and Susan are completely at odds with each other and it becomes clear that the mediation is at an impasse. At this point Inez suggests that they each meet separately with her in what is called a private caucus. Private caucuses are often used when mediation sessions become contentious and stop making progress. In a private caucus, each person may express themselves fully and suggest possible solutions without fear or anxiety over how the other person will react. The mediator can then bring them together and try to reconcile the different positions. Susan and Fred each agree to have a private caucus and take turns meeting with Inez alone. When they meet again as a group, they are then able to add more options to the list of possible solutions.

Fred and Susan come up with a list of options for what to do with their house:

- Wait for four months until the end of the school year, and then sell the house during the summer.

- Wait until the children are finished with high school to sell the house. Rent a room in the house to help with the house payments.

- List the house immediately, but make the sale contingent upon allowing Susan and the children to stay in the home until the school year is over.

- Sell the house and let the kids get used to living somewhere else.

- Have Fred wait to move out until the children finish the school year in four months.

- Have Fred rent an apartment with a roomate to share expenses, which would leave Fred with more money to help Susan and the children stay in the house.

Fred and Susan also come up with a list of options for visitation and holiday schedules:

- Have the children spend alternate weeks with each parent.

- Have the children spend three days with Fred and four days with Susan.

- Have each child live with one parent and spend scheduled times together.

- Let the children sort it out based on their schedules.

- Try four days on/four days off as proposed for a specific amount of time and agree to renegotiate and/or mediate if it presents problems.

- Have the children spend part of each holiday with each parent, unless one parent wants to take the children to visit friends or family out of town. In that case, work out an every-other-year scenario. If Susan takes them to Cleveland one year for Christmas, for example, Fred will have the option of taking them to visit his family for the next Christmas.

- Have the children alternate between parents every two weeks during summer vacation.

5. Reaching an Agreement and Putting It In Writing

After considering all the options, Fred and Susan agree that they will list the house immediately, but make the sale contingent upon Susan and the children staying in the home until the school year is over. Fred will find an apartment where he will live alone. For visitation and holiday schedules, they will try four days on/four days off for a specific amount of time and agree to renegotiate and or mediate if it does not work. Inez drafts a written agreement which is reviewed and signed by both Fred and Susan.

H. Translating the Mediation Results Into Court Papers

If mediation is successful and an agreement is reached, this agreement can be put in writing and incorporated into the divorce papers or included as an attachment. (Often, an agreement will be both incorporated into the divorce papers and included as an attachment.) Your mediator should be able to help you draft the agreement to comply with any court rules. At that point, you can continue with your divorce on your own with the help of this book. See Chapter 8, Section D, for a sample mediated agreement and instructions on how to incorporate this information into your petition and decree.

If your divorce had already become contested by the time you attended mediation, you will have to show the court that your divorce is again uncontested by filing a Stipulated Decree with both of your signatures and supporting documents that show you have reached an agreement. This process is covered in the forms section, Chapter 12, Section A.

If mediation is unsuccessful and an agreement is not reached, you are free to try mediation again, with a different mediator if you so choose. Trying and failing to reach a mediated agreement does not prevent you from trying again. If your disagreements persist, or if you choose not to try mediation, you can hire attorneys and fight it out in court—a situation that can be very costly, both financially and emotionally.

COURT ORDERED MEDIATION

DISPUTE	COURT ORDERED	PRIVATE
Custody	x	
Visitation	x	x
Property Division		x
Debt Division		x
Other		x

COUNTY COURT SPECIFICS

COUNTY	HAVE MEDIATION	PARENTING CLASS
Baker	none	none
Benton	yes	none
Clackamas	yes	yes
Clatsop	none	none
Columbia	none	none
Coos	none	starting
Crook	yes	none
Curry	none	none
Deschutes	yes	none
Douglas	yes	none
Gilliam	yes	none
Grant	none	none
Harney	none	none
Hood River	yes	none
Jackson	yes	starting
Jefferson	yes	none
Josephine	yes	starting
Klamath	yes	none
Lake	none	none
Lane	yes	none
Lincoln	none	none
Linn	yes	none
Malheur	yes	yes
Marion	yes	yes
Morrow	none	none
Multnomah	yes	yes, as part of mediation
Polk	yes	yes
Sherman	yes	none
Tillamook	yes	none
Umatilla	none	none
Union	yes	none
Wallowa	none	none
Wasco	none	none
Washington	yes	yes, as part of mediation
Wheeler	none	none
Yamhill	yes	yes ∎

Property and Debt Division

A. Determining Which Property Is Marital Property	7/2
1. Separate Property	7/2
2. Marital Property	7/3
3. The Fine Line Between Separate and Marital Property	7/3
4. Disclosing Assets and Debts to Your Spouse	7/3
B. Dividing Marital Property	7/4
1. Dividing Personal Property	7/4
2. Dividing Real Estate	7/5
C. Dividing Debts of the Marriage	7/7
1. Determining Which Debts Are Marital Debts	7/7
2. Dividing Marital Debts	7/8
3. Enforcing Marital Debt Repayment Agreements	7/9

Since you are getting an uncontested divorce (otherwise you will need help beyond this book), you and your spouse must decide what is to be done with the property and debts of the marriage. In divorce parlance, this is called dividing your property. Dividing property is covered in Sections A and B. Dividing debts is discussed in Section C.

In Oregon, divorcing couples must divide marital property and debt in a way that is fair, or equitable, to each person. Unlike states that follow the law of community property and require their judges to award each party half of the marital property, Oregon follows the rule of equitable distribution, which anticipates that property should be divided fairly, but not necessarily 50-50. However, a 50-50 split is assumed to be a fair distribution and a court will not interfere with such an arrangement. If, however, a court thinks a proposed property division is unfair, it may reject it and not sign the divorce decree. So in Oregon, couples are free to divide marital property and debts by whatever ratio they want as long as the distribution doesn't appear to be unfair to one spouse.

Example: *Jane and Hassan have two cars, a house, various bank accounts and household goods. They have decided to sell the house, divide the equity, split the bank accounts, divide the household goods and each keep the car they drive. Since the division is more or less 50-50 there would be no basis for the court to interfere.*

Example: *Raeleen and Billy have two cars, a boat, a house, various bank accounts and miscellaneous household goods. Their proposed property division gives everything to Billy except for one car, which Raeleen will keep. The court could decide that this division is unfair to Raeleen and reject the divorce papers.*

If your papers are rejected they will be accompanied by a letter of explanation. If you do not understand the problem or if you feel the division of property and debts is fair (equitable) regardless of what the judge thinks, call the judge's office for a clarification. If you still don't understand or don't agree with the judge's decision, you should see an attorney or try to come up with a new division that moves towards what the judge seems to want.

A. Determining Which Property Is Marital Property

Before you can divide the property of the marriage, you must decide which property qualifies as such. Property that you or your spouse own individually—separate property—is not divided, only marital property is. So after your property division is complete, you'll keep all of your separate property, plus some share of the marital property.

1. Separate Property

Since it's not always easy to determine what property is marital property, let's look first at separate property, which does not count as marital property. Separate property generally includes:

- property owned by a spouse before the marriage,
- property inherited by a spouse either before or during the marriage,
- property given as a gift specifically to one spouse (including gifts given by the other spouse),
- property owned in only one spouse's name.

Property purchased by one spouse for that spouse's sole use, such as a camera purchased by the husband as part of his photography hobby would be the husband's separate property. However, property that is purchased for the use of both spouses, such as furniture in the home, would generally be considered property of the marriage.

2. Marital Property

Property of the marriage is generally defined as:

- property that is owned by both spouses together,

- property owned in both spouses' names (where there is a title document, as in stocks or real estate),

- part of the property owned by one spouse that the other spouse contributed to during the marriage (such as by paying for major repairs for a house that had been owned by the other spouse before the marriage).

Working as a homemaker can be considered to be a contribution to property, which can make household property marital property, even if the property is held in the other spouse's name (ORS 107.105). If one of you is a wage earner and the other spouse is a homemaker, see an attorney for help in determining an equitable property division. Information on hiring attorneys is covered in Chapter 15.

Example: *Susan and Jay own their house in both of their names. Susan has a car and a bank account solely in her name. Jay has a motorcycle and bank account solely in his name. Susan's car and bank account are her separate property. Jay's motorcycle and bank are his separate property. The only property of the marriage is the house, which is thus the only asset to be divided in the divorce.*

3. The Fine Line Between Separate and Marital Property

Often, property has no title and is not owned in anyone's name. Many household items are owned this way, things such as appliances or furniture that were perhaps bought with cash out of a joint bank account. This type of property can become a problem to divide if memories and opinions about its ownership differ.

Generally, if you keep cash and investments in individual, not joint, accounts and the deposits for those accounts come from your wages, those accounts are your separate property. If, however, one spouse is a homemaker and does not work outside the home, his or her contribution to the household can count towards that property and make it property of the marriage, thus entitling them to a share at divorce. And retirement accounts accumulated during the marriage also are subject to division at divorce.

If you have a life insurance policy with a cash value, the cash may be an asset to be divided. These types of policies are called universal life, whole life or savings life insurance. By contract, term life insurance has no cash value, meaning that you can't borrow against it. If one spouse is a homemaker his or her contribution may entitle the spouse to a share of the life insurance value. If both spouses work outside the home and each maintain their own life insurance policies, each policy would be considered separate property and each spouse would keep their own.

4. Disclosing Assets and Debts to Your Spouse

Many couples share knowledge about their finances as part of their marriage. Many others delegate the financial affairs to one spouse, leaving the other spouse pretty much in the dark. As part of a divorce, you and your spouse must disclose to each other everything you know about your property and debts (ORS 107.089).

If you and your spouse are filing the papers together (as co-petitioners) you can sign a waiver of the disclosure requirement. If you do sign the waiver, you must realize that you are giving up your right to find out financial information about your spouse as well as your right to penalize your spouse for failing to disclose hidden assets.

If you are filing the divorce papers alone and having your spouse served, you should be sure to disclose any assets that your spouse might wish to claim as his or her own. The penalty for not doing so is substantial. Intentional concealment of significant assets can leave you open to asset seizure and redistribution for up to ten years. This means that your ex-spouse could take you back to court and prove that you purposefully hid assets that he or she was rightfully entitled to in the divorce. If you lose, the court can take that property and give it all to your ex-spouse.

A notice for disclosure (and instructions on how to use it) is included in the forms section on page 12/16.

Example: *Scott has been secretly investing money. When he divorces Justine, he doesn't mention these investments in the divorce papers. Scott is guilty of intentional concealment of these investments. If Justine finds out about them, she could have the court seize those assets and have some or all of them turned over to her.*

B. Dividing Marital Property

Once you sort out your separately owned property from the property of the marriage, the next task is to divide the marital property. This is fairly straightforward when tangible property items such as furniture, record collections, cars, boats, artworks, antiques and jewelry are involved. Either you divvy up the items in a way that seems fair to both of you, or you agree to sell certain items and to split the proceeds.

Intangible property items such as investments, businesses and pensions can be much more troublesome. Real estate can also be difficult to divide. For help in dividing real estate and intangible property items, a good resource is *Divorce and Money* by Violet Woodhouse and Victoria F. Collins (Nolo Press). *Divorce and Money* also covers the tax consequences of the division of various types of property. If you need to divide these types of assets, you will need an attorney to help you draft any resulting agreement, which may then be included with the divorce forms from this book as an attachment.

I. Dividing Personal Property

Your personal property is everything that is not attached to land: your cars, bank accounts, furniture, artwork, appliances, businesses, recreational vehicles, household goods, investments, retirement plans, copyrights, patents, boats and tools. Your house, on the other hand, is considered real property, not personal property.

Your divorce forms will have a section for listing the property that will go to each spouse. In filling out this section, be as specific as you feel you need to be. If you and your spouse have an agreement on property division and trust each other to honor it, or if you have already divided your personal property, you probably do not need to worry about drafting a highly specific property division arrangement. In any case, remember this rule: the more specific your arrangement, the more enforceable it is.

Example: *Vanessa and Raymond separated five years ago. At that time Vanessa took all her separate property, which included household goods and her car. They divided the joint bank account and never owned a house. Five years after their separation, they file for divorce. Since the property has already been divided, they have no need to include information about property division in the divorce papers.*

Example: *Theo and Liv have reached an uneasy agreement about who gets what pieces of personal property. Liv is afraid that Theo will not live up to his agreement to let her have the home computer, the laser printer and two Persian rugs. To make sure that she gets what she was promised, she makes sure to include these items (and all the other items* *they agreed upon) in the property division section of the divorce petition. She includes descriptions of each item, as well as the serial numbers of the computer and laser printer. If Theo later tries to renege, she can refer to this part of the divorce decree to enforce their agreement.*

When You Might Need an Attorney

As emphasized earlier, you should use this book if you and your spouse are in agreement or if your spouse will not fight the divorce. Sometimes, a spouse that did not contest a divorce becomes uncooperative after the divorce is final, such as by refusing to give you certain property items awarded in the divorce decree. If so, you may need another court order to get your property.

If you have significant assets in joint ownership with your spouse and are concerned about your spouse taking these assets before there is a court order to divide them, you can get a temporary order to freeze accounts. If you need to get court orders for transferring property or to freeze assets, you will need to hire an attorney. See Chapter 15 for how to hire an attorney.

2. Dividing Real Estate

If you and your spouse own a house as property of the marriage, you will need to take several important items of information into account before dividing it. Issues such as tax liability, the condition of the house, any separate property contributions that one spouse made to the house and the importance of the house to any children of the marriage need to be carefully considered before deciding what to do with a marital house.

To fully understand these and other issues involved in dividing real property in a divorce, read *Divorce and Money* by Violet Woodhouse and Victoria F. Collins (Nolo Press), or see an attorney or other professional such as a real estate broker or an accountant. Below, we'll briefly look at the most common ways divorcing couples deal with the family home.

a. Sell home—Divide equity equally

Most freqently, divorcing couples settle the division of the house by selling it and dividing the equity equally. Equity is what is left after the costs of sale, mortgages and other debts against the house are deducted from the sale price.

Figuring Equity: An Example

House value	$110,000.
mortgage	-60,000.
costs of sale and broker's commission	-10,000.
equity =	$ 40,000.

In the above example, the couple would each take $20,000, which is half the total equity of their house.

b. Sell home—Divide equity unequally

Sometimes it would not be fair to divide equity in a home equally. For example, if one spouse's separate property had been used for the downpayment, or to improve the house, or if one spouse had owned the house before the marriage, fairness would dictate that

that spouse should receive a larger share of the equity, or at least get reimbursed for his or her contribution.

Whenever you are dividing real estate, check with a tax professional—or read *Divorce and Money* (Nolo Press)—on the consequences of the division. It's particularly important to understand that taxes will be owed on any profit you make from selling real estate unless certain criteria are met, such as buying another house within two years. Sometimes it may make more sense to wait to sell the house in order to minimize the tax liability incurred by the sale. For instance, if you or the other spouse will soon turn 55, you will be entitled to a one-time capital gains exemption on the sale of your home. So in that case you would wait until the magic year is reached.

c. Hold on to the home

If you or the other spouse want to keep the home—perhaps because the real estate market is weak or because it would be best for your children—there are several ways you might proceed. Depending on how much equity there is in the home, one spouse may wish to:

- buy out the other spouse by swapping other marital property for the other spouse's interest in the house;

- take out a home equity loan to pay off the other spouse;

- refinance the home and use part of the proceeds to buy out the other spouse; or

- defer the sale until a later time, such as two years from date of your divorce decree, or upon your youngest child reaching the age of 18.

d. Protecting yourself against a bankruptcy filing

If your spouse agrees to pay you for your share of the house and then files for bankruptcy, your spouse could end up with the house and you with nothing. This is because bankruptcy discharges (gets rid of) certain categories of debt, which can include debts owed by one spouse to the other as the result of a divorce.

While bankruptcy laws do not allow someone to escape child support or alimony obligations, other obligations such as those arising from property division at divorce may be discharged unless the judge is persuaded to rule differently. To make absolutely sure that your spouse's later bankruptcy won't interfere with your right to receive payments for your share of the house, you can either:

- keep your name on the deed until you have been paid in full, or

- before your divorce is final, have your spouse sign a trust deed in your favor to secure the obligation.

A trust deed is a transfer of legal title (ownership) of a property to a trustee as security for the performance of certain obligations, such as paying debts. A bank or other entity must be named as trustee to ensure the deed's validity. You can obtain a trust deed on your own, without a lawyer. Standard forms for trust deeds are available in stationary stores. After having your spouse sign it, record it at the recorder's office in the county where the property is located. The trust deed gives you what's known as a lien on the property, and even if your husband files for bankruptcy, your lien will survive and entitle you to foreclose against the property after the bankruptcy is finished or, if you can wait, get paid when the property is ultimately sold.

Be Realistic

Remember, you and your spouse will each have to cover expenses that the two of you used to cover together: utility bills, phone bills, house or rent payments, food budgets, etc. Keeping the house if it took two incomes to afford it in the first place may not be practical or even possible.

Example: Gigi and Franklin have a gorgeous house in the West Hills. He works as a stock broker and she owns an art gallery. They want to keep the house so Gigi and the children can continue to live there, but they realize it just isn't possible. The art business has its ups and downs and doesn't provide an entirely reliable income. Even with help from Franklin, the house payments and other expenses of keeping the house will be more than Gigi can afford. They decide to sell the house and divide the equity.

If you and your spouse own more than one piece of real estate, the division of the property is too complex to explain in this book. If you have multiple real estate holdings, you should see an attorney, as well as a tax preparer or CPA to help you with the tax ramifications. See Chapter 15 for how to hire an attorney.

C. Dividing Debts of the Marriage

When filing for divorce you must divide the debts of the marriage as well as the property. Just like property, any debts you have accumulated during your marriage will be debts either in your name alone, your spouse's name alone or in both of your names jointly. It will be helpful when dividing the debts to first determine which category they fall into: yours, mine or ours.

1. Determining Which Debts Are Marital Debts

Except for family purchases and medical bills (see Subsection b below), you are liable only for debts incurred in your name. You both are responsible for any debts incurred in both your names as well as for family medical bills and family purchases.

Creditors' Rights

Regardless of how you and your spouse divide your debts, your divorce does not change any agreements with creditors. This means that despite whatever payment arrangements are made as part of the divorce, you are still liable for any debts in your name. Any debts in both your and your spouse's names will continue to be the responsibility of both of you, and both of you will be liable for the whole amount. For instance, if you list in your divorce papers that you and your spouse will each pay one-half of a joint debt, that does not mean that you are liable only to the creditor for that half. If your spouse defaults on the debt, the creditor can come to you for payment of the whole amount and list damaging information on both of your credit reports.

a. Separately owned debts

A debt is generally separately owned if it is held only in one name, even if that debt was incurred after the marriage. Credit cards held in only one name (provided that the other spouse does not have charging privileges), student loans, personal loans, lines of credit and car loans, for example, all can be and often are separately owned. The exception to this rule is when the debt arises from family medical bills or family purchases. These types of debts are discussed below.

b. Marital debts

Any debts incurred in both spouses' names are considered to be debts of the marriage. Credit cards, home or car loans in both names, for example, would be considered marital debts and both spouses would be liable for paying the balances.

In addition, debts arising from family medical bills or family purchases are considered to be marital debts, *even if they are in only one spouse's name.* In Oregon you have a duty to care for your immediate family's medical needs. You can be held financially liable for your spouse's and your children's medical bills even if your name does not appear on them. Similarly, married couples in Oregon are jointly liable for all family purchases. Examples of family purchases include home furniture, appliances or family dinners at restaurants. So, for instance, if one spouse could not get a credit card and all family purchases were made on the other spouse's credit, both spouses—not just the one with the credit card—would be liable.

If you and your spouse disagree over whether certain debts are separate or joint, you should see an attorney.

2. Dividing Marital Debts

Once you have determined which debts are marital debts, the next step is to divide them between you and your spouse. If you and your spouse are able to agree on how to divide your debts, the court is very unlikely to intervene unless the arrangement is obviously unfair to one person, or if the judge suspects that a spouse has been coerced into the agreement.

When dividing debts of the marriage, you will probably end up with one of the following arrangements:

a. Paying off the debts

This is a feasible option when there is a house, significant assets, stocks or deposit accounts which can be sold for cash.

b. Refinancing the debts

In some cases you can refinance a debt in order to remove your or your spouse's liability for it. This is a good option, for example, when one spouse agrees to pay off a debt that has the other spouse's name on it.

Example: *While married, Bob and Donna jointly got a loan to buy a new car. Now that they are divorcing, Donna agrees to take over the payments and will keep the car for herself. Bob wants to buy his own car, but his liability for the first car is preventing him from getting another loan. Donna gets a new loan in her own name and uses it to pay off the old loan so that Bob is no longer liable for her car.*

c. Dividing responsibility for the debts

You and your spouse can make an agreement as to which debts will be paid by each of you. For instance, the spouse with the higher income may agree to pay all or most of the joint debts in exchange for the other spouse receiving less property.

3. Enforcing Marital Debt Repayment Agreements

Even if you and the other spouse agree on how your debts are to be paid, there is still the issue of what happens if your ex-spouse fails to deliver. One way to protect yourself in the case that your ex-spouse does fail to pay his or her promised share of debts is to obtain a judgment against the spouse as part of your divorce. A judgment constitutes a final order by the court that the judgment debtor (the person who owes the debt in the judgment) is indebted to the other person (the judgment creditor) for the amount of the judgment. If the judgment debtor fails to honor his or her commitment to pay all or a portion of the marital debts—thereby leaving the judgment creditor on the hook to the marital debt creditors—the judgment allows the judgment creditor to be reimbursed from the judgment debtor's assets and income (subject to limitations on judgment collection imposed on judgment creditors by Oregon law).

Example: *Tony filed for divorce and included a money judgment against Annette for $5,000, consisting of:*

- *$3,000, which he and Annette borrowed from her mother and which Annette agreed to repay,*
- *$1,000 owed to a dentist for work on Annette's teeth, and*
- *$1,000 to Sears for payment on their joint account.*

Tony agreed to pay the other joint credit card debt and a hospital bill totaling $5,000. The reason for the judgment is that Annette's track record for taking care of her debts has not been good. Sure enough, Tony ends up paying Annette's bills. But because he has a money judgment against her for that amount, he can collect the money from her without going back to court (assuming he can find property to collect against).

Chapter 11 tells you exactly what to put in your divorce papers to obtain a judgment as part of your divorce.

Effect of Judgment on Credit

Although the judgment is a good way to protect yourself against the possibility of the other spouse not paying his or her share of the marital debt, it will show up on the other spouse's credit record, most likely impacting that spouse's credit rating. In some cases this won't be a major factor in the other spouse's ability to meet his or her obligations under the divorce decree. However, if the other spouse depends on his or her good credit to run a business or otherwise remain solvent, you might be shooting yourself in the foot by including the judgment in your divorce. Simply put, the more your ex-spouse needs good credit to comply with the divorce decree, the less desirable a judgment is.

If your ex-spouse files for bankruptcy after the divorce, it's likely that you will be on the hook for the entire marital debt. Also, you probably won't be able to go after your ex-spouse for reimbursement unless you file a petition in the bankruptcy court asking the judge to exempt the obligation from the bankruptcy. If bankruptcy becomes an issue in your case, see a lawyer. (Hiring a lawyer is covered in Chapter 15.)

Unfortunately, divorce and bankruptcy often go hand in hand. If you and your spouse are deeply in debt, filing bankruptcy together before you file for divorce may be a strategy for dealing with the debts. For additional information read *How to File for Bankruptcy*, Nolo Press. ∎

Child Custody and Visitation

A. Do Your Best to Reach Agreement	8/2
1. The Mediation Option	8/3
2. If You Just Can't Agree	8/3
3. What It Means to Be a Non-Custodial Parent	8/3
B. Identifying Marital Children	8/4
C. Making Custody and Visitation Arrangements	8/5
1. Determining Custody	8/5
2. Understanding Visitation	8/7
D. Putting Your Agreement in Writing	8/8

If you have any children of the marriage who are still minors, it is very important to understand the material in this chapter. Oregon defines a minor as anyone who is under age 18, or is under 21 and a "child attending school," defined in Oregon as being enrolled at least half-time plus one credit. If you don't have minor marital children, then you can skip to Chapter 10.

Deciding who will have custody (who the children will live with) and when the other parent can visit the marital children are the issues most likely to cause a divorce to be contested and the parents' pocketbooks to be drained in lengthy court battles. This is both unfortunate and unnecessary—unfortunate in that the children are almost always the losers when the parents fight in court, and unnecessary in that there are many tools available to help parents resolve their disagreements and cooperate sufficiently to provide the children with a stable and healthy post-divorce relationship with both parents.

This chapter will discuss the issues you will need to consider and the decisions you will have to make in arriving at custody and visitation arrangements for your children. As with the rest of this book, this chapter addresses the set of issues involved in an uncontested divorce—if you and your spouse are not in agreement on child custody or visitation, you will need to seek additional help outside this book. If you and your spouse cooperate, you can use this chapter to prepare you for the tasks involved in arriving at a custody and visitation arrangement and having it included in your divorce decree.

The Costs of Courtroom Battles

In addition to benefiting your children, reaching agreement on the children issues—custody, visitation and support—is good for your economic health as well. If you want to fight about any of these issues, you'll most likely need an attorney to represent you in court, at considerable expense.

A. Do Your Best to Reach Agreement

If you reach an agreement on custody and visitation, the court usually will abide by your decision. Judges seldom interfere with custody matters in uncontested divorces. As we repeatedly stress, it is far better for your family to agree on this issue than to fight it out in court. If a fight seems inevitable now, allow some time to pass before entering into a heated custody battle; time can sometimes heal the worst of emotional wounds and may help you focus on the needs of the children.

Turning a Contested Divorce Back Into an Uncontested One

If a dispute over the children caused your divorce to become contested, but you later reached an agreement (on your own or after mediation)—your divorce can become uncontested again and you will be able to proceed with the help of this book. See Chapter 4, Section J, for more information on stipulated decrees, and Chapters 12 and 13 on filling out and filing them.

1. The Mediation Option

In some cases, it may not be practical to wait to file your papers until things have cooled off—perhaps your spouse is abusive or you need a temporary order for child support. In those situations, mediation may be the answer. If you haven't already read Chapter 6, do so now if you see a custody or visitation fight looming in your future.

If your situation is highly volatile, you may be better off seeing an attorney to help you file for a restraining order or for temporary custody. Ultimately you will have to be the judge of how much help you need and when you need it, but if you have a choice in the matter you should never risk your safety or that of your children just to save the cost of legal fees. (See Chapter 15 for information on hiring an attorney.)

2. If You Just Can't Agree

If mediation fails and you and your spouse cannot reach an agreement about your children on your own, you will have to present your case in court in front of a judge. For that, we recommend an attorney. Read about hiring attorneys in Chapter 15.

Why Court Doesn't Work For Custody Disputes

Courtroom custody battles can be complicated and highly adversarial, as each parent tries to prove that he or she is the better parent, or that the other parent is unfit. Once a custody dispute reaches the stage of litigation, both parents lose a great deal of control over the outcome. Custody and visitation arrangements will be decided by a judge, based on what the judge—not you or your spouse—thinks is in the best interest of the children. Unsurprisingly, parents often disagree with judges as to what is in their children's best interest. We can't stress it enough: You and your children will be far better off if you reach an agreement with your spouse rather than putting the question to a judge to decide.

3. What It Means to Be a Non-Custodial Parent

Many people fight tooth-and-nail for custody because they believe that as non-custodial parents, they will literally lose their children. Fortunately, this is rarely true. Except in some cases where domestic, child or substance abuse is involved, Oregon law favors any arrangement that allows both parents to maintain a strong relationship with their children. If you and your spouse are cooperating on custody issues, you can define the scope and frequency of the non-custodial parent's visitation with or without the help of mediation or by using the book *Child Support: Building Parenting Agreements That Work* by Mimi Lyster (Nolo Press).

Also, both custodial and non-custodial parents have certain rights regarding their children (ORS 107.154). These include the right to:

- inspect and receive school records, and to consult with school staff concerning the children's welfare and education.

- inspect and receive governmental agency and law enforcement records for the children.
- consult with any healthcare provider, and to inspect and receive medical, dental and psychological records.
- authorize emergency medical, dental, psychological, psychiatric or other health care for the children if the custodial parent is, for all practical purposes, unavailable.
- apply to be the children's guardian ad litem, conservator or both in a court.

B. Identifying Marital Children

A divorcing couple must reach custody and visitation agreements only for what the court calls children of the marriage, or marital children. If a divorcing couple has children living with them but these children do not qualify as children of the marriage, then custody, visitation and support agreements are not necessary. So the first question to consider in dealing with any children during divorce is whether they are children of the marriage.

Generally speaking, if your children were born during the marriage they are legally presumed to be children of the marriage. If your children were born before you married, but both parents completed and filed a Joint Affidavit of Paternity with the state, the children will be considered marital children. By filing a Joint Affidavit of Paternity, the father's name will be added to the birth certificate. You can file the affidavit either before or after you marry the child's other parent. If you need to file a Joint Affidavit of Paternity, call the Oregon State Health Division, Vital Records Unit, to obtain the form.

Example: *Sam and Rissa were not married when they had baby Joey. When Joey was a few months old, Sam and Rissa married. Then they filed a Joint Affidavit of Paternity to add Sam's name to the birth certificate. Joey is a child of the marriage.*

Example: *Meg and Hayden had baby Theresa before they got married. At the time of Theresa's birth they signed a Joint Affividavit of Paternity, so that Hayden's name appeared on the birth certificate when it was first issued. Meg and Hayden married each other a year later. Theresa is a child of the marriage.*

If your children were born during your marriage, but your husband is not the father of the children, the children are not children of the marriage. However, unless you name the biological father in your divorce papers the court will presume that your husband is the father and that the children are marital children.

Marital children do not always need to be the biological children of you and your spouse. If you and your spouse adopted children during your marriage, these children are children of the marriage. Or if one spouse had biological children with a different parent, and the current spouse legally adopted these children (a stepparent adoption), then the children are marital children.

Example: *Suko had Jimmy before she married David. Once Suko and David were married, David adopted Jimmy. Jimmy is a child of the marriage.*

If the wife is pregnant at the time of the divorce and the husband is the father of the child, that child will be considered a child of the marriage and should be included in all provisions for the children. Unless declared otherwise, the husband is presumed to be the father. If the husband is not the father, the child (once born) will not be a child of the marriage. In that case, the biological father should be listed in your divorce papers to give the court notice that the husband is not the father. (More detailed instructions are included in the forms section.)

Now that we've looked at what makes a child a child of the marriage, consider the question from the other side. A child is not of the marriage if all of the following are true:

- the child was not born during the marriage,
- the child was not adopted during the marriage, and

- the child was not acknowledged by the father with a Joint Affidavit of Paternity.

Example: *Karin had a daughter, Megan, before she met Steven. A few years later, Karin met and married Steven. Steven never adopted Megan. Megan is not a child of the marriage.*

If there are minor children by a father other than the husband, or if a divorcing wife is pregnant and the husband is not the father, see an attorney. (See Chapter 15 on hiring attorneys.)

C. Making Custody and Visitation Arrangements

Here we briefly address the basic options available under Oregon law for child custody and visitation arrangements. Most often, divorcing parents in Oregon agree that one parent will have sole custody while the other parent will have visitation rights. Even in the standard sole custody/visitation model, however, there can be a broad range of visitation schedules or other specific arrangements. Keep in mind that there are many different ways you and your spouse can raise your children while living in separate households.

1. Determining Custody

At its basic level, custody of a child means the right to care for and control that child. Included in this concept is the right to make major decisions affecting the child such as choosing a school or making medical treatment decisions. One parent can have sole custody, custody may be shared jointly or, if there are multiple children, custody can be split between the parents.

a. Sole custody

When the right of control over a child is given to one parent, that parent is said to have sole custody of the child and is referred to as the custodial parent. It's definitely the right of control that's important, not the amount of time the children spend with the custodial parent, although most often the children live predominantly with the custodial parent and are visited at regular intervals by the non-custodial parent. More specifically, the custodial parent is responsible for the day-to-day care of the children and enjoys ultimate decision-making authority, including choosing a school or childcare provider, making medical treatment decisions and arranging for the child's religious education. The most common visitation schedule for a non-custodial parent is alternate weekends and alternate holidays.

> **Is There a Preference for Mothers?**
>
> Some people think that judges deciding custody disputes are biased in favor of mothers. Oregon laws (ORS 107.137), however, state that no preference shall be given to the mother over the father only because she is the mother. This being said, the younger the child, the more likely it is that custody will be given to the mother.

b. Joint custody

As its name implies, in joint custody arrangements each parent shares some of the custodial rights and responsibilities. There are two types of joint custody: joint legal custody and joint physical custody.

- Joint physical custody and joint legal custody

If you share joint legal custody with your ex-spouse, you both will have an equal say in major decisions regarding the upbringing of the children, including their education, health care and religious instruction.

If you share joint physical custody with your ex-spouse, your children will spend a significant amount of time with each of you, and each of you will control the children when they are with you. Joint physical custody obviously requires close cooperation between parents, and courts are often unwilling to grant it unless the circumstances indicate that the parents are capable of such cooperation. One such circumstance is the ability of the parents to agree on all child-related issues. And so, if you and the other parent are able to accomplish an uncontested divorce (which means you have reached agreement on all important issues), the court is unlikely to intervene if you opt for joint physical custody.

Example: *Jose and Marie live in different states. Under their joint physical and joint legal custody agreement, the children spend eight months with Jose and four months with Marie. Jose and Marie communicate well and share all important school, medical and health decisions. Day-to-day child-rearing decisions are made by the parent with whom the children are living at that time.*

Example: *Kieko and Jim live in the same city. They have two children, Tori, age nine, and Aubrey, age 15. Under the joint legal and joint physical custody agreement, both children spend Sunday through Wednesday evening with Kieko, and Thursday through Saturday nights with Jim. The parents continue to jointly parent as they did before the divorce, consulting each other on all important decisions and making sure that their day-to-day child-rearing decisions are consistently enforced in their respective households.*

- Joint legal custody and sole physical custody

Probably the most common joint custody arrangement is where one parent has sole physical custody and both parents share joint legal custody. This means that one parent—the custodial parent—raises the children while the other parent visits them, but the non-custodial parent shares in major decision-making about the children's health, education and welfare.

Example: *LeRoy and Tanya live with their mother Donna and spend one night during the week and one day and night during the weekend with their father, John. John also gets the kids every other Christmas, Easter and Fourth of July. Donna consults with John about all major decisions involving the children.*

c. Split custody

If you have more than one child, you can have a split custody arrangement in which each parent has sole custody of at least one child. It is also possible to have split physical custody with joint legal custody in both parents. Each parent has visitation with the children not in his or her custody. Visitation is often arranged so the siblings can spend time together. There are a number of reasons why a split custody arrangement might be best for a family: for instance, if one parent cannot support all the children, even with child support from the other parent, a split custody arrangement might be financially easier to manage. Sometimes older children wish to live with one parent, say the father, but the younger siblings want to stay with the mother.

Example: *Sue and George have three children: Justin, Jason and Annette. Justin and Jason, 15-year-old twin boys, live with their father. Annette—age 6—lives with her mother. Neither parent could afford a house large enough for all the children, and Jason needs his father who he has always been closest to. All the children spend weekends and holidays together.*

Most experts believe that children are better off living together than apart. For that reason, split custody is relatively rare and not to be encouraged. However, in some cases it remains the best remedy.

2. Understanding Visitation

As stressed earlier, the courts want both you and your spouse to maintain as strong a relationship with the children as possible under the circumstances. For this reason, visitation is routinely granted to the non-custodial parent in a traditional sole custody arrangement. If you and your spouse agree upon some kind of visitation schedule, the court will almost never intervene in your arrangement. Visitation can vary with what you and the other parent want and what your schedules will allow.

Examples of Visitation Arrangements

- Frank and Michelle live in the same neighborhood. The children spend the after-school and evening hours with Frank, then go to Michelle's house for the night.

- Jaime and Anita live in different states. Their children live with Jaime in Oregon. Anita has visitation for six weeks of summer and two weeks at Christmas with the children.

- Rebecca and Richard live in neighboring towns. The children spend every other weekend and every other holiday with Rebecca, and live with Richard. This is often called "standard visitation."

When working out a custody and visitation arrangement—sometimes called a parenting plan—with your spouse, you may find that outlining a visitation schedule can be complicated. This is not to say that visitation arrangements are particularly difficult to make, but there are many details to consider, such as what time of day the children will visit, who will drive the children back and forth, who will pay for gas or how the children will get to school.

Since many visitation arrangements contain many small but important details, many divorcing couples choose to draft parenting plan agreements that specifically outline visitation schedules and all other particulars. Drafting a detailed parenting plan is a good way to avoid the conflicts that often arise regarding visitation. The more specific a visitation agreement is, the more enforceable it will be. Section D below discusses the various ways you can approach drafting a parenting plan agreement.

There are a number of issues to consider when making visitation arrangements.

a. Needs of the child

If a parent has not regularly taken care of a child overnight, changed a young child's diapers, given a child baths or prepared meals for the child, you might want to limit visits accordingly. You could have the child visit the non-custodial parent during daytime only, for instance, when meals and diapers will be less of an issue. If the child is a nursing baby, visitation may be limited to short periods to fit a feeding schedule. And don't forget: Children grow, and their needs change. See the section below on anticipating changing circumstances in your visitation arrangement.

b. Costs of travel for visitation

If you live far away from the other parent, visitation costs can be expensive. The cost of visitation is not figured into the child support formula. If travel costs will be high, be sure to explain in your visitation agreement how these costs will be met.

c. Transportation to and from visitation

When discussing or deciding visitation schedules be sure to include who will be responsible for picking up and delivering the children for visitation.

d. Dealing with future changed circumstances

A visitation agreement might work well right after it was written, but may fail to change and grow along with your family. Even a once amicable arrangement can become strained. The addition of stepparents into your children's lives, or one parent moving to a distant city, are two of the most common reasons for your visitation agreements to become strained or disputed. One strategy for dealing with change is to include a mediation clause (see below). Another is to make sure that your agreement is written specifically and clearly—the more specific the agreement, the more enforceable it is.

e. Mediation clauses

You may wish to include a mediation clause to resolve conflicts with your spouse without resorting to court. It is becoming common to see such clauses in contracts, divorce, employment and labor agreements.

Example: *Joanne and Paul were in complete agreement on all the issues in their divorce. And even though they were still friends they knew things could change. Just in case they couldn't agree in the future they included an agreement to try mediation before asking the court to step in. They used the following language: "The parties will attempt to work together to avoid any further disputes. Should any dispute arise that cannot be resolved we agree to mediate the dispute with a mutually agreed-upon mediator. The cost of mediation shall be shared equally."*

See Chapter 6 for more information about mediation.

D. Putting Your Agreement in Writing

The divorce petition and decree will ask you to describe the arrangements you have agreed upon for custody and visitation. You can either enter this information on the petition and decree, or you can put it into a separate written agreement that can be included with the divorce papers as an attachment. Since custody and visitation matters are often complicated, many people choose to use written agreements so the arrangements can be described in detail—including the days, dates and times of visits, the exact location to pick up and drop off the children and the responsibility for expenses incurred during visits, for example.

If you choose to use a written custody and visitation agreement to attach to the divorce papers, there are a number of ways to proceed. You and your spouse could draft a written agreement on your own. The book *Child Custody: Building Agreements That Work* is an excellent guide to drafting custody and visitation agreements. Another option is to use a standard parenting time agreement if its provisions were acceptable to both of you. In the forms section of this book, you'll find a number of visitation schedules that you can include with your divorce paperwork. Finally, if you attend mediation to help you resolve conflicts over the children, a mediation settlement agreement can be used as the document describing your custody and visitation arrangements (assuming that such an agreement was reached in mediation). With any of these written agreements, be sure to include them with your divorce papers and write "See attached" in any blanks asking for custody and visitation information. (For more information on attachments, see Chapter 10, Section B, below.) ■

Child Support—What It Is, How It's Computed

A. Requesting Child Support	9/2
B. Determining Who Will Pay Child Support	9/2
C. Deviating From the Statutory Guidelines	9/3
D. Expenses Included in Child Support Calculations	9/3
1. Health Insurance	9/3
2. Child Care Expenses	9/4
3. Private School	9/4
4. Higher Education Expenses	9/4
E. Encountering Problems With Child Support Arrangements	9/4
1. Legitimate Reasons for Not Paying Full Child Support	9/5
2. Non-Legitimate Reasons for Not Paying Full Child Support	9/5
3. Enforcing Child Support Obligations	9/5
F. Before You Fill Out the Child Support Worksheets	9/6
1. Getting Help in Calculating Child Support	9/6
2. Obtaining Current Statutory Guidelines	9/6
3. Which Worksheets to Fill Out	9/6
G. Instructions for Completing the Child Support Worksheets	9/7
1. Compute Your Gross Monthly Income	9/7
2. Worksheet A (Nonjoint Child Credit Computation)	9/10
3. Worksheet B (Support Calculation—Regular Custody)	9/12
4. Worksheet C (Support Calculation—Split Custody)	9/15
5. Worksheet D (Support Calculation—Shared Custody)	9/18
6. Worksheet E (Support Computation—Child Care Credit)	9/21

Both you and your spouse are required to support your minor children after you divorce. One of you will be paying some support to the other. Who this is and the amount that he or she will have to pay will depend on your custody arrangements. (See Section B below.)

Child support is paid until a child is 18 years old. It may continue past that age if the child attends school more than half-time. If this requirement is met, child support continues until age 21 (ORS 107.108).

Oregon's divorce laws contain child support guidelines that determine how much child support must be paid. The guidelines are based on:

- what the state has figured it costs to raise a child at various income levels, and
- what type of custody arrangement you enter into.

In establishing these guidelines, the state has included allowances for shelter, utilities, food, clothing, public school expenses, transportation and other necessities. All divorcing parents must use these guidelines when filling out child support worksheets to determine how much child support will be paid.

This chapter will explain when and how to request child support, how to handle child support problems and how to deal with the state guidelines when figuring out a support amount that works for your family. The guidelines and the worksheets are included in the forms section of this book, and this chapter contains step-by-step instructions on how to use them.

A. Requesting Child Support

If you have minor children, you must request child support in your divorce Petition and fill out the child support worksheets to arrive at a support amount. This is true no matter what custody arrangements you plan to have. Although support is usually paid by a non-custodial parent to a parent with sole physical custody, that is not the only situation that requires child support to be paid. If you and your spouse will have joint or split custody, you still must request child support and use the worksheets to arrive at an amount.

If child support is requested and ordered, failure to pay the support will result in an arrearage. This arrearage is a debt that can be collected on for many years into the future—plus interest—even if the parent to receive the support agrees not to require its payment. This means that the spouse obligated to pay support under the guidelines should plan on paying the amount of support requested in the Petition.

In rare situations it is possible to request little or no support in the Petition. See Section C below.

B. Determining Who Will Pay Child Support

When one parent has sole physical custody of the children, the other parent must provide financial support. The support obligation of the custodial parent is considered to be taken care of by the custody itself.

In shared custody situations (also known as joint custody), child support is usually paid by the parent with the higher income, though the amount of time each parent spends with the children may also be a determining factor. Generally, the more time a parent spends with the children the less that parent is obliged to pay in financial support.

If custody of the children has been split between the parents, the varying custody roles of each parent will be taken into account, and one parent will end up paying the other parent an amount of support determined by the guidelines for split custody situations.

If you haven't yet figured out what custody arrangement you will have for your minor children, read Chapter 8. You will first need to determine what your custody arrangements will be before you can compute the amount of child support that one of you will have to pay to the other.

C. Deviating From the Statutory Guidelines

In some instances, you can agree with your spouse to a different amount of child support than the formula provides. The legal term for this is called "rebutting the presumption of support." If, for instance, the custodial parent has a significantly higher income than the non-custodial parent, the parents may agree that it is unnecessary for the non-custodial parent to pay the amount set by the state guidelines. The courts do not look favorably on child support arrangements that deviate from the state guidelines. If you wish to deviate from the guidelines, see an attorney or independent paralegal for assistance. See Chapter 15 for information on hiring an attorney.

D. Expenses Included in Child Support Calculations

Raising children involves many different types of expenses. In calculating your child support amount, some expenses are automatically accounted for at a standard level determined by the state, others must be calculated according to your individual expenses and others are optional.

Oregon's child support guidelines are based on a formula that accounts for a standard level of basic living expenses such as food, clothing, public school expenses and rent or mortgages. For these basic expenses, the guidelines use the same formula for everybody—with adjustments for different income levels—based upon what the state has determined is reasonable. In other words, the guidelines presume that everybody at a certain income level will have the same basic living expenses.

Other expenses such as health insurance and child care costs must also be included in your child support calculation, but unlike basic living expenses, the state has not determined a standard level for all parents. Instead, these costs are figured in at the level that the parents actually pay. The child support worksheets require you to enter these costs in figuring your child support amount.

Finally, some expenses such as tuition for college or private school are optional for parents to pay. If the parent paying child support agrees to help with optional child support expenses, this agreement should be included in the "Other Provisions" section of the divorce Petition and Decree, and possibly in the money judgment section of the Decree. Optional expenses are not included in the child support worksheets.

1. Health Insurance

All minor children of divorcing parents must be covered by health insurance, either on the parent's employer-provided policy or, if neither parent has employer-provided insurance, on a policy purchased for the children. The child support worksheets require you to figure a monthly insurance expense into the calculation. Whichever parent carries the children on their insurance policy or pays for a policy for the children is entitled to a credit against child support.

For example, if the custodial parent carries the children's insurance, then the other parent must include a portion of the expense of the insurance in their child support payment. If the non-custodial parent carries the insurance, he or she can subtract a portion of the insurance expense from their child support payment. Just how much is added or subtracted depends on the relative incomes of the parents. The actual formula and worksheets are included in Section G below.

Example: *Kevin has health insurance available through his work, and has his children added to his policy. Kevin also pays child support to the children's mother, Stacey. Having his two children covered costs Kevin an additional $75 per month which is deducted from his paycheck. Kevin is entitled to a reduction of his monthly child support payment by a portion of the $75. The amount of the credit is determined by a formula which compares his income to Stacey's income. (This formula is covered in the instructions for the child support worksheets, below.)*

2. Child Care Expenses

If a custodial parent is employed or is looking for work, daycare costs for the children must be included in the child support calculation. The child support worksheets include a form for calculating child care costs, which are then figured into the child support calculation.

Example: *Scott and Laura's children live with Laura, who works part-time. The children spend four hours a day at daycare while Laura is at work. When figuring out the amount of child support Scott must pay, they must fill out Child Support Worksheet E to determine the monthly child care costs that must be covered. This amount is then figured into the general child support formula to arrive at a monthly amount for Scott to pay.*

3. Private School

Parents are not obligated to pay for private school for their children. If you choose to, however, you and your spouse can agree to the payment of additional funds for private school tuition and other school expenses. If the parent paying child support does agree to help with private school expenses, this agreement should be included in the "Other Provisions" section of the Petition and Decree. If the receiving parent is concerned that the other parent will not live up to this agreement, he or she can include a money judgment for the agreed-upon amount in the "Judgments" section of the Decree.

Example: *Lee and Jenny have a child, Sasha, who attends private school. They agree that Lee will continue to pay for Sasha's tuition and Jenny will cover other school expenses such as books, activities and sports. They include this agreement in writing in the "Other Provisions" section of their divorce Petition and Decree. Jenny trusts that Lee will honor this agreement so she does not include a money judgment for the private school payments.*

4. Higher Education Expenses

Parents are not required to pay for their children's education beyond high school. If the parent paying support is willing to help pay for your child's college or vocational school expenses, you may include such an agreement in the "Other Provisions" section of the Petition and Decree. (See next chapter for instructions in filling out the Petition and Decree.) A judgment may also be included in the Decree to ensure the agreement can be enforced.

E. Encountering Problems With Child Support Arrangements

Unfortunately, child support is often a highly contentious issue between divorced parents, particularly when payments fall behind or stop coming altogether. Sometimes a parent who owes child support has a valid rea-

son for not paying the full amount of support ordered by the court, such as if he or she was laid off from work or suffered a serious illness. Many other times, however, the failure to pay support is unjustified.

Interference or denial of your visitation rights is not a legitimate reason for you to withhold child support payments. If your ex-spouse is not complying with your visitation agreement, there are other ways to enforce your rights. (See Section E3 below.) Failing to pay child support in this situation is often viewed harshly by judges.

1. Legitimate Reasons for Not Paying Full Child Support

If the person who owes child support suffers some circumstance that makes child support payments difficult or impossible, he or she may be able to have the support order modified. Examples of reasons to lower support that courts and the State Child Support Enforcement Division may accept are job loss, injury or serious illness. An owing parent who suffers this type of problem and is thus unable to continue making child support payments must take immediate action to modify the child support order. Modifications can be made on a temporary or permanent basis, depending on the situation. If the order is not modified and payments fall behind, the child support debt (called arrearages) will accumulate and cannot be retroactively reduced.

Example: *Tamara was paying $500 per month for child support when she lost her job. She could not find a job with a comparable rate of pay until six months later. Tamara did not ask the court for a temporary reduction in her child support obligation on the grounds of diminished income, and let her payments slide for the six months she was unemployed. Her ex-husband Joe was automatically awarded a judgment for $3,000 she owed plus interest. Since arrearages cannot be retroactively reduced, Tamara will have to pay the arrearages plus interest, even though she can show that she was unable to pay during her unemployment.*

Modifying court orders—including child support orders—after your divorce is final is covered briefly in Chapter 14. For the most part, however, modifications of divorce orders are not covered in this book. If you wish to modify your child support order after your divorce is final, read Chapter 14 and see an attorney. If child support is being collected through Support Enforcement the payor must notify Support Enforcement and follow their procedures to request a reduction.

2. Non-Legitimate Reasons for Not Paying Full Child Support

Many parents who fail to meet their child support obligations do not have legitimate reasons for not paying child support. Simply claiming that they cannot afford the payments is not in itself a valid reason that the court will accept; as described above, there generally must be a drastic change in the parent's circumstances to justify their inability to pay. In the court's view, the support of his or her children is the parent's paramount responsibility, and trying to convince the court that the parent's other needs come first is an extremely hard sell. For example, an additional financial burden associated with the purchase of a new home or car would not be considered a valid reason for a parent to lower his or her child support obligation. However, if a parent incurred a medical expense for a procedure necessary to the parent's ability to work, the court would most likely be willing to provide some temporary relief.

3. Enforcing Child Support Obligations

If child support is not being paid according to the support order, there are several methods of collection available to the parent who should be receiving the support. One is to call the Child Support Enforcement Division located in each county's district attorney's office. Support Enforcement has the power to collect child support through wage withholding and seizure of tax returns. This agency can also penalize non-payers by revoking their driver's licenses as well as other professional licenses such as electricians', plumbers' or builders' licenses. Of course, it may be counter-productive for you to have your ex-spouse's licenses revoked if that results in his or her inability to work, earn money and thus pay child support.

Another option for collecting overdue child support is to hire an attorney, an independent paralegal or collection agent to collect the debt through wage or bank garnishment, asset seizure or liens on real property, inheritances, judgments and other assets.

F. Before You Fill Out the Child Support Worksheets

In the appendix of this book you will find a set of child support worksheets, A through E, and the statutory guidelines to use when filling them out. Before you begin, carefully tear out the child support worksheets and make at least one photocopy of each before you make any marks on them. You'll be glad to have an extra copy on hand in case you make any mistakes in filling them out. You may also want to tear out the statutory guidelines so that you can make reference to them more easily as you fill out the worksheets.

1. Getting Help in Calculating Child Support

If you have an open file with the State Office of Children and Families, the Oregon State Child Support Enforcement Division may be willing to do the calculations for you. Call 503-986-6090 or call your case worker.

If you can't get help from the state, be aware that most Oregon family law attorneys and some independent paralegals have computer programs that enable them to calculate child support at reasonable rates. One such attorney is Stuart Sugarman at 503-234-2694.

If you are not in a position to pay for assistance in computing your child support but don't trust your own math skills, ask a friend who is good at math to give you a hand.

2. Obtaining Current Statutory Guidelines

Statutory child support guidelines current for 1997 are included in this book. The guidelines are reviewed by the State of Oregon and are subject to revision every two years. For updated guidelines, you can call the central state Support Enforcement Division in Salem at 503-986-6090. The Support Enforcement Division also has offices within the district attorney's offices in each county. The family law division of your local county court may also be able to provide you with current guidelines if the ones in this book are no longer current.

3. Which Worksheets to Fill Out

You will fill out only the worksheets that apply to your situation.

- Worksheet A should be filled out if either spouse is legally obligated to pay child support for non-marital minor children or either spouse lives with his or her non-marital minor children. If each spouse has a non-marital minor child that he or she lives with or pays support for, then each spouse must fill out a separate Worksheet A. If only one spouse lives with or supports a non-marital minor child, only one Worksheet A needs to be completed. If you need to review the definition of marital versus non-marital children, see Chapter 8, Section B.

- Worksheet B should be filled out if one parent will have sole physical custody of the child or children.

- Worksheet C should be filled out if custody of the children will be split between the parents.

- Worksheet D should be filled out if the parents will have shared custody of the child or children. A child must spend at least 35% of his or her nights with each parent in order for the arrangement to be considered shared custody. (See Sidebar.)

Deciding Whether You Have Shared Custody

A custody arrangement will not be considered shared if one parent's overnight time with the children is less than 35%. In that event, for the purposes of the child support calculation the arrangement would be considered a sole physical custody situation and you would use Worksheet B.

You can figure the percentage of overnight time with each parent in a few different ways. If the custody schedule is on a weekly basis, such as spending Monday afternoon through Friday afternoon with one parent and the rest of the week with the other, you could calculate what percentage of days per week is spent with each parent. If four nights are spent with one parent, then divide four by seven (the number of days in one week). The result will be a decimal number less than one, .57. Decimal numbers convert to percentages by moving the decimal point two places to the right, which would convert .57 into 57%. Calculating for the other parent who spends three days a week with the children would show that parent's percentage of time with the children to be 43%. Since each parent's portion of overnight time is at least 35%, the arrangement would be considered shared custody for purposes of calculating child support.

If your custody schedule is on a different basis, you should calculate according to the most appropriate time period. If, for instance, the children will spend the school year (nine months) with one parent and the three summer months with the other, you could calculate the portion of months per year spent with each parent. For the parent who has the children during the school year, divide nine (the number of months spent) by 12 (the number of months per year) to arrive at 75%. The parent who has the children during the summer would have them for three months, so divide three by 12 to get 25%. In this situation, the custody arrangement could not be considered joint for purposes of calculating child support, because one parent has overnight custody of the children for less than 35% of the time.

- Worksheet E should be filled out if either parent pays for daycare of marital children.

NOTE: There are 365 days in one year.
There are 52 weeks in one year.
There are 12 months in one year.

G. Instructions for Completing the Child Support Worksheets

Use the following instructions for the worksheets that apply to your situation. Some of the instructions, such as how to compute your gross monthly income, apply to everybody, and some instructions are specific to each form.

1. Compute Your Gross Monthly Income

Whichever worksheets you use, you will need to know your gross monthly income. You should compute it before you begin filling out the worksheets. Gross monthly income is your total income per month—before deductions such as taxes or insurance premiums have been taken out—from all sources. Most people will have one source of income: their wages from work. There are several ways to determine your gross monthly income.

Hourly wage

To compute gross monthly income from your hourly wage:

Multiply your hourly wage by the number of hours worked each week (usually 40, which is full-time). This is your gross weekly income. Multiply your gross weekly income by 52, which is the number of weeks in one year. This is your gross yearly income. Then divide your gross yearly income by 12, which is the number of months in one year.

Example: Jana makes $12.00 per hour and works full-time. $12.00 per hour X 40 hours per week = $480 per week. $480 per week X 52 weeks per year = $24,960 per year. $24,960 per year / 12 months per year = $2,080 per month. Jana's gross monthly income is $2,080.

Weekly income

To compute gross monthly income from weekly income:

Multiply your gross weekly income (before deductions) by 52, which is the number of weeks in one year. This is your gross yearly income. Then divide your gross yearly income by 12, which is the number of months in one year.

Example: *James makes $260 per week before deductions. $260 per week X 52 weeks per year = $13,520 per year. $13,520 per year / 12 months per year = $1,126.66 per month. James' monthly gross income is $1,126.66.*

Biweekly income

To compute gross monthly income from a biweekly check (a check issued every two weeks):

Multiply the pre-deduction amount per check by 26, which is the number of two-week periods in a year. This is your gross yearly income. Then divide the gross yearly income by 12, which is the number of months in one year.

Example: *Jonas gets a paycheck every two weeks for $850, before deductions. $850 per two-week period X 26 two-week periods per year = $22,100 per year. $22,100 per year / 12 months per year = $1,841.66. Jonas's gross monthly income is $1,841.66.*

Twice-a-month income

To compute gross monthly income if two checks are received each month—say, on the 1st and 16th of each month—simply double the pre-deduction amount.

Example: *Ali gets a paycheck twice a month for $675, before deductions. $675 twice a month X 2 = $1,350 per month. Ali's gross monthly income is $1,350.*

Annual income

To compute gross monthly income from yearly income, divide the gross yearly salary (before deductions) by 12, which is the number of months in one year.

Example: *Colleen makes $42,000 a year. $42,000 per year / 12 months per year = $3,500 per month. Colleen's gross monthly income is $3,500.*

If you or your spouse have income besides your regular paychecks from work, you must include this income in your gross monthly income. For the purpose of the child support worksheets, income includes: salaries, wages, commissions, advances, payments, forgiven debts, bonuses, dividends, severance pay, pensions, interest, honoraria, trust income, annuities, return of capital, Social Security benefits, workers' compensation benefits, unemployment benefits, disability insurance benefits, gifts, prizes and other public assistance.

Since other income may not be received as regularly as paychecks, it can be trickier to figure out how much of it you receive each month. You can use the same general rules as explained above in converting your other income into a gross monthly income figure, and then add that figure to your gross monthly income from regular wages. For example, if in addition to your regular job pay you received a $1,200 bonus one year, you would divide that $1,200 by 12, the number of months in one year, to arrive at $100 per month in bonus pay. You would then add $100 to whatever figure you had arrived at for gross monthly income from regular pay. The total would be the figure to use in the worksheets.

The following worksheets are for you to use in calculating your and your spouse's gross monthly incomes. There is space for each of you to enter your financial information. (They are not part of the child support worksheets to submit to the court.)

Gross Monthly Income Worksheet
For your work only; not for filing with court

From hourly wage:
Amount paid per hour		_____
Number of hours worked each week (usually 40)	X	_____
(Gross weekly income—regular)	=	_____
Number of weeks per year	X	52
(Gross yearly income—regular)	=	_____
Number of months per year	/	12
(Gross monthly income—regular)	=	_____
Other gross monthly income	+	_____
(Total gross monthly income)	=	_____

From weekly income:
Amount paid per week (before deductions)		_____
Number of weeks per year	X	52
(Gross yearly income)	=	_____
Number of months per year	/	12
(Gross monthly income)	=	_____
Other gross monthly income	+	_____
(Total gross monthly income)	=	_____

From biweekly income (every two weeks):
Amount paid every two weeks (before deductions)		_____
Number of two-week periods per year	X	26
(Gross yearly income)	=	_____
Number of months per year	/	12
(Gross monthly income)	=	_____
Other gross monthly income	+	_____
(Total gross monthly income)	=	_____

From twice-a-month income:
Amount paid twice a month (before deductions)		_____
	X	2
(Gross monthly income)	=	_____
Other gross monthly income	+	_____
(Total gross monthly income)	=	_____

From yearly income:
Amount paid per year		_____
Number of months per year	/	12
(Gross monthly income)	=	_____
Other gross monthly income	+	_____
(Total gross monthly income)	=	

If neither you nor your spouse has any non-marital children, you can skip the instructions for Worksheet A.

2. Worksheet A (Nonjoint Child Credit Computation)

Use this form only if you or your spouse pay child support for non-marital children (children from a prior relationship, also called nonjoint children), or have non-marital children living in one or both of your households. If neither of you support or live with non-marital children, you do not need to complete this form.

If both you and your spouse either pay child support for or live with non-marital children, you will need to do one Worksheet A for yourself and one for your spouse. If only one of you supports or lives with non-joint children, only one Worksheet A needs to be completed.

- Leave the "Support Case No. _____" at the top of the page blank.

- Check the appropriate parent box. If you are filing as a sole Petitioner, check box "Parent 1" if this form is for yourself and check box "Parent 2" if this form is for your spouse. If you are filing together as co-petitioners, always use Parent 1 for one of you (the one who fills out the forms) and Parent 2 for the other. It is important to be consistent throughout the child support worksheet forms—that is, you should always be Parent 1 and your spouse should always be Parent 2.

Item 1: Fill in gross monthly income. (See Section G1 above to figure out gross monthly income.)

If Your Spouse is Uncooperative

If your spouse is uncooperative in providing financial information for the child support calculations, you can make estimated guesses as to these figures. For your husband's income, for example, base the estimate on how much he used to make, how much others in the industry make or on his tax return from the previous year. If your spouse does not contest the divorce, the figures you provide will be used to calculate a monthly child support payment.

Item 2: Spousal support is not covered in this book. Either fill in 0 or see an attorney for additional help.

Item 3: Subtract the amount in line 2 from line 1. Enter the result here.

Item 4: Enter the number of nonjoint children. List those children's names and birthdates in the lines provided.

Item 5: Use the Oregon Scale of Basic Child Support Obligations (in Appendix C) to find the support obligation for that number of children and list it here.

The latest version of the worksheets issued by the Support Enforcement Division contains an error. The support obligation from Worksheet A, line 5, should be entered on Worksheet B, line 3. This is true despite the fact that Worksheet B, line 3, asks for the figure from Worksheet A, line 3. This is incorrect; the figure from Worksheet A, line 5—not line 3—should be entered into Worksheet B, line 3.

WORKSHEET A (NONJOINT CHILD CREDIT COMPUTATION)

Support Case No. _____

Worksheet A
Nonjoint Child Credit Computation

FOR: ☐ PARENT 1 ☐ PARENT 2

1. PARENT'S GROSS MONTHLY INCOME $_____

2. Add or subtract spousal support paid or received $_____

3. ADJUSTED GROSS INCOME $_____

4. TOTAL NUMBER OF NONJOINT CHILDREN _____
   (including children to whom parent has been ordered to pay support by prior order) (Do not include stepchildren)

   Name(s) and date(s) of birth:

   _____
   _____
   _____
   _____
   _____
   _____
   _____
   _____

5. SUPPORT OBLIGATION FOR NONJOINT CHILDREN $_____
   (using only this parent's adjusted gross monthly income from line 3; from scale in OAR 137-50-490)

SED 109A (Rev. 5/96)

Here's how to use the guidelines:

- Locate the line for your (or your spouse's) adjusted gross income on the left side of the chart.

- Locate the column for the number of non-marital children at the top of the chart. If there are more than six children, see note below.

- Find the number where the line representing your (or your spouse's) income intersects with the column representing the number of non-marital children. This is the support obligation.

NOTE: If you have more than six non-marital children, find the support obligation for six children and add 6.6% of that figure for each additional child.

If you will not use the worksheet for sole custody, you can skip the next section. For split custody arrangements, go to Section G4. For joint (shared) custody arrangements, go to Section G5.

Remember, if the percentage of overnight time a child spends with one parent is less than 35%, it is considered to be a sole custody arrangement for purposes of calculating child support. Unless you will have split custody, you must use Worksheet B to calculate child support if one parent has the child overnight less than 35% of the time.

3. Worksheet B (Support Calculation—Regular Custody)

This worksheet should be used if one parent will have sole (regular) custody of the children.

- Leave the "Support Case No. _____" at the top of the page blank.

Item 1: Fill in each spouse's gross monthly income. (See Section G1 above for how to compute gross monthly income.) The custodial column is for information about the parent who will have sole custody, and the non-custodial column is for information on the parent without custody.

Item 2: Requesting spousal support is not covered in this book. Either fill in 0 or see an attorney for additional help.

Item 3: If you or your spouse pay child support for or live with any nonjoint children (children from prior relationships), you should already have completed Worksheet A (Section G2 above). Put the figure from Worksheet A, line 5, here on line 3. Otherwise, if there are no nonjoint children involved, fill in zero.

The latest version of the worksheets issued by the Support Enforcement Division contains an error. The support obligation from Worksheet A, line 5, should be entered on Worksheet B, line 3. This is true despite the fact that Worksheet B, line 3, asks for the figure from Worksheet A, line 3. This instruction is incorrect; the figure from Worksheet A, line 5—not line 3—should be entered into Worksheet B, line 3.

Item 4: Subtract line 3 from line 1 in each column. This is the adjusted gross monthly income. Add your and your spouse's adjusted gross monthly incomes together and put the answer on line 4 in the Combined column.

Item 5: Enter the percentage each of your incomes is of your total combined income. To determine what percentage of the total combined income each of you earns, divide the individual figure for gross monthly income by the total gross monthly income. Do this for both you and your spouse. The result will be a decimal number less than one, such as .45. Decimal numbers convert to percentages by moving the decimal point two places to the right, which would convert .45 into 45%. Round up any decimal amounts of .5 or higher, and round down decimals of .4 or lower. 47.5, for instance would round up to 48; 56.4 would round down to 56.

Example: *Laura's gross monthly income is $2,200 and David's is $1,900. Adding the two incomes together results in their combined gross monthly income, $4,100. To figure out what percentage of the combined income Laura contributes, she divides 2,200 by 4,100. The result is .537. She converts that number into a percentage by moving the decimal point two places to the right, which results in 53.7%. She rounds up to 54%. For David's income, she divides 1,900 by 4,100, to get .463. This converts to 46.3%, which she rounds down to 46%.*

NOTE: Your and your spouse's percentages of income will always add up to 100%. Because of this, another way you can calculate your respective percentages is to figure out the percentage for one spouse, then simply subtract that number from 100. The difference will be the percentage for the other spouse. If Nancy calculated her percentage of income to be 49%, for example, she could figure her spouse's percentage by subtracting 49 from 100, which equals 51. Her spouse's percentage of income would be 51%.

Item 6: Look up the amount of the child support obligation on the Oregon Scale of Basic Child Support Obligations. To do this, locate the column for the number of marital children at the top of the chart. (If you have more than six children, see note below.) Locate the line for your combined adjusted gross income (from item 4) at the left side of the chart. If the combined monthly income is more than $10,000 use the amount for $10,000. Where the two lines intersect, you will have the child support obligation. Enter this number in the Combined column on item 6.

NOTE: If you have more than six marital children, find the support obligation for six children and add 6.6% of that figure for each additional child.

If you wish to pay or receive more child support than shown in the $10,000 column (or to change the child support computation for any other reason), you must convince the court to accept your proposed amount. That process is not covered in this book. You should be aware that the courts do not look favorably on any change in the formula. If you nonetheless want to strike out on your own, see an attorney.

Item 6A: If the custodial parent pays for child care so the parent can work or look for work, fill out Worksheet E to calculate the Child Care Credit. Enter the figure from Worksheet E line H in the Combined column on line 6A on Worksheet B. (Instructions for Worksheet E are provided in Section G6 below.)

Item 6B: If the children have regular medical expenses such as prescriptions or regular treatments that are not covered by insurance, enter these expenses in the Combined column on line 6B.

Item 7: Add the amounts from the Combined column of lines 6, 6A and 6B and enter the total in the Combined column on line 7.

Item 8: For each parent, multiply his or her percentage share of income (line 5) by the total child support obligation (line 7), and fill in the results for each parent on line 8.

Example: *Monica and Rick have a combined total income of $6,400 per month. Monica brings in $3,840, which makes her percentage share of income 60%. Rick brings in $2,560, which makes his percentage share 40%. Their total child support obligation for their two children, the sum of lines 6, 6A and 6B (basic child support obligation, child care costs and uninsured medical expenses), is $1,300. To figure Monica's share of the total child support obligation, she multiplies her percentage share of income (60%) by $1,300, which equals $780. Rick's share is 40% times $1,300, which equals $520.*

WORKSHEET B (SUPPORT CALCULATION—REGULAR CUSTODY)

Support Case No. _____

Worksheet B
Support Calculation—Regular Custody

	Custodial	Non-custodial	Combined
1. Gross monthly income	_____ p/m	_____ p/m	
2. Add or subtract spousal support paid or received	_____	_____	
3. Subtract credit for nonjoint child(ren) from worksheet A, line 3	_____	_____	
4. Adjusted gross monthly income	_____	_____	_____ p/m
5. Percentage share of income (each parent's line 4 income divided by combined income)	_____ %	_____ %	
6. Basic child support obligation (combined income @ # of children) (see scale)			_____
A. Child care costs			_____
B. Medical expenses (OAR 137-50-430) NOTE: DO NOT INCLUDE INSURANCE COSTS– SEE 11 BELOW			_____
7. Total child support obligation (line 6 + 6A + 6B)	_____	_____	_____
8. Each parent's child support obligation (line 5 x line 7 for each parent) ($50 minimum order)	_____	_____	
9. Monthly child support obligation (line 8 non-custodial)		_____	
10. Cost of insurance (for joint child(ren) only) in column for parent who will provide. If non-custodial providing, and line 10 is more than line 9, fill in ZERO	_____	_____	
11. Each parent's pro rata share of insurance cost (line 5 times line 10 for each parent)	_____	_____	
12. TOTAL PRESUMED CHILD SUPPORT If non-custodial provides insurance, line 9 MINUS line 11 custodial. If custodial provides insurance, line PLUS line 11 non-custodial.		_____	

Other comments or rebuttal to calculations:

Item 9: Enter the non-custodial parent's child support obligation (line 8) in the non-custodial column in line 9.

Item 10: List the cost of insurance that the parent having the children covered will pay in the column for that parent. If the non-custodial parent will pay for health insurance and the cost is more than the monthly child support obligation (line 9), enter 0.

Item 11: For each parent, multiply the percentage share of income (line 5) by the cost of insurance for the parent providing it (line 10), and enter the results in the appropriate columns.

Example: Massoud pays for his children's insurance which totals $420 per month. He and Judy have a combined monthly income of $3,200, and his percentage share of this total is 55% while Judy's percentage share is 45%. To calculate Massoud's pro rata share of insurance costs, he multiplies his percentage share of income (55%) by $420 which equals $231. Judy's share of insurance costs is 45% times $420 which equals $189.

Item 12: If the non-custodial parent is paying for the health insurance, subtract the custodial parent's share of insurance (line 11) from the child support obligation (line 9) and enter that amount here. If the custodial parent is paying for the health insurance, add his or her share (line 11) to the child support obligation (line 9) and enter that amount here. This figure is the amount of child support to be paid each month by the non-custodial parent (unless a court orders otherwise).

What If You Wish to Receive More or Pay Less?
As mentioned earlier in Section C, if you wish to pay less or receive more child support than shown in the worksheet, you must convince the court to accept your proposed amount. That process is not covered in this book. You should be aware that the courts do not look favorably on any change in the formula. If you nonetheless want to strike out on your own, see an attorney.

4. Worksheet C (Support Calculation—Split Custody)

This worksheet should be used if both spouses will have sole physical custody of one or more of the marital children.

- Leave the "Support Case No. _____" at the top of the page blank.

- At the top of the page, fill in the total number of children of the marriage. Then fill in the number of marital children who will be living with each parent. Use the Parent 1 column for your information and Parent 2 for your spouse's. Remember to be consistent throughout the worksheets—one parent should always be Parent 1 and the other should always be Parent 2.

Item 1: Fill in each spouse's gross monthly income. (See Section G1 above for how to compute gross monthly income.) Put your income in the column for Parent 1 and your spouse's income in the column for Parent 2. Be careful to put the information for the right parent in the right column.

Item 2: Requesting spousal support is not covered in this book. Either fill in 0 or see an attorney if you wish to request spousal support.

Item 3: If you or your spouse pay child support for or live with any nonjoint children (children from prior relationships), you should already have completed Worksheet A (Section G2 above). Enter the figure from Worksheet A, line 5, here on line 3. Otherwise, if there are no nonjoint children involved, fill in zero.

The latest version of the worksheets issued by the Support Enforcement Division contains an error. The support obligation from Worksheet A, line 5, should be entered on Worksheet C, line 3. This is true despite the fact that Worksheet C, line 3, asks for the figure from Worksheet A, line 3. This instruction is incorrect; the figure from Worksheet A, line 5—not line 3—should be entered into Worksheet C, line 3.

Item 4: Subtract line 3 from line 1 in each column. This is the adjusted gross monthly income. Add your and your spouse's adjusted gross monthly incomes together and put the answer on line 4 in the Combined column.

Item 5: Look up the amount of the child support obligation on the Oregon Scale of Basic Child Support Obligations. To do this, locate the column for the total number of marital children at the top of the chart. (If you have more than six children, see note below.) Locate the line for your combined adjusted gross income (from item 4) at the left side of the chart. If the combined monthly income is more than $10,000 use the amount for $10,000. Where the two lines intersect, you will have the child support obligation. Enter this number in both columns of line 5.

Note: If you have more than six marital children, find the support obligation for six children and add 6.6% of that figure for each additional child.

If you wish to pay or receive more child support than shown in the $10,000 column (or to change the child support computation for any other reason), you must convince the court to accept your proposed amount. That process is not covered in this book. You should be aware that the courts do not look favorably on any change in the formula. If you nonetheless want to deviate from the guidelines, see an attorney.

Item 6: Compute the percentage of children that will live with each parent. For example, if there are two children and each parent will live with one child, the percentage is 50%-50%. If there are three children and one will live with one parent and two with the other, the percentage is 33% for the parent with one child (1 divided by 3), and 67% for the parent with two children (2 divided by 3).

Item 7: For each parent, multiply the basic child support obligation (line 5) by the percentage of children living with that parent (line 6) to obtain the prorated basic support for each parent.

Example: *Jason and Katherine each will have one child living with them in a split custody arrangement. The percentage of children living with each parent is 50% for both Jason and Katherine. Jason and Katherine's combined gross monthly income is $2,500, so according to the Oregon Scale of Basic Child Support Obligations, their basic child support obligation is $504. Jason's prorated basic support would be calculated by multiplying the percentage of children living with him (50%) by the basic child support obligation ($504). Since Katherine also will have 50% of the children living with her, her figures will be the same as Jason's. Before multiplying, 50% would have to be converted into decimal form, which is .5. Multiplying $504 by .5 equals $252, which would be the prorated basic support for both Jason and Katherine.*

Item 8A: List the amount that each parent will pay per month to provide health insurance for the children of the marriage in each column.

Item 8B: If either parent pays for child care in order to work or look for work, you will need to complete Worksheet E to compute the Child Care Credit. If

WORKSHEET C (SUPPORT CALCULATION—SPLIT CUSTODY)

Support Case No. _____

Worksheet C
Support Calculation—Split Custody

Total joint children: _____   # children w/parent 1: _____   # children w/parent 2: _____

	Parent 1	Parent 2	Combined
1. Gross monthly income	_____ p/m	_____ p/m	
2. Add or subtract spousal support paid or received	_____	_____	
3. Subtract credit for nonjoint child(ren) from worksheet A, line 3	_____	_____	
4. Adjusted gross monthly income	_____	_____	_____ p/m
5. Basic child support obligation (apply line 4 combined income on scale for ALL joint children & list total support in each column)	_____	_____	
6. Prorated percentage (children w/each parent divided by total joint children)	_____ %	_____ %	
7. Prorated basic support for children with each parent (line 6 times line 5 for each parent)	_____	_____	

8. ADDITIONAL COSTS/EXPENSES

	Parent 1	Parent 2
A. Health insurance (place amount paid by each parent in column for that parent)	_____	_____
B. Child care as defined in OAR 137-50-420 (place amount paid by each parent in column for that parent)	_____	_____
C. Recurring medical costs as defined in OAR 137-50430 (place amount paid by each parent in column for that parent)	_____	_____

9. TOTAL SUPPORT COSTS

   A. Line 7 parent 1 plus lines 8A, 8B and 8C for parent 1 _____

   B. Line 7 parent 2 plus lines 8A, 8B and 8C for parent 2 _____

10. ALLOCATION TO PARTIES

	Parent 1	Parent 2
A. Percentage share of income (each parent's line 4 income divided by combined income)	_____ %	_____ %

   B. Parent 1 owes to parent 2 (line 10A parent 1 times line 9B) _____

   C. Parent 2 owes to parent 1 (line 10A parent 2 times line 9A) _____

11. NET OBLIGATION (if applicable)
Subtract the smaller from the larger amounts in lines 10B and 10C and place the result in the parent's column with the larger amount in line 10B or 10C. _____ _____

Other comments and rebuttals to calculations:

you both pay for child care, two Worksheets will need to be completed. See Section G6 for instructions in filling out Worksheet E. Enter the amount from Worksheet E's line H in Worksheet C, line 8B, for each parent.

Item 8C: If the children have regular medical expenses such as prescriptions or regular treatments that are not covered by insurance, enter these expenses in line 8C for whichever parent pays them.

Item 9A: Add lines 7, 8A, 8B and 8C for you (Parent 1).

Item 9B: Add lines 7, 8A, 8B and 8C for your spouse (Parent 2).

Item 10A: For each parent, enter his or her percentage share of income. To determine what percentage of the total combined income each of you earns, divide the individual figure for gross monthly income by the total gross monthly income (line 4). Do this for both you and your spouse. The result will be a decimal number less than one, such as .45. Decimal numbers convert to percentages by moving the decimal point two places to the right, which would convert .45 into 45%. Round up any decimal amounts of .5 or higher, and round down decimals of .4 or lower. 47.5, for instance would round up to 48; 56.4 would round down to 56.

Item 10B: Enter the amount Parent 1 owes Parent 2. To figure this, multiply the percentage share of income for Parent 1 (line 10A) by the amount on line 9B and enter the amount here. Convert the percentage to a decimal number before multiplying by moving the decimal point two places to the left. 45%, for instance, would convert to .45.

Item 10C: Enter the amount Parent 2 owes Parent 1. To figure this, multiply the percentage share of income for Parent 2 (line 10A) by the amount on line 9A and enter the amount here. Convert the percentage to a decimal number before multiplying by moving the decimal point two places to the left.

Item 11: Determine the net obligation by subtracting the smaller from the larger number from lines 10B and 10C. In other words, if 10B is smaller than 10C, subtract the 10B figure from 10C. If 10C is the smaller number, subtract it from 10B. If 10B and 10C are the same, that means that each parent owes the other parent the same amount, which will cancel out any obligation between them. If there is a difference between what each parent owes, enter it in line 11, in the column with the larger amount in line 10B or 10C. This is the amount of child support to be paid each month by one parent to the other.

5. Worksheet D (Support Calculation—Shared Custody)

Use this worksheet (Worksheet D) for shared custody arrangements, also called joint custody.

Remember, if the percentage of overnight time a child spends with one parent is less than 35%, it is considered to be a sole custody arrangement for purposes of calculating child support. Unless you will have split custody, you must use Worksheet B to calculate child support if one parent has the child overnight less than 35% of the time. See the sidebar in Section F above for how to compute the percent of overnight time a child spends with each parent.

- Leave the "Support Case No. _____" at the top of the page blank.

Item 1: Fill in each spouse's gross monthly income. (See Section G1 above for how to compute gross monthly income.) Use the Parent 1 column for your information and Parent 2 for your spouse's. Remember to be consistent throughout the worksheets—one parent should always be Parent 1 and the other should always be Parent 2.

Item 2: Requesting spousal support is not covered in this book. Either fill in zero, or see an attorney for additional help.

Item 3: If you or your spouse pay child support for or live with any nonjoint children (children from prior relationships), you should already have completed Worksheet A (Section G2 above). Put the figure from Worksheet A, line 5, here on line 3. Otherwise, if there are no nonjoint children involved, fill in zero.

The latest version of the worksheets issued by the Support Enforcement Division contains an error. The support obligation from Worksheet A, line 5, should be entered on Worksheet D, line 3. This is true despite the fact that Worksheet D, line 3, asks for the figure from Worksheet A, line 3. This instruction is incorrect; the figure from Worksheet A, line 5—not line 3—should be entered into Worksheet D, line 3.

Item 4: Subtract line 3 from line 1 in each column. This is the adjusted gross monthly income. Add your and your spouse's adjusted gross monthly incomes together and put the answer on line 4 in the Combined column.

Item 5: Look up the amount of the child support obligation on the Oregon Scale of Basic Child Support Obligations. To do this, locate the column for the total number of marital children at the top of the chart. (If you have more than six children, see note below.) Locate the line for your combined adjusted gross income (from item 4) at the left side of the chart. If the combined monthly income is more than $10,000 use the amount for $10,000. Where the two lines intersect, you will have the child support obligation. Enter this number in both columns of line 5.

NOTE: If you have more than six marital children, find the support obligation for six children and add 6.6% of that figure for each additional child.

If you wish to pay or receive more child support than shown in the $10,000 column (or to change the child support computation for any other reason), you must convince the court to accept your proposed amount. That process is not covered in this book. You should be aware that the courts do not look favorably on any change in the formula. If you nonetheless want to change the amount, see an attorney.

Item 6: Multiply the amount on line 5 by 1.5 and enter the result for each parent. The state presumes it costs one and a half times as much to raise children in two households.

Item 7: Enter the percentage of overnight time the children will be with each parent. See the Sidebar on page 9/7 for help in making this calculation. Remember, if either percentage is below 35%, you'll need to use Worksheet B.

Item 8: Enter the prorated basic support for each parent. To obtain this figure, for each parent multiply the basic support amount (line 6) by the percentage of time that parent will have custody of the children (line 7).

Item 9A: List the amount that each parent will pay each month to provide health insurance for the children of the marriage in each column.

WORKSHEET D (SUPPORT CALCULATION—SHARED CUSTODY)

Support Case No. _____

Worksheet D
Support Calculation—Shared Custody

	Parent 1	Parent 2	Combined
1. Gross monthly income	_____ p/m	_____ p/m	
2. Add or subtract spousal support paid or received	_____	_____	
3. Subtract credit for nonjoint child(ren) from worksheet A, line 3	_____	_____	
4. Adjusted gross monthly income	_____	_____	_____ p/m
5. Basic child support obligation (apply line 4 combined income on scale for all joint children and list total support in each column)	_____	_____	
6. Basic support (line 5) times 1.5	_____	_____	
7. Percentage of time child(ren) will be in custody of each parent IF ONE PARENT'S PERCENT = LESS THAN 35, DO NOT USE THIS WORKSHEET. INSTEAD USE THE REGULAR CUSTODY WORKSHEET (WORKSHEET B)	_____ %	_____ %	
8. Prorated basic support for children (line 7 times line 6 for each parent)	_____	_____	

9. ADDITIONAL COSTS/EXPENSES

	Parent 1	Parent 2
A. Health insurance (place amount paid by each parent in column for that parent)	_____	_____
B. Child care as defined in OAR 137-50-420 (place amount paid by each parent in column for that parent)	_____	_____
C. Recurring medical costs as defined in OAR 137-50-430 (place amount paid by each parent in column for that parent)	_____	_____

10. TOTAL SUPPORT/COSTS

   A. Line 8 for parent 1 plus lines 9A, 9B and 9C for parent 1 _____

   B. Line 8 for parent 2 plus lines 9A, 9B and 9C for parent 2 _____

11. ALLOCATION TO PARTIES

   A. Percentage share of income (each parent's line 4 income divided by combined income)   _____ %   _____ %

   B. Parent 1 owes to parent 2 (line 11A parent 1 times line 10B) _____

   C. Parent 2 owes to parent 1 (line 11A parent 2 times line 10A) _____

12. NET OBLIGATION (if applicable)
    Subtract the smaller from the larger amounts in lines 11B and 11C and place the result in the parent's column with the larger amount in line 11B or 11C   _____   _____

Other comments and rebuttals to calculations:

Item 9B: If either parent pays for child care in order to work or look for work, you will need to complete Worksheet E to compute the Child Care Credit. If you both pay for child care, two Worksheets will need to be completed. See Section G6 for instructions in filling out Worksheet E. Enter the amount from Worksheet E's line H into line 9B for each parent.

Item 9C: If the children have regular medical expenses such as prescriptions or regular treatments that are not covered by insurance, enter these expenses in line 9C for whichever parent pays them.

Item 10A: Add lines 8, 9A, 9B and 9C for Parent 1.

Item 10B: Add lines 8, 9A, 9B and 9C for Parent 2.

Item 11A: For each parent, enter his or her percentage share of income. To determine what percentage of the total combined income each of you earns, divide the individual figure for gross monthly income by the total gross monthly income (line 4). Do this for both you and your spouse. The result will be a decimal number less than one, such as .45. Decimal numbers convert to percentages by moving the decimal point two places to the right, which would convert .45 into 45%. Round up any decimal amounts of .5 or higher, and round down decimals of .4 or lower. 47.5, for instance would round up to 48; 56.4 would round down to 56.

Item 11B: Enter the amount Parent 1 owes Parent 2. Multiply the percentage share of income for Parent 1 (line 11A) by the amount on line 10B and enter the amount here. Convert the percentage to a decimal number before multiplying by moving the decimal point two places to the left; 45%, for instance, would convert to .45.

Item 11C: Enter the amount Parent 2 owes Parent 1. Multiply the percentage share of income for Parent 2 (line 11A) by the amount on line 10A and enter the amount here. Convert the percentage to a decimal number before multiplying by moving the decimal point two places to the left.

Item 12: Determine the net obligation by subtracting the smaller from the larger number from lines 11B and 11C. In other words, if 11B is smaller than 11C, subtract the 11B figure from 11C. If 11C is the smaller number, subtract it from 11B. If 11B and 11C are the same, that means that each parent owes the other parent the same amount, which will cancel out any obligation between them. If there is a difference between what each parent owes, enter it in line 12, in the column with the larger amount in line 11B or 11C. This is the amount of child support to be paid each month by one parent to the other.

6. Worksheet E (Support Computation—Child Care Credit)

If either parent pays for child care in order to work or to look for work, you must fill out this form. If you both pay for daycare you must each fill out this form separately. If you both need to fill out this form, be sure to make a copy of it while it is still blank.

Item A: Do you or your spouse, whichever is the custodial parent, pay for child care to be able to work or look for work? If not, do not fill out this form. If yes, proceed.

Item B: Is the child 12 years old or less or disabled? If not, do not fill out this form. If yes, proceed.

Item C: List one month's child care cost. Figure out your monthly child care costs based on how you pay for child care, either hourly, daily or weekly.

Example: *Tony pays $2.00 per hour and works 140 hours a month.*

$2.00 X 140 = $280.00 per month

Example: *Rachel pays $80 per week for child care. There are an average of 4.33 weeks per month.*

$80 X 4.33 = $346.40 per month

WORKSHEET E (SUPPORT COMPUTATION—CHILD CARE CREDIT)

Support Case No. _____

Worksheet E
Child Care Credit

When calculating the basic child support obligation, credit is given for actual, reasonable costs incurred on behalf of any *joint* child(ren) under OAR 137-50-420. The amount of the credit is the gross child care expense minus the federal and state income tax credit. Use the formula below.

A. Does the custodial parent pay child care for a joint child to enable the parent to work or seek employment?
If yes, proceed. If no, stop here.

B. Is the child 12 years old or less, or if older, is the child disabled and not able to care for itself?
If yes, proceed. If no, stop here.

C. What is the monthly cost of child care? $_____ [C]

D. If there is only one joint child, enter the lesser of C or $200.
If there are two or more children, enter the lesser of C or $400. $_____ [D]

E. Find the custodial parent's income below on the Federal Tax Credit Table. Using the percentage of tax credit corresponding with the parent's income, multiply the percentage by D above. This amount is the federal monthly child care credit. Enter on line at right. $_____ [E]

F. Find the custodial parent's income on Oregon's tax credit table below. Using the percentage of tax credit corresponding with the parent's income, multiply the percentage by D above. This amount is the Oregon monthly child care credit. Enter on line at right. $_____ [F]

G. Add together E and F. Enter on the line at right. $_____ [G]

H. Subtract line G from C to arrive at net child care cost. Enter result on line at right. $_____ [H]

Federal Tax Credit Table

Gross Monthly Income			Tax Credit %
$ 0	to	833	.30
834	to	1,000	.29
1,001	to	1,166	.28
1,167	to	1,333	.27
1,334	to	1,500	.26
1,501	to	1,666	.25
1,667	to	1,833	.24
1,834	to	2,000	.23
2,001	to	2,166	.22
2,167	to	2,333	.21
2,334	to	9,999	.20

Oregon Tax Credit Table

Gross Monthly Income			Credit %
$ 0	to	416	.30
417	to	833	.15
834	to	1,250	.08
1,251	to	2,083	.06
2,084	to	2,916	.05
2,917	to	3,750	.04

Monthly Child Care Costs Worksheet
(not to be filed with court)

Using hourly rate:

Amount paid per hour   _____
Number of hours worked
  each month   X _____
                      = _____

Using daily rate:

Amount paid per day   _____
Number of days per month   X   30
                      = _____

Using weekly rate:

Amount paid per week   _____
Number of weeks per month X 4.33
                      = _____

Item D: If there is one child, fill in $200 or the monthly child care cost from line C, whichever is smaller. If there are two or more children, fill in $400 or the monthly child care cost from line C, whichever is smaller.

Item E: Multiply line D by your federal tax credit. To find your federal tax credit, use the Federal Tax Credit Table found at the bottom left of Worksheet E. Find the tax credit % that corresponds to your gross monthly income. (See Section G1 above on how to figure your gross monthly income.) Multiply the tax credit % amount by the amount on line D. List this result on line E.

Item F: Multiply line D by your Oregon tax credit. To find your Oregon tax credit, use the Oregon Tax Credit Table at the bottom right of Worksheet E. Find the credit % that corresponds to your gross monthly income. (See Section G1 above on how to figure your gross monthly income.) Multiply the credit % amount by the amount on line D. List this result on line F.

Item G: Add E and F together and enter the sum on line G.

Item H: Subtract line G from line C (the two numbers in boxes) to get the child care credit. Fill in this number on line H. ■

The Forms

A. Which Forms to Use 10/2
      Co-Petitioner Divorce Forms 10/3
      Petitioner/Respondent Divorce Forms 10/3

B. Tips for Filling In the Forms 10/4
    1. Make enough copies before you start. 10/4
    2. Print or type the forms. 10/4
    3. Be consistent. 10/4
    4. Use your married names. 10/4
    5. Use attachments when necessary. 10/4

C. Signing and Notarizing the Forms 10/5
    1. Where to Sign 10/5
    2. Notarizing the Forms 10/5

In the previous chapters, we discussed the various issues that you can expect to encounter when going through a divorce. These issues—most notably property and debt division, child custody and visitation and child support—will likely take a fair amount of time and effort for you and your spouse to resolve, either on your own or with the help of a professional such as a mediator or an attorney. Resolving these issues is a separate task from filling out the divorce paperwork, which is the subject of the following chapters. You should make every effort to come to agreements on all issues in your divorce before actually filling out and filing a divorce Petition, which will be explained in detail in Chapters 11 through 13. This chapter provides general instructions for filling out forms for either kind of divorce, co-petitioner or petitioner/respondent.

The instructions for completing the paperwork involved in an Oregon divorce are based on the assumption that you and your spouse are in agreement on all issues in your divorce. If you're having trouble reaching agreement, or if disputes arise after you've already filed the divorce paperwork, the procedures outlined in this book may become delayed or more complex, and you will need to refer to other sections of the book or other resources for help in how to proceed. Remember: it's never too late to resolve differences with your spouse, and once you do so your divorce will proceed much more smoothly, according to the steps outlined in the following chapters.

A. Which Forms to Use

In the Appendix of this book, you'll find two sets of forms, one for co-petitioner divorces, and one for petitioner/respondent divorces. You will use one set or the other. If you and your spouse are in agreement on all the issues and are both willing to sign the papers, choose the set marked Co-Petitioner and follow the instructions in Chapter 11. If you want to file for divorce alone and have your spouse served with the papers, choose the set marked Petitioner/Respondent and follow the instructions in Chapter 12.

If you think your spouse will fight you in court on any of the issues in your divorce, you should seek the help of an attorney. You should not try to represent yourself with the help of this book in a contested divorce. (See Chapter 2 above on the difference between contested and uncontested divorces.) If, however, your divorce was contested, but you were then able to resolve the dispute outside the courtroom, your divorce may become uncontested again, and you can proceed with the help of this book.

Each set of forms contains all the forms you'll need for the type of divorce you're getting, either a co-petitioner divorce or a petitioner/respondent divorce. The following lists show all the forms required for each type of divorce. Forms marked with asterisks are necessary only for some couples; for instance, child support worksheets will be required only if you have children.

Co-Petitioner Divorce Forms

AFFIDAVIT APPLICATION FOR DECREE

AFFIDAVIT OF COMPLIANCE WITH U.C.C.J.A. *

AFFIDAVIT REQUESTING WAIVER OF NINETY-DAY WAITING PERIOD *

CERTIFICATE OF DOCUMENT PREPARATION

CERTIFICATE OF RESIDENCY

CHILD SUPPORT WORKSHEETS *

DECREE OF DISSOLUTION OF MARRIAGE AND JUDGMENT

MOTION AND ORDER FOR WAIVER OF NINETY-DAY WAITING PERIOD *

PETITION FOR DISSOLUTION OF MARRIAGE

PROPERTY SETTLEMENT (FOR REAL PROPERTY) *

SUPPORT ORDER ABSTRACT *

VITAL RECORDS (NOT INCLUDED IN APPENDIX; SEE SAMPLE ON PAGE 11/13)

WAIVER OF DISCLOSURE

Petitioner/Respondent Divorce Forms

AFFIDAVIT OF COMPLIANCE WITH U.C.C.J.A. *

AFFIDAVIT OF PROOF OF SERVICE

AFFIDAVIT REQUESTING WAIVER OF 90-DAY WAITING PERIOD *

AFFIDAVIT SUPPORTING DECREE OF DISSOLUTION WITHOUT A HEARING

CERTIFICATE OF DOCUMENT PREPARATION

CERTIFICATE OF RESIDENCY

CHILD SUPPORT WORKSHEETS *

COMPLIANCE WITH DISCLOSURE

DECREE OF DISSOLUTION OF MARRIAGE AND JUDGMENT

MOTION AND ORDER FOR WAIVER OF 90-DAY WAITING PERIOD *

PETITION FOR DISSOLUTION OF MARRIAGE

PETITIONER'S AFFIDAVIT, MOTION AND ORDER FOR DEFAULT DECREE

PROPERTY SETTLEMENT (FOR REAL PROPERTY) *

STIPULATED DECREE OF DISSOLUTION OF MARRIAGE AND JUDGMENT *

SUMMONS FOR DISSOLUTION OF MARRIAGE

SUPPORT ORDER ABSTRACT *

VITAL RECORDS (NOT INCLUDED IN APPENDIX; SEE SAMPLE ON PAGE 12/13)

> **How Can I Tell Which Form Is Which?**
>
> The name of the form will always be printed to the right of your name in the caption, and at the bottom left of the form. For instance, CERTIFICATE OF RESIDENCY in capital letters will appear to the right of your and your spouse's names on that form. CERTIFICATE OF RESIDENCY is also printed at the bottom left side of the form.

Find the correct set of forms for your divorce, and carefully tear them from the book. Photocopy at least one complete set to use as worksheets before you actually mark on any of the forms.

B. Tips for Filling In the Forms

The following advice applies to everyone doing their own divorce, whether as co-petitioners or petitioner/respondent, whether you have children or don't.

1. Make enough copies before you start.

Be sure to make photocopies of the blank set of forms before writing on them. Everyone makes mistakes, and you'll be glad to have extra copies on hand in case you enter something incorrectly. (You'll also need to make copies of the forms after filling them out—we'll cover that in Chapter 13.)

2. Print or type the forms.

You are not required to type the forms, although many courts prefer that they be typed. If you type your forms, use a typeface that is at least size 10 pica (most typewriters come with this size of letters). If you do not have a typewriter, you may be able to use one at a local library. Or, you may hire an independent paralegal or a typing service to do the typing for you. (See Chapter 15 for Other Resources.) If you do not type your forms, be sure to print neatly and legibly.

3. Be consistent.

When filling out your divorce papers, you'll find yourself entering the same information a number of times in different places. It's very important that you be consistent throughout the paperwork, and always enter the exact same information every time you are asked for it. Your name, for example, should always be the same each time it appears in the paperwork. If you use a middle initial, use it every time you enter your name. If you enter a full name such as Theodore Smith in one blank, don't use the shortened name Ted Smith in a different blank.

4. Use your married names.

Use the names you have been using while married. For instance, if the wife took her husband's name during the marriage, she should use that same name in the papers. If she kept her maiden name, she should use that name in the papers. You do not have to use full names but it is recommended to do so. Most importantly, be consistent. Many people use their full legal first and last name and just a middle initial.

5. Use attachments when necessary.

The amount of space given in various sections of the forms is limited. If you need more space—for example, when listing your personal property—enter "See attached" in the space provided on the form and use another sheet of paper for the information. Attachments are also commonly used when longer agreements such as parenting plans have been drafted. If you have mediated some or all aspects of your divorce, you usually will emerge from the mediation with a written agreement. When information from such a written agreement—except for child support information (see Sidebar)—is required in the forms, enter "See attached" and be sure to include a copy of that agreement with the form. Label the top of every attachment with an easy to understand title, for example: "Wife's Personal Property," or "Parenting Plan."

Be sure to include a copy of each attachment with every copy of the Petition and Decree, not just with the original. Staple the individual pages of the attachment together, and use a paper clip to attach it to the Petition and to the Decree.

> **You Must Transfer Child Support Information Onto the Forms**
>
> If child support is a part of your divorce, the blanks for child support information on the Petition and Decree forms must be filled in, even though the same information is included on the attached child support worksheets and sometimes in a mediated agreement. Transfer the child support information from the worksheets (and any other attached agreements) onto the Petition and Decree. Do not write "See attached" in the blanks where child support information is requested, or your papers may be rejected.

C. Signing and Notarizing the Forms

Many forms require signatures after being filled out, and some must be signed in front of a notary (notarized). For this reason, we recommend that after you fill out a form, set it aside without signing it until all forms have been filled out. At that point, you can go through the completed forms, pull out the ones that need to be notarized, and take them all together to a notary. The rest of the forms that don't need notarizing can then be signed. At the end of each set of instructions for filling out the forms you'll find a list of which forms need to be notarized and which don't. The instructions for each form also tell you whether or not notarization is necessary.

1. Where to Sign

All of the forms have an X next to any required signature. On most co-petitioner forms, there will be spaces for both spouses to sign. A few co-petitioner forms, however, only require one signature. If only one signature is required on a co-petitioner form, either you or your spouse can sign. For the co-petitioner forms that require only one signature, one spouse usually ends up signing all of them, but there is no rule against each spouse signing some of them.

If you are filing alone, you will be the only one signing the papers. You should sign everywhere there is an X.

2. Notarizing the Forms

Some of the forms, both co-petitioner and petitioner/respondent forms, must be signed in front of a notary. You can tell which ones need notarization because they include the following section after the space provided for the signature(s):

SUBSCRIBED AND SWORN to before me this

_____ day of _____, 19_____.

_____

Notary Public for Oregon

My Commission expires: _____, 19_____.

A notary usually charges a small fee and will check your identification to verify that you are in fact who you say you are. Notaries are often available at mailbox service businesses, title companies, secretarial services and independent paralegal offices. Some court clerks are notaries. You might be able to have your documents notarized for free at your bank, place of employment or possibly by a friend who is a notary. And you can always find a notary by looking in the Yellow Pages.

If you and your spouse sign the papers together in front of a notary, you will need only one notary section to be filled out. If you sign the papers separately, at different times or places, you will need to have a notary section filled out at the time of each spouse's signature. An extra notary statement is included in the appendix for this purpose, or the notary may provide their own form. If you and your spouse will sign the papers at different times, be sure that you both have enough copies of the extra notary form so that you can do all the necessary notarizations. ■

Filling Out Co-Petitioner Forms

A. Form-by-Form Instructions 11/2
    Form 1: Certificate of Residency 11/2
    Form 2: Certificate of Document Preparation 11/2
    Form 3: Petition for Dissolution of Marriage 11/2
    Form 4: Affidavit of Compliance With U.C.C.J.A. 11/8
    Form 5: Decree of Dissolution of Marriage 11/8
    Form 6: Support Order Abstract 11/10
    Form 7: Property Settlement 11/10
    Form 8: Vital Records 11/12
    Forms 9 & 10: 90-Day Waiver Forms 11/14
    Form 9: Motion and Order for Waiver of Ninety-Day Waiting Period 11/14
    Form 10: Affidavit Requesting Waiver of Ninety-Day Waiting Period 11/14
    Form 11: Affidavit Application for Decree 11/14
    Form 12: Waiver of Disclosure 11/15

B. After You've Completed the Forms 11/15

A. Form-by-Form Instructions

If you are filing alone and using the petitioner/respondent forms, jump ahead to Chapter 12.

This chapter covers all the forms that co-petitioners will need to file. Most forms have a caption, one or more numbered sections and a signature area.

Take a deep breath, get out your pen (or typewriter) and begin.

Form 1: Certificate of Residency

- Fill in the blanks on the caption. On the first blank line fill in the name of the county in which you are filing. Enter your name, then your spouse's name, in the two blanks below "In the Matter of the Marriage of." It is particularly important to be consistent and accurate when filling out the captions. Always use the same version of the same name; for example, don't use the name Mike Greene in one caption and Michael Greene on another. Leave the blank on the right side following "No." empty. This is for your case number which will be filled in later.

  Section 1: Fill in your name. (Remember, be consistent.)

- Skip to the bottom of the form and fill in your name, address and phone number in the area headed "Submitted by:".

- Set this form aside for signing later. You do not need to sign this in front of a notary.

Form 2: Certificate of Document Preparation

- Fill in the caption. (See above instructions for Certificate of Residency for help in filling out the caption.)

  Section 1: If you complete the forms yourself without any help from an independent paralegal or typing service, check box (a). If you pay for help from an independent paralegal or typing service, check box (b) and fill in the name of the company or person that helped you. If a friend helps you but they don't charge money then check (a).

- Set this form aside for completion later. This form must be signed in front of a notary.

Form 3: Petition for Dissolution of Marriage

- Fill in the caption. (See above instructions for Certificate of Residency for help in filling out the caption.)

  Section 1: There are no blanks to fill in. If the statement in this paragraph is not true, then technically you don't have grounds for a divorce. See an attorney for how to proceed.

  Section 2: There are no blanks to fill in. If the statement in this paragraph is not true (that is, if there are other actions pending in other courts) you'll need to see a lawyer.

  Section 3: Check the statement that applies to you and your spouse, either (a), (b) or both. Either you or your spouse must be a resident for you to be able to file for divorce in Oregon.

  Section 4: In this section fill in information about your marital children.

- **4-a:** Fill in the number of marital children that are still minors or are attending school. For the purposes of this and most other divorce forms, a "child attending school" must be under age 21 and enrolled in school at least half time plus one credit. Fill in the names, addresses, Social Security numbers and birthdates for these children. If you do not have minor children of the marriage, write "none." For more on children of the marriage, see Chapter 8.

- **4-b:** If the wife is pregnant check the box "is currently pregnant" and put the baby's due date on the next line. If not pregnant, check the blank "is not currently pregnant" and fill in N/A (for Not Applicable) on the blank line.

Section 5: In this section fill in the custody and visitation arrangements you have made if you have any minor children.

- **5-a:** If there are no minor children of the marriage or children attending school, check box (a). You can then skip ahead to Section 9.

- **5-b:** If you have a separate parenting plan or mediation agreement covering custody and visitation, check box (b) and include your attachment. The rest of sections 5, 6 and 7 can be answered by filling in "See attached parenting agreement."

- **5-c:** If you do not have a separate parenting plan or mediation agreement, fill in your proposed custody arrangement in this space. For each child this will be:

    - sole custody to one of the parents, or
    - sole physical custody to one of the parents and joint legal custody to both parents, or
    - joint physical custody and joint legal custody to both parents.

For more on what these custody labels mean, see Chapter 8.

Examples:

Sole Custody

4. a. There have been two child(ren) born to Petitioners (before or during the marriage), or adopted by them.

5. c. The custody of the minor child(ren) shall be awarded as follows:

James Tyler Jeffries to Jennifer Rae Jeffries

Justin Samuel Jeffries to Jennifer Rae Jeffries

Joint Legal and Joint Physical Custody

4. a. There have been two child(ren) born to Petitioners (before or during the marriage), or adopted by them.

5. c. The custody of the minor child(ren) shall be awarded as follows:

LeRoy Thomas Jones—Joint Legal and Physical Custody

Tanya Marie Jones—Joint Legal and Physical Custody

Joint Legal and Sole Physical Custody

4. a. There has been one child born to Petitioners (before or during the marriage), or adopted by them.

5. c. The custody of the minor child(ren) shall be awarded as follows:

LeRoy Thomas Jones—Joint Legal Custody, Sole Physical custody with Dolores Marie Jones

Split Custody

4. a. There have been three child(ren) born to Petitioners (before or during the marriage), or adopted by them.

5. c. The custody of the minor child(ren) shall be awarded as follows:

Justin Mark Simms—Legal and Physical Custody with Mark Steven Simms

Jason Matthew Simms—Legal and Physical Custody with Mark Steven Simms

Annette Sara Simms—Legal and Physical Custody with Roberta Hayward-Simms

---

- **5-d:** If you do not have a separate parenting plan or mediation agreement, fill in your proposed visitation arrangement in this space. If your visitation or parenting time arrangement is outlined in an attachment, write in this space "See attached parenting agreement" and attach:

    - a copy of one of the visitation or parenting time schedules which are included with the book, or
    - a copy of a parenting agreement that resulted from using *Child Custody: Building Agreements That Work* (Nolo Press), or
    - a mediation settlement agreement.

Example:

5. d. Visitation or parenting time with the child(ren) shall be as follows:

Rachel Lenore Loftin and Ricky Ray Loftin shall spend the after school and evening hours, from 3:00 p.m. to 7:30 p.m. with their father, Frank James Loftin and overnight, from 7:30 p.m. to 3:00 p.m. with their mother, Michelle Leigh Loftin. Each parent shall have the children every other weekend and holiday according to the attached schedule. If at any time the parents cannot agree on a visitation or parenting time schedule, we agree to attend mediation.

5. d. Visitation or parenting time with the child(ren) shall be as follows:

Ian James Smith and Michael Tyler Smith shall live with Paul Nolan Smith and Paul shall have physical custody. Paul Nolan Smith and Joanne Marie Smith have joint legal custody. The children shall spend from Friday at 3:30 p.m. to Sunday at 6:00 p.m. with Joanne Marie Smith, and every other holiday and the second weekend per month also with Joanne Marie Smith.

The parties will attempt to work together to avoid any further disputes. Should any dispute arise that cannot be resolved we agree to mediate the dispute with a mutually agreed-upon mediator. The cost of mediation shall be shared equally.

In the Appendix there are several visitation or parenting time arrangements and schedules you can use. Or, you can write your own.

Section 6: Fill in the name of the parent who will provide health insurance and the name of the parent who will pay uninsured medical expenses.

Section 7: Fill in the name of the parent who will claim the children for tax purposes. If you are splitting the tax benefit—that is, each parent is claiming one or more different children—state which children are being claimed by which parent.

Section 8: This section has four blanks. In the first blank, enter the name of the parent who will be paying child support, then in the next blank fill in the name of the parent who will receive child support. Enter the amount of child support to be paid each month, and the date child support should begin.

Use Chapter 9 to compute the amount of child support to be paid. For the date child support will begin, most people fill in the word "decree," meaning that child support will begin on the date the Decree is signed by the judge. If you would rather specify a date that child support is to begin, fill in that specific date.

Even if you have attached a mediated agreement specifying child support arrangements, make sure you enter this information into the divorce forms themselves. Attaching the agreement is not enough—you must transfer the information onto the divorce papers. And make sure that the information you enter is exactly the same as in the attachment. Failing to enter child support information into the Petition or entering information that conflicts with an attachment may cause your papers to be rejected.

Section 9: This section is for information about your marital property.

- **9-a:** If there is no personal property of the marriage, check box (a). You can then skip to Section 10.

- **9-b:** If you have marital property that has not yet been divided, check box (b) and list the property in lines 9c and 9d.

- **9-c** is for listing the property that will go to the husband.

- **9-d** is for listing the property that will go to the wife.

If you need more room than the lines provide, write "See attached" in the space and use a separate sheet to list your property. Make sure the attachment is clearly labeled and be sure to include it with your papers. The next chapter will cover the specifics of assembling all the forms and attachments. See Chapter 10, Section B5 for more on attachments.

If you're not sure if property is marital property, see Chapter 7, Section A.

Listing Property in Your Divorce Papers

The main reason to list the property to be divided in the divorce Petition is to have the arrangement in writing, which may be helpful if your spouse later disputes the property division. So depending on your circumstances and on how much you trust your spouse, you may decide not to list any property at all or you might list specific items with detailed descriptions and serial numbers.

If you trust your spouse or you have already divided and received your property, you can state "mutually divided" instead of listing specifics. If you do want to list items so as to avoid confusion—especially when there is a lot of property to divide—you need to be only as specific as you think is necessary for you and your spouse to carry out your arrangement.

Example:

Judy and Steve Jones reach a property division agreement, and they trust each other to honor it. They divide the bulk of their property on their own but enter in the divorce Petition the most valuable property items, just to make sure they don't have any misunderstandings over the division. They fill out their Petition as follows:

9. b. The personal property of the marriage shall be divided as follows:

9. c. The husband shall be awarded the following property:

All household goods in his possession, except for the property awarded to Judy Jones, listed below.

9. d. The wife shall be awarded the following property:

Magnavox 18-inch television, blue couch and loveseat, 1992 Ford Bronco.

If you do not trust your spouse, you should specifically identify the property division in the divorce Petition. That way, if your spouse tries to get more property than was agreed to, you can ask the court to enforce the written arrangement. This is especially important if your share of any property is still in your spouse's possession.

Example:

After Vanessa and Robert Stevenson file for divorce, Vanessa moves out of their house with only what fits in her car. She is afraid that she will not get the share of property Robert agreed to when they discussed property division. When they fill out the co-petitioner divorce papers, she is sure to list the items that each person will get, including descriptions and serial numbers. Her Petition, in part, looks like this:

9. b. The personal property of the marriage shall be divided as follows:

9. c. The husband shall be awarded the following personal property:

Tan and black 1995 Range Rover, license TAK-124, vehicle identification number B234M78236. Oil painting of fruit still life in gilt frame, purchased at Alexis Gallery, October, 1994.

9. d. The wife shall be awarded the following personal property:

Maple Edwardian armoire, purchased at the Water Street Antique Mall in June, 1993. Silver 1994 Lexus, license GKZ-512, vehicle identification number J235T29875.

Bank Accounts and Investments

If you and your spouse have not already divided your personal assets such as bank accounts, certificates of deposit (CDs) or other investments, it is important to list the name of the bank, the account number and the approximate balance for each asset. Remember, if the account is jointly owned, your spouse can withdraw any or all of its funds. See Chapter 7, Sections B and C on dividing property and debts, and Chapter 5, Section A, on assets that should be divided as quickly as possible once you've decided to divorce.

DMV Transfers. If a car is adequately described in the property section of the divorce Petition and Decree, the Department of Motor Vehicles may transfer ownership solely on the basis of a certified copy of the divorce Decree. When describing the vehicle in Section 9, include the make, model and year, and the Vehicle Identification Number or license; for example: 1992 Ford Bronco, license #JLT-345, title #HP-2579K90.

Section 10: If there is no real property of the marriage, or if you have already divided it, check box (a). If you do have real property which still must be divided, check box (b) ("The parties own the real property on the attached real property settlement agreement") and attach a property settlement. Real property settlement forms are included in the Appendix, and instructions for filling them out are included below.

If you need more information about real property, see Chapter 7.

Section 11: There are no blanks to fill in.

Section 12: Enter information about marital debts in this section.

- **12-a:** If there are no debts of the marriage, check the box (a). You can then go to Section 13.

- **12-b:** If you do have debts to divide, check box (b) ("The debts of the marriage shall be divided as follows:") and list the debts in lines 12c and 12d.

- **12-c** is for debts that the husband will pay.

- **12-d** is for debts that the wife will pay.

When listing debts, include the creditor name, the account number and the amount due.

Example:

Nordstrom	#455-0977-3	$560
Sears	#344-567-9008	$400
Dr. Miller	#345-7889	$600
First Mortgage Co.	#87-907867	$72,000

For more information about how to divide debts, see Chapter 7.

Making Sure Debts Are Paid

If you or your spouse is supposed to pay debts of the marriage and you want extra protection in case he or she doesn't live up to the agreement, you can obtain a judgment against your spouse, which is essentially a court order for him or her to pay the debt. To obtain a judgment, you must ask for one in your Petition and Decree. In the Petition, enter one of the following clauses in Section 14, "Other Provisions":

The husband is awarded a judgment against the wife in the sum of $_____. The wife can satisfy this judgment by paying off the following debts: [List the debts here.] After the debts have been paid the husband shall sign a satisfaction of judgment form for the wife to file.

or:

The wife is awarded a judgment against the husband in the sum of $_____. The husband can satisfy this judgment by paying off the following debts: [List the debts here.] After the debts have been paid the wife shall sign a satisfaction of judgment form for the husband to file.

Read Chapter 7 for a more detailed discussion of debt judgments.

Section 13: If the wife wants to change her name to her maiden name or to another name, on the first line fill in the wife's current name. On the second line fill in the name the wife wants. If the wife does not want to change her name fill in N/A for Not Applicable.

Section 14: Use this space if you wish to include other provisions in your divorce that do not seem to fit elsewhere. Examples of other issues you might want to cover include insurance policies, mediation agreements, debt judgments and private school tuition for children.

Whatever other provisions you include in this space, be sure to list them on both the Petition and the Decree.

Examples:

14.

Lester Green shall maintain the life insurance policy that is currently in effect, policy number AB-12349876, with a face value of not less than $50,000, and shall keep Andrew Green named as the irrevocable beneficiary to insure Lester Green's child support obligations. During the term of the obligation to maintain insurance, Lester Green shall furnish Barbara Green, upon request, a copy of such policy or other evidence that the proper life insurance is in force, with the appropriate beneficiary designation in effect.

14.

Ethan Harris shall pay the premiums to maintain Susan Harris on Aetna health insurance including medical/dental and vision, for a period of five years from the date of Decree.

14.

If a dispute arises that cannot be resolved, we agree to mediate the dispute with a mutually agreed-upon mediator. The cost of mediation shall be shared equally.

14.

Both parents, Jamie Shavers and Stephanie Shavers, agree that the children shall attend private school until the end of junior high school. Jamie Shavers agrees to pay half the costs of private school for the children in addition to the child support payments calculated in the child support worksheets.

Section 15: Fill in all the requested information. If you don't know some of this information you can still proceed with your divorce. Fill in "Unknown" if you don't know. For the wife's former names, enter her maiden name first, then any other names she has used. For the place of marriage, enter the city and state.

- Set this form aside for signing and dating later. This form must be signed in front of a notary.

Congratulations! You have finished the most difficult form!

Form 4: Affidavit of Compliance With U.C.C.J.A.

You only need to complete this form if you have minor children of the marriage or children attending school. If you do not have minor children of the marriage you can skip this form. (See Chapter 8 for more on children of the marriage.)

- Fill in the caption. (See instructions for Certificate of Residency for help in filling out the caption.) At the bottom of the caption, fill in the name of the county in which you are signing this form. It will often be the same county that you entered at the top of the caption.

Section 1: Enter your name in the first blank and your spouse's name in the second blank.

Section 2: List your children's current address. If they have lived anywhere else in the past five years, list the places they lived and the dates they lived there. If they lived with anyone other than yourself or your spouse during the past five years, list that person's name and present address. If you need more space, use an attachment. (See Chapter 10, Section B5, on attachments.)

- Set this form aside for signing later. It will need to be notarized.

Form 5: Decree of Dissolution of Marriage

The Decree is the form that the judge will sign granting your divorce, awarding custody and visitation or parenting time and dividing property and debts. It will be the document that officially establishes your divorce.

The most important thing to keep in mind when filling out the Decree is that it must match the Petition. If any information you enter in the Decree conflicts with information you included in the Petition, the court may not sign the Decree. If you list two cars and a boat in the Petition, you must list two cars and a boat in the Decree. If you list three children in the Petition, all three children must be listed in the Decree.

- Fill in the caption. (See instructions for Certificate of Residency for help in filling out the caption.)

Section 1: Do not fill in the date in Section 1 until after you file the Petition. After the Petition is filed, fill in the date you filed it.

Section 2: Leave this blank for the judge to fill in.

Section 3 is a reminder that your will, once your divorce is final, will be invalid as it applies to your spouse. If you wish to make a new will, read *Nolo's Will Book* by Denis Clifford (Nolo Press) or use Nolo's WillMaker software.

Section 4 should match the information in Section 4 of the Petition.

Section 5 should match the information in Section 5 of the Petition. Be sure to include another copy of any attachments included with the Petition.

Section 6 should match the information in Section 6 of the Petition.

Section 7 should match the information in Section 7 of the Petition.

Section 8 should match the information in Section 8 of the Petition. Be sure to include another copy of the child support worksheets included with the Petition.

Section 9 should match the information in Section 9 of the Petition. Be sure to include another copy of any attachments included with the Petition.

Section 10 should match the information in Section 10 of the Petition. Be sure to include another copy of any real property settlement included with the Petition.

Section 12 should match the information in Section 12 of the Petition. Be sure to include another copy of any attachments included with the Petition.

Section 13 should match the information in Section 13 of the Petition.

Section 14 should match the information in Section 14 of the Petition. Be sure to include another copy of any attachments included with the Petition.

Requesting Judgments

By filling in either judgment section, you are requesting the court to order a judgment to be created against your spouse or yourself. If you have minor children, it is mandatory to request a child support judgment. Money judgments to cover debts are optional.

Section 15: This section is for information on child support payments if you have minor children of the marriage. You must fill in the information for a child support judgment if you have minor marital children. Make sure this information is identical to the information in Section 8 of the Decree and Petition.

- **15-a:** Judgment Creditor: List the person who will be receiving child support on behalf of the children. If there are no children fill in N/A for not applicable.
- **15-b:** Judgment Debtor: List the name of the person paying child support.
- **15-c:** Principal Amount of Judgment: Fill in the amount to be paid each month.

Section 16: This section is for any money judgment you requested in the Petition.

Money judgments (sometimes called debt division judgments) are optional; you may fill in the information for a judgment if you want to obtain one to protect yourself in case your spouse does not pay the debts as agreed. See Section 12 of the Petition above for more information about requesting money judgments.

- **16-a:** Judgment Creditor: Fill in the name of the spouse who will benefit from the debts being paid.
- **16-b:** Judgment Debtor: Fill in the name of the spouse who will be paying the debts.
- **16-c:** Principal Amount of Judgment: Fill in the amount of the judgment (the total of the debts to be paid).

Example:

16.

a. JUDGMENT CREDITOR: JAMIE LOU REED

b. JUDGMENT DEBTOR: ANTHONY JOSEPH CARILLO

c. PRINCIPAL AMOUNT OF JUDGMENT: $5,000

d. INTEREST OWED TO DATE OF JUDGMENT: Nine percent (9%) per annum.

- Leave the date blank for the judge to fill in.

Section 17: The Notice of Income Withholding is a statement that is required when child support is involved in a divorce. The statement explains that child support can be withheld from wages if the person who owes the support is more than 30 days late with payment.

Section 18: Enter all the requested information. Make sure the information is identical with the information in the relevant data section (Section 15) of the Petition.

- You have finished your Decree. Set it aside. You will not sign this form; the judge signs it to grant your divorce.

Form 6: Support Order Abstract

You only need to complete this form if you have minor children of the marriage or children attending school. If you do not have minor children of the marriage you can skip this form. (See Chapter 8 for more on children of the marriage.)

This form contains mostly the same information as the relevant data sections of the Petition and Decree which you have already completed.

- The caption on this form is slightly different from the other captions in that it asks for additional information. At the top, fill in your county. Then fill in your and your spouse's names, addresses, Social Security numbers, birthdates and genders. Leave the spaces on the right side for the case number and the date of order blank.

- Enter the date and the place of your marriage (city and state).

- For the date of separation, enter the date you and your spouse stopped continuously living together. The place of separation is the last place (city and state) you lived together before you moved apart. If you are still living together, list N/A for not applicable.

- **Obligor:** Fill in the name of the person who will be paying child support.

- **Obligor's Employer's name/address:** Fill in the name and address of the employer of the person paying support. If the person paying support is unemployed, list N/A.

- In the blank after "Pmt $" enter the total amount of child support to be paid each month. This number should be the same as on the Money Judgment for Child Support in the Decree. On the blank after "Next Due Date" fill in the date child support is due, which also should match the figure in the Money Judgment for Child Support in the Decree. On the "Arrearage $" blank, fill in the amount of overdue child support payments, if any. Since child support generally does not start until after the divorce is final, most people will fill in 0.

- The lines under the headings "Beneficiary(ies), Birthdate, Relationship, SS#, Amount, Limit," are for information about your children. Enter the requested information for each of your minor children. The children's names go under "Beneficiary." Under "Relationship," enter either "Daughter" or "Son." For the "Amount" column, divide the total child support to be paid each month by the total number of minor children of the marriage and enter that amount in this column for each child. "Statutory" has already been entered under the "Limit" column.

- Set the form aside. You will not sign this form; only the judge will date and sign it.

Form 7: Property Settlement

The Property Settlement form is only for real estate. If you do not own any real estate, you can skip this form.

If you own real estate, you must complete a Property Settlement form. You may also draft a written settlement for your personal property, but you would not use this particular form for that purpose. A mediator or attorney may be able to help you draft your own personal property settlement, or you could use the book *Divorce and Money* to help you. See above Chapter 7 on personal property division.

The first step is to decide which Property Settlement applies to your situation. Either you will sell the property (usually, the family home) and divide the equity between the two of you, or one of you will sell your interest in the property to the other. If you are unsure about how to divide the real property, see Chapter 7.

Choose the appropriate form, either the settlement in which the property is sold, or the settlement in which one spouse transfers his or her share to the other spouse. We call the settlement in which the property is sold Property Settlement (A), and the other arrangement Property Settlement (B).

Property Settlement (A): Selling the Property and Dividing the Equity

- Fill in the caption.

Section 1: Enter each spouse's share of the equity. For example, if you are dividing the equity equally, enter: "50% to Joe Jones and 50% to Kate Jones."

Section 2: In the blanks following "The property is commonly described as:" fill in the address of the property. In the blanks following "And legally described as:" fill in the legal description of the property. You must get the property's legal description from an actual deed for the property—not from your property taxes or other papers where the description has been abbreviated and may not be acceptable.

- Set this form aside for signing and dating later. This form must be signed in front of a notary.

Property Settlement (B): Transferring Ownership to One Spouse

- Fill in the caption.

Section 1: Enter the name of the spouse who will keep the property in the first blank. In the second blank, fill in the other spouse's name, the one who is giving up his or her share of the property.

Section 2: In the blanks following "The property is commonly described as:" fill in the address of the property. In the blanks following "And legally described as:" fill in the legal description of the property. You must get the property's legal description from an actual deed for the property—not from your property taxes or other papers where the description has been abbreviated and may not be acceptable.

Section 3: In the first blank, enter the name of the spouse who will keep the property. In the second blank, enter the name of the spouse who is giving up his or her share of the property.

- Set this form aside for signing and dating later. This form must be signed in front of a notary.

The Following Examples Show the Most Common Ways That Legal Descriptions Are Given

Lot 3, Block 45
Ironwood Subdivision
Hillsboro, Oregon
County of Washington

or:

Beginning at an iron pipe on the West line of that certain tract of land conveyed by John Metzger and Joline Metzger to J.S. Barnum and Nellie Barnum on January 4, 1922, and continuing East to County Road X...[extended description of coordinates, landmarks, measurements]...thence South to the point of beginning.

or:

The North 40 feet of the East 30 feet of Lot 2, according to the duly filed plat of REDWOOD, in the City of Portland, filed January 21, 1936, in Plat Book 1178, Page 48, Records of the County of Multnomah and State of Oregon.

If the legal description you find for your property does not resemble any of the examples given above, you may need additional help to determine the correct legal description to use. Call the county property tax office, a title company, a realtor or even the holder of your mortgage.

Form 8: Vital Records

This form is required for all divorces. We have included a sample form in this chapter for your reference, though you will have to obtain an original of this form from your local courthouse. The Vital Records form cannot be provided as a tear-out form in this book because it contains carbons and an orange stripe that the court uses for filing purposes. Call your county courthouse to find out where to get one; a list of phone numbers and addresses is included on page 13/15.

The Vital Records form asks mostly for relevant data such as names, addresses, Social Security numbers and birthdates. The answers to most of the questions are self-explanatory, though here are some tips on the less obvious questions.

Item 15: Fill in the number of minor children of the marriage, including children attending school. (For more information on children of the marriage, see Chapter 8.)

Item 16: Since you are filing as co-petitioners, check "Both."

Item 17: Since you are getting your own divorce without being represented by an attorney, fill in "None" in items 17a and 18a, and N/A for "not applicable" in items 17b and 18b.

Items 19 through 27: Leave these boxes blank for the court to fill in.

Item 29b: Enter the date the last marriage for the husband ended. You can approximate if you don't know the exact date.

Item 29d: Enter the date the last marriage for the wife ended. You can approximate if you don't know the exact date.

Item 30a: You may decline to enter the husband's race. If you do, fill in "refused."

Item 30b: You may decline to enter the wife's race. If you do, fill in "refused."

- You do not need to sign this form. It will be signed by a court official.

Filling Out Co-Petitioner Forms

Vital Records

OREGON DEPARTMENT OF HUMAN RESOURCES
HEALTH DIVISION
Vital Records Unit

RECORD OF DISSOLUTION OF MARRIAGE, OR ANNULMENT

CO. FILE NO. _____
136- _____ State File Number

TYPE OR PRINT PLAINLY IN BLACK INK

HUSBAND
1. HUSBAND'S NAME (FIRST) (MIDDLE) (LAST)
2. RESIDENCE OR LEGAL ADDRESS — STREET AND NUMBER — CITY OR TOWN — COUNTY — STATE
3. SOCIAL SECURITY NUMBER (Optional)
4. BIRTHPLACE (State or Foreign Country)
5. DATE OF BIRTH (Month, Day, Year)

WIFE
6a. WIFE'S NAME (First, Middle, Last)
6b. MAIDEN SURNAME
7. FORMER LEGAL NAMES (IF ANY) (1) (2) (3)
8. RESIDENCE OR LEGAL ADDRESS — STREET AND NUMBER — CITY OR TOWN — COUNTY — STATE
9. SOCIAL SECURITY NUMBER (Optional)
10. BIRTHPLACE (State or Foreign Country)
11. DATE OF BIRTH (Month, Day, Year)

MARRIAGE
12a. PLACE OF THIS MARRIAGE–CITY, TOWN OR LOCATION
12b. COUNTY
12c. STATE OR FOREIGN COUNTRY
13. DATE OF THIS MARRIAGE (Month, Day, Year)
14. DATE COUPLE LAST RESIDED IN SAME HOUSEHOLD (Month, Day, Year)
15. NUMBER OF CHILDREN UNDER 18 IN THIS HOUSEHOLD AS OF THE DATE IN ITEM 14. Number _____ ☐ None
16. PETITIONER ☐ Husband ☐ Wife ☐ Both

ATTORNEY
17a. NAME OF PETITIONER'S ATTORNEY (Type / Print)
17b. ADDRESS (Street and Number or Rural Route Number, City or Town, State, Zip Code)
18a. NAME OF RESPONDENT'S ATTORNEY (Type / Print)
18b. ADDRESS (Street and Number or Rural Route Number, City or Town, State, Zip Code)

DECREE
19. MARRIAGE OF THE ABOVE NAMED PERSONS WAS DISSOLVED ON: (Month, Day, Year)
20. TYPE OF DECREE ☐ DISSOLUTION OF MARRIAGE ☐ ANNULMENT
21. DATE DECREE BECOMES EFFECTIVE (Month, Day, Year)
22. NUMBER OF CHILDREN UNDER 18 WHOSE PHYSICAL CUSTODY WAS AWARDED TO: Husband _____ Wife _____ Joint (Husband / Wife) _____ Other _____ ☐ No children
23. COUNTY OF DECREE
24. TITLE OF COURT
25. SIGNATURE OF COURT OFFICIAL
26. TITLE OF COURT OFFICIAL
27. DATE SIGNED (Month, Day, Year)

ORS 432.010 REQUIRED STATISTICAL INFORMATION. THE INFORMATION BELOW WILL NOT APPEAR ON CERTIFIED COPIES OF THE RECORD.

	22. NUMBER OF THIS MARRIAGE–First, Second, etc. (Specify below)	29. IF PREVIOUSLY MARRIED, LAST MARRIAGE ENDED		30. RACE–American Indian, Black, White, etc. (Specify below)	31. EDUCATION (Specify only highest grade completed)	
		By Death, Divorce, Dissolution, or Annulment (Specify below)	Date (Month, Day, Year)		Elementary / Secondary (0-12)	College (1-4 or 5+)
HUSBAND	28a.	29a.	29b.	30a.	31a.	
WIFE	28b.	29c.	29d.	30b.	31b.	

THE PETITIONER OR LEGAL REPRESENTATIVE OF THE PETITIONER IS RESPONSIBLE FOR COMPLETING THE PERSONAL INFORMATION ON THIS FORM AND SHALL PRESENT THIS FORM TO THE CLERK OF THE COURT WITH THE PETITION.
IN ALL CASES THE COMPLETED RECORD SHALL BE A PREREQUISITE TO THE GRANTING OF THE FINAL DECREE.

45-5 (1/95)

ORIGINAL–VITAL RECORDS COPY

Forms 9 & 10: 90-Day Waiver Forms

If you do not want to have the 90-day waiting period waived, you can skip ahead to the instructions for Form 11.

Certain forms must be filed if you want the judge to sign your divorce Decree without having to wait out the 90-day waiting period. (See Chapter 3 for more on waiting periods and 90-day waivers.) If you want the 90-day waiting period waived, you will need to fill out the Motion and Order for Waiver of Ninety-Day Waiting Period and the Affidavit Requesting Waiver of Ninety-Day Waiting Period.

Form 9: Motion and Order for Waiver of 90-Day Waiting Period

- Fill in the caption. (See instructions for Certificate of Residency for help in filling out the caption.)
- Leave the date and the lower signature line blank for the judge to sign.
- Set the form aside for signing later. It does not need to be notarized.

Form 10: Affidavit Requesting Waiver of 90-Day Waiting Period

- Fill in the caption. (See instructions for Certificate of Residency for help in filling out the caption.) At the bottom of the caption, fill in the county you are filing in. This will be the same as the county you entered just above at the top of the caption.

Section 1: Fill in your name and then your spouse's name.

Section 2: Fill in the reason you and your spouse cannot resolve your differences. Some of the reasons commonly used are:

We have attended marriage counseling that has failed.

I am moving to another state and my spouse will remain in Oregon.

We have established separate lives.

My spouse is abusive and I have a restraining order.

Section 3: List the emergency reason affecting a third party why you need a 90-day waiver. Some of the reasons commonly used are:

I am refinancing my house (or buying a home) and need the divorce to be final to qualify for the financing.

I need child support to be ordered by the court.

I am pregnant and am planning to marry the father.

I have been seeing a therapist and they suggest that I finalize my divorce to lower my stress level which has been affecting my children and their conduct at school.

- Set the form aside for signing later. This form must be signed in front of a notary.

Form 11: Affidavit Application for Decree

In this form you are swearing under penalty of perjury that the information you have entered on the forms is true. It is these facts that justify the court to grant a divorce and the other relief requested in the forms.

- Fill in the caption. (See instructions for Certificate of Residency for help in filling out the caption.) At the bottom of the caption, fill in the name of the county in which you are signing this form. It will often be the same county that you entered at the top of the caption.

Section 1: List your name and your spouse's name.

Section 2: There are no blanks to fill in. You are swearing under oath that neither you nor your spouse are on active military duty. If you or your spouse is in the military, you can still get a divorce but you will need a waiver from the military. Ask the legal department of your military unit to provide you with a waiver. Attach it to this form and cross out Section 2.

Section 3: Fill in the city, state and county in which you were married. Enter the date of your marriage.

Section 4: There are no blanks to fill in. If the statement in this paragraph is not true (that is, if there are other actions pending in other courts) you'll need to see a lawyer.

Section 5: There are no blanks to fill in. If the statement in this paragraph is not true, then technically you don't have grounds for a divorce. See an attorney for how to proceed.

Section 6: Fill in the name of the parent or other person whom the children have been living with for the past six months. Fill in the city and state where the children have been living for the past six months.

Section 7: Fill in your name ("Petitioner"), your gross monthly income and your employer's name ("source of that income is:"). Starting with the next blank for "Petitioner," enter the same information for your spouse.

Sections 8 and 9: There are no blanks to fill in. These sections state your belief in the reasonableness of your proposed property and debt division. If either of you disagree with these statements, see a mediator or attorney.

Section 10: If the wife is seeking to change her name, enter the wife's current name on the first blank. Fill in the wife's proposed new name (usually her maiden name) on the next blank If the wife does not want to change her name fill in N/A for not applicable.

- Set this form aside for signing later. This form must be signed in front of a notary.

Form 12: Waiver of Disclosure

The purpose of the Waiver of Disclosure form is to let the court know that you have provided your spouse with a copy of the asset disclosure notice required by ORS 107.089. A copy of the asset disclosure notice is included in the Appendix for you to use.

- Fill in the caption. (See instructions for Certificate of Residency for help in filling out the caption.)
- Set this form aside for signing later. It must be signed in front of a notary.

B. After You've Completed the Forms

After all the forms have been filled out, they must be signed by you and, depending on the form, by your spouse. Some of the forms require signing in front of a notary. (See Chapter 10 above for more information on signing and notarizing the forms.) When you have finished filling out your forms, separate them on the basis of which ones need notarizing and which ones need your (and maybe your spouse's) signature (see list below). Then, once you've signed and notarized all the appropriate forms you'll be ready to organize them for filing with the court. Organizing and filing the forms are covered in Chapter 13.

The forms for co-petitioner filers that must be signed in front of a notary are:

- CERTIFICATE OF DOCUMENT PREPARATION
- PETITION FOR DISSOLUTION OF MARRIAGE
- AFFIDAVIT OF COMPLIANCE WITH U.C.C.J.A.
- PROPERTY SETTLEMENT
- AFFIDAVIT REQUESTING WAIVER OF NINETY-DAY WAITING PERIOD
- AFFIDAVIT APPLICATION FOR DECREE
- WAIVER OF DISCLOSURE

The forms that must be signed by you—and sometimes your spouse—without being notarized are:

- CERTIFICATE OF RESIDENCY
- MOTION AND ORDER FOR WAIVER OF NINETY-DAY WAITING PERIOD

The forms that are signed by the court are:

- DECREE OF DISSOLUTION OF MARRIAGE AND JUDGMENT
- SUPPORT ORDER ABSTRACT
- VITAL RECORDS FORM
- MOTION AND ORDER FOR WAIVER OF NINETY-DAY WAITING PERIOD (THE ORDER PORTION)

Forms that are not signed by anyone:

- CHILD SUPPORT WORKSHEETS

If you are filing as co-petitioners and have finished filling out, signing and notarizing all the forms described in this chapter, you can skip ahead to Chapter 13 for instructions on organizing and filing your paperwork. ■

Filling Out Petitioner/Respondent Forms

A. Form-by-Form Instructions 12/2
    Form 1: Certificate of Residency 12/2
    Form 2: Certificate of Document Preparation 12/2
    Form 3: Petition for Dissolution of Marriage 12/2
    Form 4: Affidavit of Compliance With U.C.C.J.A. 12/8
    Form 5: Decree of Dissolution of Marriage 12/8
    Form 6: Support Order Abstract 12/10
    Form 7: Property Settlement 12/11
    Form 8: Vital Records 12/12
    Forms 9 & 10: 90-Day Waiver Forms 12/14
    Form 9: Motion and Order for Waiver of Ninety-Day Waiting Period 12/14
    Form 10: Affidavit Requesting Waiver of Ninety-Day Waiting Period 12/14
    Form 11: Summons for Dissolution of Marriage 12/15
    Form 12: Affidavit Proof of Service 12/15
    Form 13: Petitioner's Affidavit, Motion and Order for Default Decree 12/15
    Form 14: Affidavit Supporting Decree of Dissolution Without a Hearing .. 12/16
    Form 15: Compliance With Disclosure 12/16
    Form 16: Stipulated Decree of Dissolution of Marriage and Judgment 12/16

B. After You've Completed the Forms 12/17

A. Form-by-Form Instructions

This section covers all the forms that petitioners filing alone will need to file. (See Chapter 11 if you and your spouse are signing the papers and filing together.) Take a deep breath, get out your pen (or typewriter) and begin.

Form 1: Certificate of Residency

- Fill in the blanks on the caption. On the first blank line fill in the name of the county in which you are filing. Enter your name in the blank for Petitioner, and your spouse's name in the blank for Respondent. It is particularly important to be consistent and accurate when filling out the captions. Always use the same version of the same name; for example, don't use the name Mike Greene in one caption and Michael Greene on another. Leave the blank on the right side following "No." empty. This is for your case number which will be filled in later.

    Section 1: Fill in your name. (Remember, be consistent.)

- Skip to the bottom of the form and fill in your name, address and phone number in the area headed "Submitted by:".

- Set this form aside for signing later. You do not need to sign this in front of a notary.

Form 2: Certificate of Document Preparation

- Fill in the caption. (See above instructions for Certificate of Residency for help in filling out the caption.)

    Section 1: If you complete the forms yourself without any help from an independent paralegal or typing service, check box (a). If you pay for help from an independent paralegal or typing service, check box (b) and fill in the name of the company or person that helped you. If a friend helps you but they don't charge money then check (a).

- Set this form aside for completion later. This form must be signed in front of a notary.

Form 3: Petition for Dissolution of Marriage

- Fill in the caption. (See instructions for Certificate of Residency for help in filling out the caption.)

    Section 1: There are no blanks to fill in. If the statement in this paragraph is not true, then technically you don't have grounds for a divorce. See an attorney for how to proceed.

    Section 2: There are no blanks to fill in. If the statement in this paragraph is not true (that is, if there are other actions pending in other courts) you'll need to see a lawyer.

    Section 3: Check the statement that applies to you and your spouse, either (a), (b) or both. Either you or your spouse must be a resident for you to be able to file for divorce in Oregon.

    Section 4: In this section fill in information about your marital children.

- **4-a:** Fill in the number of marital children that are still minors or are attending school. For the purposes of this and most other divorce forms, a "child attending school" must be under age 21 and enrolled in school at least half time plus one credit. Fill in the names, addresses, Social Security numbers and birthdates for these children. If you do not have children of the marriage, write "none." For more on children of the marriage, see Chapter 8.

- **4-b:** If the wife is pregnant check the box "is currently pregnant" and put the baby's due date on the next line. If not pregnant, check the blank "is not currently pregnant" and fill in N/A (for Not Applicable) on the blank line.

    Section 5: In this section fill in the custody and visitation arrangements you propose if you have any minor children.

- **5-a:** If there are no minor children of the marriage or children attending school, check box (a). You can then skip to Section 9.

- **5-b:** If you have a separate parenting plan or mediation agreement covering custody and visitation, check box (b) and include your attachment. The rest of sections 5, 6 and 7 can be answered by filling in "See attached parenting agreement."

- **5-c:** If you do not have a separate parenting plan or mediation agreement, fill in your proposed custody arrangement in this space. For each child this will be:
  - sole custody to one of the parents, or
  - sole physical custody to one of the parents and joint legal custody to both parents, or
  - joint physical custody and joint legal custody to both parents.

  For more on what these custody labels mean, see Chapter 9.

Examples:

Sole Custody

4. a. There have been two child(ren) born to Petitioners (before or during the marriage), or adopted by them.

5. c. The custody of the minor child(ren) shall be awarded as follows:

James Tyler Jeffries to Jennifer Rae Jeffries

Justin Samuel Jeffries to Jennifer Rae Jeffries

Joint Legal and Joint Physical Custody

4. a. There have been two child(ren) born to Petitioners (before or during the marriage), or adopted by them.

5. c. The custody of the minor child(ren) shall be awarded as follows:

LeRoy Thomas Jones—Joint Legal and Physical Custody

Tanya Marie Jones—Joint Legal and Physical Custody

Joint Legal and Sole Physical Custody

4. a. There has been one child born to Petitioners (before or during the marriage), or adopted by them.

5. c. The custody of the minor child(ren) shall be awarded as follows:

LeRoy Thomas Jones—Joint Legal Custody, Sole Physical custody with Dolores Marie Jones

Split Custody

4. a. There have been three child(ren) born to Petitioners (before or during the marriage), or adopted by them.

5. c. The custody of the minor child(ren) shall be awarded as follows:

Justin Mark Simms—Legal and Physical Custody with Mark Steven Simms

Jason Matthew Simms—Legal and Physical Custody with Mark Steven Simms

Annette Sara Simms—Legal and Physical Custody with Roberta Hayward-Simms

- **5-d:** If you do not have a separate parenting plan or mediation agreement, fill in your proposed visitation arrangement in this space. If your visitation or parenting time arrangement is outlined in an attachment, write in this space "See attached parenting agreement" and attach:
  - a copy of one of the visitation or parenting time schedules which are included with the book, or
  - a copy of a parenting agreement that resulted from using *Child Custody: Building Agreements That Work* (Nolo Press), or
  - a mediation settlement agreement.

Example:

5. d. Visitation or parenting time with the child(ren) shall be as follows:

Rachel Lenore Loftin and Ricky Ray Loftin shall spend the after school and evening hours from 3:00 p.m. to 7:30 p.m. with their father, Frank James Loftin, and overnight from 7:30 p.m. to 3:00 p.m. with their mother, Michelle Leigh Loftin. Each parent shall have the children every other weekend and holiday according to the attached schedule. If at any time the parents cannot agree on a visitation or parenting time schedule, we agree to attend mediation.

5. d. Visitation or parenting time with the child(ren) shall be as follows:

Ian James Smith and Michael Tyler Smith shall live with Paul Nolan Smith and Paul shall have physical custody. Paul Nolan Smith and Joanne Marie Smith have joint legal custody. The children shall spend from Friday at 3:30 p.m. to Sunday at 6:00 p.m. with Joanne Marie Smith, and every other holiday and the second weekend per month also with Joanne Marie Smith.

The parties will attempt to work together to avoid any further disputes. Should any dispute arise that cannot be resolved we agree to mediate the dispute with a mutually agreed-upon mediator. The cost of mediation shall be shared equally.

In the Appendix there are several visitation or parenting time arrangements and schedules to choose from. Or, you can write your own.

Section 6: Fill in the name of the parent who will provide health insurance and the name of the parent who will pay uninsured medical expenses.

Section 7: Fill in the name of the parent who will claim the children for tax purposes. If you are splitting the tax benefit—that is, each parent is claiming one or more different children—state which children are being claimed by which parent.

Section 8: This section has four blanks. In the first blank, enter the name of the parent who will be paying child support, then in the next blank fill in the name of

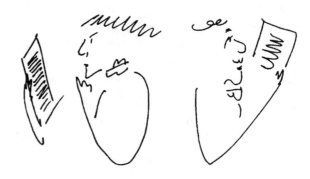

the parent who will receive child support. Enter the amount of child support to be paid each month, and the date child support should begin.

Use Chapter 9 to compute the amount of child support to be paid. For the date child support will begin, most people fill in the word "decree," meaning that child support will begin on the date the Decree is signed by the judge. If you would rather specify a date that child support is to begin, fill in that specific date.

Even if you have attached a mediated agreement specifying child support arrangements, make sure you enter this information into the divorce forms themselves. Attaching the agreement is not enough—you must transfer the information onto the divorce papers. And make sure that the information you enter is exactly the same as in the attachment. Failing to enter child support information into the Petition or entering information that conflicts with an attachment may cause your papers to be rejected.

Section 9: This section is for information about your marital property.

- **9-a:** If there is no personal property of the marriage, check box (a). You can then skip to Section 10.

- **9-b:** If you have marital property that has not yet been divided, check box (b) and list the property in lines 9c and 9d.

- **9-c** is for listing the property that will go to the husband.

- **9-d** is for listing the property that will go to the wife.

If you need more room than the lines provide, write "See attached" in the space and use a separate sheet to list your property. Make sure the attachment is clearly labeled and be sure to include it with your papers. The next chapter will cover the specifics of assembling all the forms and attachments. See Chapter 10, Section B5, for more on attachments.

If you're not sure if property is marital property, see Chapter 7, Section A.

Listing Property in Your Divorce Papers

The main reason to list the property to be divided in the divorce Petition is to have the arrangement in writing, which may be helpful if your spouse later disputes the property division. So depending on your circumstances and on how much you trust your spouse, you may decide not to list any property at all or you might list specific items with detailed descriptions and serial numbers.

If you trust your spouse or you have already divided and received your property, you can state "mutually divided" instead of listing specifics. If you do want to list items so as to avoid confusion—especially when there is a lot of property to divide—you need to be only as specific as you think is necessary for you and your spouse to carry out your arrangement.

Example:

Judy and Steve Jones reach a property division agreement, and they trust each other to honor it. They divide the bulk of their property on their own but enter in the divorce Petition the most valuable property items, just to make sure they don't have any misunderstandings over the division. They fill out their Petition as follows:

9. b. X The personal property of the marriage shall be divided as follows:

9. c. The husband should be awarded the following property:

All household goods in his possession, except for the property awarded to Judy Jones, listed below.

9. d. The wife should be awarded the following property: Magnavox 18-inch television, blue couch and loveseat, 1992 Ford Bronco.

If you do not trust your spouse, you should specifically identify the property division in the divorce Petition. That way, if your spouse tries to get more property than was agreed to, you can ask the court to enforce the written arrangement. This is especially important if your share of any property is still in your spouse's possession.

Example:

After Vanessa files for divorce from Robert, Vanessa moves out of their house with only what fits in her car. She is afraid that she will not get the share of property Robert agreed to when they discussed property division. When she fills out the divorce papers, she is sure to list the items that each person will get, including descriptions and serial numbers. Her Petition, in part, looks like this:

9. b. X The personal property of the marriage shall be divided as follows:

9. c. The husband should be awarded the following personal property:

Tan and black 1995 Range Rover, license TAK-124, vehicle identification number B234M78236. Oil painting of *fruit still life in gilt frame, purchased at Alexis Gallery, October, 1994.*

9. d. The wife should be awarded the following personal property:

Maple Edwardian armoire, purchased at the Water Street Antique Mall in June, 1993. Silver 1994 Lexus, license GKZ-512, vehicle identification number J235T29875.

Bank Accounts and Investments

If you and your spouse have not already divided your personal assets such as bank accounts, certificates of deposit (CDs) or other investments, it is important to list the name of the bank, the account number and the approximate balance for each asset. Remember, if the account is jointly owned, your spouse can withdraw any or all of its funds. See Chapter 7, Sections B and C, on dividing property and debts, and Chapter 5, Section A, on assets that should be divided as quickly as possible once you've decided to divorce.

DMV Transfers: If a car is adequately described in the property section of the divorce Petition and Decree, the Department of Motor Vehicles may transfer ownership solely on the basis of a certified copy of the divorce Decree. When describing the vehicle in Section 9, include the make, model and year, and the Vehicle Identification Number or license; for example: 1992 Ford Bronco, license #JLT-345, title #HP-2579K90.

Section 10: If there is no real property of the marriage, or if you have already divided it, check box (a). If you do have real property which still must be divided, check box (b) ("The parties own the real property on the attached real property settlement agreement") and attach a property settlement. Real property settlement forms are included in the Appendix, and instructions for filling them out are included below.

If you need more information about real property, see Chapter 7.

Section 11: There are no blanks to fill in.

Section 12: Enter information about marital debts in this section.

- **12-a:** If there are no debts of the marriage, check the box (a). You can then go to Section 13.
- **12-b:** If you do have debts to divide, check box (b) ("The debts of the marriage shall be divided as follows:") and list the debts in lines 12c and 12d.
- **12-c** is for debts that the husband will pay.
- **12-d** is for debts that the wife will pay.

When listing debts, include the creditor name, the account number and the amount due.

Example:

Nordstrom	#455-0977-3	$560.
Sears	#344-567-9008	$400.
Dr. Miller	#345-7889	$600.
First Mortgage Co.	#87-907867	$72,000.

For more information about how to divide debts, see Chapter 7.

Making Sure Debts Are Paid

If you or your spouse is supposed to pay debts of the marriage and you want extra protection in case he or she doesn't live up to the agreement, you can obtain a judgment against your spouse, which is essentially a court order for him or her to pay the debt. To obtain a judgment, you must ask for one in your Petition and Decree. In the Petition, enter one of the following clauses in Section 14, "Other Provisions":

The husband is awarded a judgment against the wife in the sum of $_____. The wife can satisfy this judgment by paying off the following debts: [List the debts here.] After the debts have been paid the husband shall sign a satisfaction of judgment form for the wife to file.

or:

The wife is awarded a judgment against the husband in the sum of $_____. The husband can satisfy this judgment by paying off the following debts: [List the debts here.] After the debts have been paid the wife shall sign a satisfaction of judgment form for the husband to file.

Read Chapter 7 for a more detailed discussion of debt judgments.

Section 13: If the wife wants to change her name to her maiden name or to another name, on the first line fill in the wife's current name. On the second line fill in the name the wife wants. If the wife does not want to change her name fill in N/A for Not Applicable.

Section 14: Use this space if you wish to include other provisions in your divorce that do not seem to fit elsewhere. Examples of other issues you might want to cover include insurance policies, mediation agreements, debt judgments and private school tuition for children.

Whatever other provisions you include in this space, be sure to list them on both the Petition and the Decree.

Examples:

14.

Lester Green shall maintain the life insurance policy that is currently in effect, policy number AB-12349876, with a face value of not less than $50,000, and shall keep Andrew Green named as the irrevocable beneficiary to insure Lester Green's child support obligations. During the term of the obligation to maintain insurance, Lester Green shall furnish Barbara Green, upon request, a copy of such policy or other evidence that the proper life insurance is in force, with the appropriate beneficiary designation in effect.

14.

Ethan Harris shall pay the premiums to maintain Susan Harris on Aetna health insurance including medical/dental and vision, for a period of five years from the date of Decree.

14.

If a dispute arises that cannot be resolved, we agree to mediate the dispute with a mutually agreed-upon mediator. The cost of mediation shall be shared equally.

14.

Both parents, Jamie Shavers and Stephanie Shavers, agree that the children shall attend private school until the end of junior high school. Jamie Shavers agrees to pay half the costs of private school for the children in addition to the child support payments calculated in the child support worksheets.

Section 15: If you are requesting a fee deferral, indicate which person will be responsible to pay the fee. By checking one of the boxes you are asking the judge for a judgment in the amount of the filing fee against either yourself or your spouse.

NOTE: Obtaining Fee Deferrals. Each county has its own forms and procedures for obtaining a fee deferral.

Checking one of the boxes on the Petition is not sufficient to request a fee deferral. Call your county courthouse to find out how to apply for one. (See Note in Chapter 13, Section B2 for more information.)

Section 16: Fill in all the requested information. If you don't know some of this information you can still proceed with your divorce. Fill in "Unknown" if you don't know. For the wife's former names, enter her maiden name first, then any other names she has used. For the place of marriage, enter the city and state.

- Set this form aside for signing and dating later. This form must be signed in front of a notary.

Congratulations! You have finished the most difficult form!

Form 4: Affidavit of Compliance With U.C.C.J.A.

You only need to complete this form if you have minor children of the marriage or children attending school. If you do not have minor children of the marriage you can skip this form. (See Chapter 8 for more on children of the marriage.)

- Fill in the caption. (See instructions for Certificate of Residency for help in filling out the caption.) At the bottom of the caption, fill in the name of the county in which you are signing this form. It will often be the same county that you entered at the top of the caption.

Section 1: Enter your name in the blank.

Section 2: List your children's current address. If they have lived anywhere else in the past five years, list the places they lived and the dates they lived there. If they lived with anyone other than yourself or your spouse during the past five years, list that person's name and present address. If you need more space, use an attachment. (See Chapter 10, Section B5 on attachments.)

- Set this form aside for signing later. It will need to be notarized.

Form 5: Decree of Dissolution of Marriage

The Decree is the form that the judge will sign granting your divorce, awarding custody and visitation or parenting time and dividing property and debts. It will be the document that officially establishes your divorce.

The most important thing to keep in mind when filling out the Decree is that it must match the Petition. If any information you enter in the Decree conflicts with information you included in the Petition, the court may not sign the Decree. If you list two cars and a boat in the Petition, you must list two cars and a boat in the Decree. If you list three children in the Petition, all three children must be listed in the Decree.

- Fill in the caption. (See instructions for Certificate of Residency for help in filling out the caption.)

Section 2: Leave this blank for the judge to fill in.

Section 3 is a reminder that your will, once your divorce is final, will be invalid as it applies to your spouse. If you wish to make a new will, read *Nolo's Will Book* by Denis Clifford (Nolo Press) or use Nolo's WillMaker software.

Section 4 should match the information in Section 4 of the Petition.

Section 5 should match the information in Section 5 of the Petition. Be sure to include another copy of any attachments included with the Petition.

Section 6 should match the information in Section 6 of the Petition.

Section 7 should match the information in Section 7 of the Petition.

Section 8 should match the information in Section 8 of the Petition. Be sure to include another copy of the child support worksheets included with the Petition.

Section 9 should match the information in Section 9 of the Petition. Be sure to include another copy of any attachments included with the Petition.

Section 10 should match the information in Section 10 of the Petition. Be sure to include another copy of any real property settlement included with the Petition.

Section 12 should match the information in Section 12 of the Petition. Be sure to include another copy of any attachments included with the Petition.

Section 13 should match the information in Section 13 of the Petition.

Section 14 should match the information in Section 14 of the Petition. Be sure to include another copy of any attachments included with the Petition.

Section 15: Check the appropriate box. If you requested a fee deferral from your county court and filing fees were deferred, enter the name of the person who will be responsible for paying the filing fee. If you enter your name, be sure to put it in the blank before "Petitioner," and if you enter your spouse's name, put it in the blank before "Respondent." Enter the amount of the filing fee that will have to be paid. (See above Note on Obtaining Fee Deferrals.)

Requesting Judgments

By filling in any of the judgment sections, you are requesting the court to order a judgment to be created against your spouse or yourself. If you have minor children, it is mandatory to request a child support judgment. Money judgments to cover debts are optional, as are judgments to cover filing fees that were deferred.

Section 16: This section is for information on child support payments if you have minor children of the marriage. You must fill in the information for a child support judgment if you have minor marital children. Make sure this information is identical to the information in Section 8 of the Decree and Petition.

- **16-a:** Judgment Creditor: List the person who will be receiving child support on behalf of the children. If there are no children fill in N/A for not applicable.

- **16-b:** Judgment Debtor: List the name of the person paying child support.

- **16-c:** Principal Amount of Judgment: Fill in the amount to be paid each month. This is the figure from your child support worksheets.

Section 17: This section is for any money judgment you requested in the Petition.

Money judgments (sometimes called debt division judgments) are optional; you may fill in the information for a judgment if you want to obtain one to protect yourself in case your spouse does not pay the debts as agreed. See Section 12 of the Petition above for more information about requesting money judgments.

- **17a:** Judgment Creditor: Fill in the name of the spouse who will benefit from the debts being paid.

- **17b:** Judgment Debtor: Fill in the name of the spouse who will be paying the debts.

- **17c:** Principal Amount of Judgment: Fill in the amount of the judgment (the total of the debts to be paid).

Example:

17.

a. JUDGMENT CREDITOR: JAMIE LOU REED

b. JUDGMENT DEBTOR: ANTHONY JOSEPH CARILLO

c. PRINCIPAL AMOUNT OF JUDGMENT: $5,000

d. INTEREST OWED TO DATE OF JUDGMENT: *Nine percent (9%) per annum.*

- Leave the date blank for the judge to fill in.

Section 18: This section is for a judgment for filing fees if you requested and were granted a fee deferral. If you did obtain a fee deferral from your county courthouse, fill in this section.

- **18-b:** Judgment Debtor: Fill in the name of the spouse who will be responsible for paying the filing fee.

- **18-c:** Principal Amount of Judgment: Fill in the amount of the filing fee.

- Leave the date blank for the judge to fill in.

Section 19: The Notice of Income Withholding is a statement that is required when child support is involved in a divorce. The statement explains that child support can be withheld from wages if the person who owes the support is more than 30 days late with payment.

Section 20: Enter all the requested information. Make sure the information is identical with the information in the relevant data section (Section 16) of the Petition.

- You have finished your Decree. Set it aside. You will not sign this form; the judge signs it to grant your divorce.

Form 6: Support Order Abstract

You only need to complete this form if you have minor children of the marriage or children attending school. If you do not have minor children of the marriage you can skip this form. (See Chapter 8 for more on children of the marriage.)

This form contains mostly the same information as the relevant data sections of the Petition and Decree which you have already completed.

- The caption on this form is slightly different from the other captions in that it asks for additional information. At the top, fill in your county. Then fill in your and your spouse's names, addresses, Social Security numbers, birthdates and genders. Remember that you are the petitioner and your spouse is the respondent. Leave the spaces on the right side for the case number and the date of order blank.

- Enter the date and the place of your marriage (city and state).

- For the date of separation, enter the date you and your spouse stopped continuously living together. The place of separation is the last place (city and state) you lived together before you moved apart. If you are still living together, list N/A for not applicable.

- **Obligor:** Fill in the name of the person who will be paying child support.

- **Obligor's Employer's name/address:** Fill in the name and address of the employer of the person paying support. If the person paying support is unemployed, list N/A.

- In the blank after "Pmt $" enter the total amount of child support to be paid each month. This number should be the same as on the Money Judgment for Child Support in the Decree. On the blank after "Next Due Date" fill in the date child support is due, which also should match the figure in the Money Judgment for Child Support in the Decree. On the "Arrearage $" blank, fill in the amount of overdue child support payments, if any. Since child support generally does not start until after the divorce is final, most people will fill in 0.

- The lines under the headings "Beneficiary(ies), Birthdate, Relationship, SS#, Amount, Limit," are for information about your children. Enter the requested information for each of your minor children. The children's names go under "Beneficiary." Under "Relationship," enter either "Daughter" or "Son." For the "Amount" column, divide the total child support to be paid each month by the total number of minor children of the marriage and enter that amount in this column for each child. "Statutory" has already been entered under the "Limit" column.

- Set the form aside. You will not sign this form, only the judge will date and sign it.

Form 7: Property Settlement

The Property Settlement form is only for real estate. If you do not own any real estate, you can skip this form.

If you own real estate, you must complete a Property Settlement form. You may also draft a written settlement for your personal property, but you would not use this particular form for that purpose. A mediator or attorney may be able to help you draft your own personal property settlement, or you could use the book *Divorce and Money* to help you. See above Chapter 7 on personal property division.

The first step is to decide which Property Settlement applies to your situation. Either you will sell the property (usually, the family home) and divide the equity between the two of you, or one of you will sell your interest in the property to the other. If you are unsure about how to divide the real property, see Chapter 7.

Choose the appropriate form, either the settlement in which the property is sold, or the settlement in which one spouse transfers his or her share to the other spouse. We call the settlement in which the property is sold Property Settlement (A), and the other arrangement Property Settlement (B).

Property Settlement (A): Selling the Property and Dividing the Equity

- Fill in the caption.

Section 1: Enter each spouse's share of the equity. For example, if you are dividing the equity equally, enter: "50% to Joe Jones and 50% to Kate Jones."

Section 2: In the blanks following "The property is commonly described as:" fill in the address of the property. In the blanks following "And legally described as:" fill in the legal description of the property. You must get the property's legal description from an actual deed for the property—not from your property taxes or other papers where the description has been abbreviated and may not be acceptable.

- Set this form aside for signing and dating later. This form must be signed in front of a notary.

Property Settlement (B): Transferring Ownership to One Spouse

- Fill in the caption.

Section 1: Enter the name of the spouse who will keep the property in the first blank. In the second blank, fill in the other spouse's name, the one who is giving up his or her share of the property.

Section 2: In the blanks following "The property is commonly described as:" fill in the address of the property. In the blanks following "And legally described as:" fill in the legal description of the property. You must get the property's legal description from an actual deed for the property—not from your property taxes or other papers where the description has been abbreviated and may not be acceptable.

Section 3: In the first blank, enter the name of the spouse who will keep the property. In the second blank, enter the name of the spouse who is giving up his or her share of the property.

- Set this form aside for signing and dating later. This form must be signed in front of a notary.

The Following Examples Show the Most Common Ways That Legal Descriptions Are Given

Lot 3, Block 45
Ironwood Subdivision
Hillsboro, Oregon
County of Washington

or:

Beginning at an iron pipe on the West line of that certain tract of land conveyed by John Metzger and Joline Metzger to J.S. Barnum and Nellie Barnum on January 4, 1922, and continuing East to County Road X...[extended description of coordinates, landmarks, measurements] ...thence South to the point of beginning.

or:

The North 40 feet of the East 30 feet of Lot 2, according to the duly filed plat of REDWOOD, in the City of Portland, filed January 21, 1936, in Plat Book 1178, Page 48, Records of the County of Multnomah and State of Oregon.

If the legal description you find for your property does not resemble any of the examples given above, you may need additional help to determine the correct legal description to use. Call the county property tax office, a title company, a realtor or even the holder of your mortgage.

Form 8: Vital Records

This form is required for all divorces. We have included a sample form in this chapter for your reference, though you will have to obtain an original of this form from your local courthouse. The Vital Records form cannot be provided as a tear-out form in this book because it contains carbons and an orange stripe that the court uses for filing purposes. Call your county courthouse to find out where to get one; a list of phone numbers and addresses is included in Chapter 13, Section F.

Filling Out Petitioner/Respondent Forms 12/13

Vital Records

OREGON DEPARTMENT OF HUMAN RESOURCES
HEALTH DIVISION
Vital Records Unit
RECORD OF DISSOLUTION OF MARRIAGE, OR ANNULMENT

136- State File Number

CO. FILE NO. _____

TYPE OR PRINT PLAINLY IN BLACK INK

HUSBAND
1. HUSBAND'S NAME (FIRST)   (MIDDLE)   (LAST)
2. RESIDENCE OR LEGAL ADDRESS   STREET AND NUMBER   CITY OR TOWN   COUNTY   STATE
3. SOCIAL SECURITY NUMBER (Optional)
4. BIRTHPLACE (State or Foreign Country)
5. DATE OF BIRTH (Month, Day, Year)

WIFE
6a. WIFE'S NAME (First, Middle, Last)
6b. MAIDEN SURNAME
7. FORMER LEGAL NAMES (IF ANY)   (1)   (2)   (3)
8. RESIDENCE OR LEGAL ADDRESS   STREET AND NUMBER   CITY OR TOWN   COUNTY   STATE
9. SOCIAL SECURITY NUMBER (Optional)
10. BIRTHPLACE (State or Foreign Country)
11. DATE OF BIRTH (Month, Day, Year)

MARRIAGE
12a. PLACE OF THIS MARRIAGE–CITY, TOWN OR LOCATION
12b. COUNTY
12c. STATE OR FOREIGN COUNTRY
13. DATE OF THIS MARRIAGE (Month, Day, Year)
14. DATE COUPLE LAST RESIDED IN SAME HOUSEHOLD (Month, Day, Year)
15. NUMBER OF CHILDREN UNDER 18 IN THIS HOUSEHOLD AS OF THE DATE IN ITEM 14.   Number _____ ☐ None
16. PETITIONER   ☐ Husband   ☐ Wife   ☐ Both

ATTORNEY
17a. NAME OF PETITIONER'S ATTORNEY (Type / Print)
17b. ADDRESS (Street and Number or Rural Route Number, City or Town, State, Zip Code)
18a. NAME OF RESPONDENT'S ATTORNEY (Type / Print)
18b. ADDRESS (Street and Number or Rural Route Number, City or Town, State, Zip Code)

DECREE
19. MARRIAGE OF THE ABOVE NAMED PERSONS WAS DISSOLVED ON: (Month, Day, Year)
20. TYPE OF DECREE   DISSOLUTION OF MARRIAGE ☐   ANNULMENT ☐
21. DATE DECREE BECOMES EFFECTIVE (Month, Day, Year)
22. NUMBER OF CHILDREN UNDER 18 WHOSE PHYSICAL CUSTODY WAS AWARDED TO:
   Husband _____ Wife _____
   Joint (Husband / Wife) _____ Other _____
   ☐ No children
23. COUNTY OF DECREE
24. TITLE OF COURT
25. SIGNATURE OF COURT OFFICIAL
26. TITLE OF COURT OFFICIAL
27. DATE SIGNED (Month, Day, Year)

ORS 432.010 REQUIRED STATISTICAL INFORMATION. THE INFORMATION BELOW WILL NOT APPEAR ON CERTIFIED COPIES OF THE RECORD.

	22. NUMBER OF THIS MARRIAGE– First, Second, etc. (Specify below)	29. IF PREVIOUSLY MARRIED, LAST MARRIAGE ENDED		30. RACE–American Indian, Black, White, etc. (Specify below)	31. EDUCATION (Specify only highest grade completed)	
		By Death, Divorce, Dissolution, or Annulment (Specify below)	Date (Month, Day, Year)		Elementary / Secondary (0-12)	College (1-4 or 5+)
HUSBAND	28a.	29a.	29b.	30a.	31a.	
WIFE	28b.	29c.	29d.	30b.	31b.	

THE PETITIONER OR LEGAL REPRESENTATIVE OF THE PETITIONER IS RESPONSIBLE FOR COMPLETING THE PERSONAL INFORMATION ON THIS FORM AND SHALL PRESENT THIS FORM TO THE CLERK OF THE COURT WITH THE PETITION.
IN ALL CASES THE COMPLETED RECORD SHALL BE A PREREQUISITE TO THE GRANTING OF THE FINAL DECREE.

45-5 (1/95)

ORIGINAL–VITAL RECORDS COPY

The Vital Records form asks mostly for relevant data such as names, addresses, Social Security numbers and birthdates. The answers to most of the questions are self-explanatory, though here are some tips on the less obvious questions.

Item 15: Fill in the number of minor children of the marriage, including children attending school. (For more information on children of the marriage, see Chapter 8.)

Item 16: Since you are filing as a solo petitioner, check the box for either husband or wife, whichever one you are.

Item 17: Since you are getting your own divorce without being represented by an attorney, fill in "None" in items 17a and 18a, and N/A for "not applicable" in items 17b and 18b.

Items 19 through 27: Leave these boxes blank for the court to fill in.

Item 29b: Enter the date the last marriage for the husband ended. You can approximate if you don't know the exact date.

Item 29d: Enter the date the last marriage for the wife ended. You can approximate if you don't know the exact date.

Item 30a: You may decline to enter the husband's race. If you do, fill in "refused."

Item 30b: You may decline to enter the wife's race. If you do, fill in "refused."

- You do not need to sign this form. A court official will sign it.

Forms 9 & 10: 90-Day Waiver Forms

If you do not want to have the 90-day waiting period waived, you can skip ahead to the instructions for Form 11.

Certain forms must be filed if you want the judge to sign your divorce Decree without having to wait out the 90-day waiting period. The 90-day period begins on the day your spouse is served. (See Chapter 12 for more on waiting periods and 90-day waivers.) If you want the 90-day waiting period waived, you will need to fill out the Motion and Order for Waiver of Ninety-Day Waiting Period and the Affidavit Requesting Waiver of Ninety-Day Waiting Period.

Form 9: Motion and Order for Waiver of 90-Day Waiting Period

- Fill in the caption. (See instructions for Certificate of Residency for help in filling out the caption.)
- Leave the date and the lower signature line blank for the judge to sign.
- Set the form aside for signing later. It does not need to be notarized.

Form 10: Affidavit Requesting Waiver of 90-Day Waiting Period

- Fill in the caption. (See instructions for Certificate of Residency for help in filling out the caption.) At the bottom of the caption, fill in the county you are filing in. This will be the same as the county you entered just above at the top of the caption.

Section 1: Fill in your name.

Section 2: Fill in the reason you and your spouse cannot resolve your differences. Some of the reasons commonly used are:

We have attended marriage counseling that has failed.

I am moving to another state and my spouse will remain in Oregon.

We have established separate lives.

My spouse is abusive and I have a restraining order.

Section 3: List the emergency reason affecting a third party why you need a 90-day waiver. Some of the reasons commonly used are:

I am refinancing my house (or buying a home) and need the divorce to be final to qualify for the financing.

I need child support to be ordered by the court.

I am pregnant and am planning to marry the father.

I have been seeing a therapist and they suggest that I finalize my divorce to lower my stress level which has been affecting my children and their conduct at school.

- Set the form aside for signing later. This form must be signed in front of a notary.

Form 11: Summons for Dissolution of Marriage

- Fill in the caption. (See instructions for Certificate of Residency for help in filling out the caption.)

- On the first line after the caption, fill in your spouse's name after "TO:" then the address where you are having them served. If you are having them served at a place other than their home—such as the place where he or she works or regularly visits (a bar, a friend's house, their parent's house)—use that address.

- In the paragraph after the heading "NOTICE TO RESPONDENT: READ THESE PAPERS CAREFULLY" there is a blank where you should enter the address of the courthouse in the county you are filing in. See Chapter 13, Section F, for a complete list of addresses of county courthouses.

- Skip the signature section and fill in your address in the next blanks.

- Fill in the Identifying Information About the Respondent section if the person serving your spouse does not know your spouse. This makes it easier for the server to recognize your spouse. Remember, you cannot serve the papers yourself.

- Set this form aside for signing later. It does not need to be notarized.

Form 12: Affidavit of Proof of Service

- Fill in the caption. (See instructions for Certificate of Residency for help in filling out the caption.) At the bottom of the caption, leave the blank after "County of" empty. The person who serves your spouse will fill this in.

- Leave the rest of this form blank for the person who serves your spouse to fill in.

When the server fills it in:

Bottom of Caption: Server fills in the county they are signing the form in.

Section 1: Server fills in their name.

Section 2: Server enters the state they live in.

Section 3: Server fills in the date they served your spouse with the papers, the county they served your spouse in and their name.

- Server signs in front of a notary and returns the form to you.

Form 13: Petitioner's Affidavit, Motion and Order for Default Decree

- Fill in the caption. (See instructions for Certificate of Residency for help in completing the caption.) At the bottom of the caption, fill in the county where you are signing the form. This will usually be the same as the county you entered just above at the top of the caption.

Section 1: Fill in your name.

Section 2: After your spouse has been served, fill in the date and the county (and state if your spouse was served in another state) in which your spouse was served. This section states that you had your spouse served, and that he or she did not file an answer with the court. Therefore you are asking the court to sign the order of default stating that your spouse has not answered. Skip to the MOTION section.

MOTION section: Enter your address on the blanks.

- Leave the rest blank for the judge to sign and date.

- Set this form aside for signing later. It needs to be signed in front of a notary.

Form 14: Affidavit Supporting Decree of Dissolution Without a Hearing

The Affidavit Supporting Decree of Dissolution Without a Hearing is a request that the court grant your divorce without a hearing. All petitioners must file this form with their divorce if they want their divorce to be granted without a courtroom hearing.

NOTE: This form is also required if your divorce became contested, but you then resolved your differences and continued with an uncontested divorce. In that case, you would need to file a Stipulated Decree (explained below) along with the Affidavit Supporting Decree of Dissolution Without a Hearing signed by both you and your spouse. Instructions for filing the Affidavit in conjunction with a Stipulated Decree are included below.

- Fill in the caption. (See instructions for Certificate of Residency for help in filling out the caption.) At the bottom of the caption, fill in the county where you are signing the form. This will usually be the same as the county you entered just above at the top of the caption.

Section 1: Fill in your name.

Section 2: Fill in the date of your marriage and the city and state where it took place.

Section 3: Fill in the date you and your spouse stopped living together. If you still live together fill in N/A for "not applicable."

Section 7: List your children's current address. If they have lived anywhere else in the past five years, list the places they lived and the dates they lived there. If they lived with anyone other than yourself or your spouse during the past five years, list that person's name and present address. If you need more space, use an attachment. (See Chapter 10, Section B5, on attachments.)

Section 9: Enter your spouse's (Respondent's) gross monthly income (before taxes), and his or her occupation. If you do not know your spouse's income or occupation, fill in "unknown" in each blank. Then enter the same information for yourself: your gross monthly income and occupation.

- Set this form aside for signing later. It does not require your spouse's signature but it must be signed in front of a notary. (Both your and your spouse's signatures are required if you submit the Affidavit along with a Stipulated Decree. See Form 16 below for information on filing this form in conjunction with a Stipulated Decree.)

Form 15: Compliance With Disclosure

The purpose of the Compliance With Disclosure form is to let the court know that you have provided your spouse with a copy of the asset disclosure notice required by ORS 107.089.

- Fill in the caption. (See instructions for Certificate of Residency for help in filling out the caption.)

- Set this form aside to sign later. It must be signed in front of a notary.

Form 16: Stipulated Decree of Dissolution of Marriage and Judgment

Fill out a Stipulated Decree only if your spouse filed an answer to your Petition—making your divorce contested—but then you reached agreement with your spouse, and you want to make your divorce uncontested again. The Stipulated Decree along with the Affidavit Supporting Decree of Dissolution Without a Hearing—signed by both you and your spouse—show the court that you and your spouse have resolved your differences and intend to proceed with an uncontested divorce.

The Stipulated Decree asks for basically the same information as the Decree for a petitioner/respondent divorce. The main difference is that both you and your spouse need to sign the Stipulated Decree. The purpose of requiring both signatures is to show that you have in fact resolved the differences that originally led to the divorce becoming contested.

Follow the instructions for filling out the petitioner/respondent Decree except, before you submit the Stipulated Decree to the court, both you and your spouse sign it. It does not need to be notarized. Remember to include any and all agreements, attachments or child support worksheets that you included with your Decree.

If you file a Stipulated Decree, you must both sign the Affidavit Supporting Decree of Dissolution Without a Hearing in front of a notary. Except for the requirement that both spouses sign this form, the instructions for filling it out are the same as if your divorce had never become contested. See Form 14 above for instructions in filling out the Affidavit Supporting Decree of Dissolution Without a Hearing.

B. After You've Completed the Forms

After all the forms have been filled out, they must be signed by you and, depending on the form, by your spouse. Some of the forms require signing in front of a notary. (See Chapter 10 above for more information on signing and notarizing the forms.) When you have finished filling out your forms, separate them on the basis of which ones need notarizing and which ones need your (and maybe your spouse's) signature (see list below). Then, once you've signed and notarized all the appropriate forms you'll be ready to organize them for filing with the court. Organizing and filing the forms are covered in Chapter 13.

The forms for petitioner/respondent filers that must be signed in front of a notary are:

- CERTIFICATE OF DOCUMENT PREPARATION
- PETITION FOR DISSOLUTION OF MARRIAGE
- AFFIDAVIT OF COMPLIANCE WITH U.C.C.J.A.
- AFFIDAVIT REQUESTING WAIVER OF NINETY-DAY WAITING PERIOD
- PROPERTY SETTLEMENT
- PETITIONER'S AFFIDAVIT, MOTION AND ORDER FOR DEFAULT DECREE
- AFFIDAVIT SUPPORTING DECREE OF DISSOLUTION WITHOUT A HEARING
- COMPLIANCE WITH DISCLOSURE

The forms that must be signed by you without being notarized are:

- CERTIFICATE OF RESIDENCY
- MOTION AND ORDER FOR WAIVER OF NINETY-DAY WAITING PERIOD
- SUMMONS FOR DISSOLUTION OF MARRIAGE
- STIPULATED DECREE OF DISSOLUTION OF MARRIAGE AND JUDGMENT (SPOUSE MUST ALSO SIGN)

The forms that are signed by the court are:

- DECREE OF DISSOLUTION OF MARRIAGE AND JUDGMENT
- SUPPORT ORDER ABSTRACT
- PETITIONER'S AFFIDAVIT, MOTION AND ORDER FOR DEFAULT DECREE (THE ORDER PORTION)
- VITAL RECORDS FORM
- MOTION AND ORDER FOR WAIVER OF NINETY-DAY WAITING PERIOD (THE ORDER PORTION)
- STIPULATED DECREE OF DISSOLUTION OF MARRIAGE AND JUDGMENT (THE ORDER AND JUDGMENT PORTIONS)

Forms that are not signed by anyone:

- CHILD SUPPORT WORKSHEETS

Forms that are signed by your process server in front of a notary:

- AFFIDAVIT OF PROOF OF SERVICE

When to Sign the Forms Some judges are very particular about when the forms are signed. In particular, solo petitioners should not sign any forms that request a default Decree or a waiver of waiting periods until the time limit for the respondent to answer has expired. You should wait to have the forms Petitioner's Motion and Order for Default Decree, Affidavit Supporting Decree of Dissolution Without a Hearing and Affidavit Requesting Waiver of Ninety-Day Waiting Period (if used) signed until 30 days after your spouse has been served. Otherwise you will state to the court that your spouse was served and didn't respond even before the deadline has passed for him or her to do so. ∎

Filing the Forms

A. Filing Instructions for Co-Petitioners	13/2
1. Making Copies	13/2
2. Assembling the Forms and Attachments	13/3
3. Filing the Forms	13/4
4. Filing First-Step Papers	13/4
5. Filing Second-Step Papers	13/4
B. Filing Instructions for Solo Petitioners	13/5
1. Making Copies	13/5
2. Assembling the Forms and Attachments	13/6
3. Filing the First-Step Papers	13/7
4. Serving First-Step Papers on Spouse	13/8
5. If You Use a Stipulated Decree	13/11
6. Filing Second-Step Papers	13/11
C. Deadlines	13/12
D. Dealing With Problems With Your Papers	13/13
E. Documents Issued by the Court	13/13
1. Continuation of Health Insurance Coverage	13/13
2. Notice of Dismissal (Multnomah County only)	13/14
3. Notice of Judgment	13/14
4. Signed Decree of Dissolution of Marriage and Judgment	13/14
F. Filing Fees by County	13/14

Once you and your spouse, or you alone, have filled out, signed and notarized all the necessary forms, you will be ready to tackle the final task of obtaining a divorce—filing the forms with the court.

There are two basic steps to filing your divorce papers. The first step involves filing your Petition and a number of other forms that lay out your request for a divorce. We will refer to these papers as first-step papers. After the first-step papers have been filed, you may need to have your spouse served (if you are a solo petitioner) or you may have to wait for a specified waiting period. Then, both co-petitioners and solo petitioners will file another set of papers, which we'll call the second-step papers. After the second-step papers have been filed, the judge will sign the Decree which will become official 30 days later.

This chapter will walk you step by step through filing the papers involved in an Oregon divorce once they have been filled out, signed and, if necessary, notarized. If you have not completed all your forms or still need to sign or notarize any of them, refer to the previous chapter for instructions.

This chapter contains two sets of instructions: one for co-petitioners, and one for petitioners filing alone. For each type of divorce, we'll go through the filing requirements step by step. We'll start with instructions for co-petitioners.

If you are a petitioner filing alone, you can skip ahead to Section B on page 13/7 for instructions on how to file your completed paperwork.

A. Filing Instructions for Co-Petitioners

The following instructions are for spouses who have filled out, signed and notarized their divorce papers together.

1. Making Copies

After all the forms have been filled out and signed, you will need to make copies of them. You should keep the copies separate from the originals.

NOTE: Not all co-petitioners will use all of the forms referred to in these instructions. If you are not using a certain form such as child support worksheets or 90-day waiver papers, just ignore the instructions pertaining to them. Be sure, however, that you file all the forms that are mandatory for an Oregon divorce. Refer to Chapter 10, Section A, if you are unsure about whether you must file a particular form.

You will need the following total number of copies of each completed form:

2　Affidavit Application for Decree

2　Affidavit of Compliance With U.C.C.J.A.

2　Affidavit Requesting Waiver of 90-Day Waiting Period

2　Affidavit Supporting Decree of Dissolution Without a Hearing

2　Certificate of Document Preparation

2　Certificate of Residency

4　Decree of Dissolution of Marriage and Judgment; 5 if filing in Multnomah County

2　Motion and Order for Waiver of 90-Day Waiting Period

2　Petition for Dissolution of Marriage

5　Support Order Abstract

2　Waiver of Disclosure

- 4 Child Support Worksheets; 5 if filing in Multnomah County
- 4 Property Settlement (for real property); 5 if filing in Multnomah County
- 4 Copies of any other attachments (such as mediated agreements, lists of personal property that were too long for the forms, other clauses that were too long for the forms or lengthy parenting arrangements); 5 if filing in Multnomah County.

(The Vital Records form has a number of pages with carbons and does not need to be copied.)

2. Assembling the Forms and Attachments

You should now have a number of copies of each of your forms, plus the originals. For the most part, the copies are for your records. The originals (plus a few copies) will be filed with the court in two steps which will be explained below.

Once you've made all the necessary copies, you will have to organize the copies and the originals into sets. Each set may not contain exactly the same documents as another set, so be careful to organize them and file them according to the following instructions.

a. Make two sets for your records

First, assemble two sets of copies (not originals)—one for you and one for your spouse. Include one copy of every form, including attachments. You and your spouse will keep these sets for your records. You should each put your set in a safe place.

NOTE: Normally, attachments should be included with all copies of the Petition and Decree. However, for your and your spouse's personal records, we're instructing you to include just one copy of each attachment per set, rather than to include one for the Petition and another one for the Decree.

b. Make a set to file with the court

After you've made a set of copies for both you and your spouse, there will be a few copies of documents left over, plus all the originals. These will eventually be filed with the court. You should staple together all the pages that are part of each individual form, whether it's a copy or an original. For example, the Petition has six pages, so staple all those pages together. The Decree has six pages, so staple those pages together. Do not, however, staple forms to each other, such as stapling the Decree to the Petition, or the original Decree to a copy of the Decree. Each individual form should remain separate from the others.

Next, you'll divide the originals (and the few extra copies) into two sets: one first-step set, and one second-step set. Each set will be filed with the court at separate times.

First-Step Papers

Group together the following documents, in order:

1. Vital Records (original)
2. Petition and any attachments (originals)
3. Certificate of Residency (original)
4. Certificate of Document Preparation (original)
5. Motion and Order for Waiver of 90-Day Waiting Period (original; if used)
6. Affidavit Requesting Waiver of 90-Day Waiting Period (original; if used)
7. Waiver of Compliance (original).

If there are children of the marriage, also include:

8. Child Support Worksheets (original)
9. Support Order Abstract (original plus one copy)
10. Affidavit of Compliance With U.C.C.J.A. (original).

Put these documents aside for filing. Section A3 below will explain how and when to file these papers.

Second-Step Papers

Group together the following documents, in order:

1. Affidavit Application for Decree (original)

2. Decree (original), plus 2 copies, 3 if filing in Multnomah County, and any attachments for each. Use the originals of the attachments to attach to the original Decree, and copies of the attachments to attach to the copies of the Decree.

3. Self-Addressed Stamped Envelope

4. Two copies of Support Order Abstract.

Put these documents aside for filing. Section A3 below will explain how and when to file these papers.

3. Filing the Forms

After the completed forms have been organized according to the above instructions, you should be ready to file them with the court. You will file some of the forms at one time, and the rest of the forms a short while later.

a. You can file by mail or in person

All divorces can be filed either in person or by mail. If you file your first step in person, you may file the second step by mail, and vice versa. The differences between the two ways of filing are mostly minor and should not impact the outcome of your case. Most people base their decision on which method they find the most convenient.

If you file in person, the court clerk will look through the papers to make sure that you have arranged everything in the right order. You pay the filing fee with cash or a money order, or a personal check if that court accepts them. The clerk will assign you a case number and stamp it on your forms. If you bring along your second-step forms, the clerk will stamp the case number on those forms as well.

One advantage to filing in person is that the court clerk will look over your papers and let you know immediately if something is missing or otherwise unacceptable. This can help prevent delays in your case. Also, you will get your case number right away and have it entered onto your second-step papers for you—rather than having to wait for it to be mailed to you and having to enter it onto your papers yourself. On the other hand, traveling to the courthouse, finding parking, and perhaps waiting in line can all be inconvenient. You'll have to decide for yourself which method of filing you prefer.

4. Filing First-Step Papers

If you file by mail, send the first-step papers (listed above) to your county Circuit Court. (You'll find a list of county courthouses and addresses at the end of this chapter.) Don't forget to include a money order or a personal check (call the court ahead of time to see if they accept personal checks) for the filing fee. Also, if you include a self-addressed stamped envelope (SASE), the court clerk will mail you a receipt for the filing fee with your case number written on it. Otherwise, you'll have to call the court to get your case number and you won't receive a receipt for the filing fee. Put the divorce papers, the check or money order and the SASE into a large manila envelope and mail it to the courthouse. Once you know your case number, you should write it on all the remaining papers in the caption where you see "No. _____" to the right of your names. Your first step of filing will then be complete.

If you file your papers in person, go to your county's Circuit Court. If the county you are filing in has a family law office you will probably be directed to file your papers in that room of the courthouse. The court clerk will look over your papers and collect the filing fee. He will then assign you a case number. If you bring your second-step papers with you the court clerk will stamp the case number on them for you. That will complete the first step of filing.

5. Filing Second-Step Papers

Unless a 90-day waiver is granted, you must wait 90 days from filing the first-step papers to file your second-step papers. If you are not requesting a 90-day waiver or if the judge did not grant you one, wait 90 days from filing the first-step papers, then file in person or mail the second-step forms. (Second-step papers are listed above.) If the court clerk didn't stamp the case number on your second-step forms, be sure you enter the case number on all remaining papers.

If you have requested a waiver of the 90-day waiting period, you may file your second-step papers as soon as you know the judge granted the 90-day waiver. To find out if the judge signed the waiver, wait a week or two and call the court. Give the clerk your case number and ask if the judge granted the 90-day waiver. If the judge did, you may file your second-step papers either in person or by mail. If the judge did not grant you the waiver you must wait 90 days from filing the first step to file the rest of the papers.

NOTE: If you are requesting a waiver of the 90 days, you can try filing all your papers at one time rather than breaking the filing down into two steps. However, some judges and clerks do not like this kind of efficiency and may reject a portion of the papers until the judge actually grants the 90-day waiver.

After you file the second-step papers, you should receive the Decree signed by the judge in about two to three weeks. The signed Decree is the document that officially establishes your divorce, but it will not become final until 30 days after the judge signed it. At that point, 30 days after the Decree was signed, you and your spouse will be officially divorced.

B. Filing Instructions for Solo Petitioners

The following instructions are for petitioners who are filing their divorce papers alone, and having their spouses served.

1. Making Copies

After all the forms have been filled out and signed, you will need to make copies of them. You should keep the copies separate from the originals.

NOTE: Not all petitioners will use all of the forms referred to in these instructions. If you are not using a certain form such as child support worksheets or 90-day waiver papers, just ignore the instructions pertaining to them. Be sure, however, that you file all the forms that are mandatory for an Oregon divorce. Refer to Chapter 10, Section A, if you are unsure about whether you must file a particular form.

Petitioners filing alone will need the following total number of copies of each completed form:

- 2 Affidavit of Compliance With U.C.C.J.A.
- 1 Affidavit of Proof of Service
- 1 Affidavit Requesting Waiver of 90-Day Waiting Period
- 1 Affidavit Supporting Decree of Dissolution Without a Hearing
- 1 Certificate of Document Preparation
- 1 Certificate of Residency
- 1 Compliance With Disclosure
- 3 Decree of Dissolution; 4 if filing in Multnomah County
- 1 Motion and Order for Waiver of 90-Day Waiting Period
- 1 Notice of Disclosure
- 2 Petition for Dissolution of Marriage
- 1 Petitioner's Motion and Order for Default Decree
- 2 Summons for Dissolution of Marriage
- 3 Support Order Abstract
- 3 Stipulated Decree of Dissolution of Marriage and Judgment; 4 if filing in Multnomah County
- 4 Child Support Worksheets; 5 if filing in Multnomah County

4 Property Settlement (for real property); 5 if filing in Multnomah County

4 Copies of any other attachments (such as mediated agreements, lists of personal property that were too long for the forms, other clauses that were too long for the forms or lengthy parenting arrangements); 5 if filing in Multnomah County.

(The Vital Records form has a number of pages with carbons and does not need to be copied.)

2. Assembling the Forms and Attachments

You should now have a number of copies of each of your forms, plus the originals. For the most part, the copies are for your records. The originals (plus a few copies) will be filed with the court in two steps which will be explained below.

Once you've made all the necessary copies, you will have to organize the copies and the originals into sets. Each set may not contain exactly the same documents as another set, so be careful to organize them and file them according to the following instructions.

a. Make a set of copies for your records

First, assemble a set of copies (not originals) for yourself. Include one copy of every form. You will keep this set for your records. Put your set in a safe place.

NOTE: Normally, attachments should be included with all copies of the Petition and Decree. However, for your personal records, we're instructing you to include just one copy of each attachment, rather than to include one for the Petition and another one for the Decree.

b. Make a set to be served on your spouse

Next, put together a set of forms that will be served on your spouse. (The details of serving your spouse are covered below in Section B4.) Group together the following documents in order:

1. Summons (copy)

2. Petition and any attachments (copies)

3. Child Support Worksheets (copies; if there are children)

4. Affidavit of Compliance With U.C.C.J.A. (copy; if there are children)

5. Notice of Disclosure (copy).

On the copy of the Petition to be served on your spouse, make sure to attach copies of any and all attachments such as property settlements, parenting agreements, mediated agreements or other sheets you attached if you ran out of room on the forms. See Chapter 10, Section B5, for more information about attachments.

c. Make a set to file with the court

After you've made a set of copies for yourself and for serving your spouse, there will be a few copies of documents left over, plus all the originals. You should staple together all the pages that are part of each individual form. For example, the Petition has six pages, so staple all those pages together. The Decree has seven pages, so staple those pages together. Do not, however, staple forms to each other, such as stapling the Decree to the Petition, or the original Decree to a copy of the Decree. Each individual form should remain separate from the others.

Next, you'll divide the originals (and the few extra copies) into two sets to file with the court: one first-step set, and one second-step set. Each set will be filed with the court at separate times.

First-Step Papers

Group together the following documents, in order:

1. Vital Records (original)

2. Petition for Dissolution of Marriage and any attachments (original)

3. Certificate of Residency (original)

4. Certificate of Document Preparation (original)

5. Fee Deferral papers from your county courthouse (original; if used).

If there are children of the marriage, also include:

6. Child Support Worksheets (original)
7. Support Order Abstract (original)
8. Affidavit of Compliance With U.C.C.J.A. (original).

NOTE: Obtaining Fee Deferrals. Each county has its own forms and procedures for obtaining a fee deferral. Call your county courthouse to find out how to apply for one. If you obtain and fill out the fee deferral forms ahead of time, you can include them with the first-step papers as described above. However, oftentimes a petitioner will not obtain the fee deferral forms until she is at the courthouse ready to file her first-step papers. If you do not get the fee deferral forms until you go to the courthouse to file your first-step papers, just ask the court clerk there what to do. Once you complete whatever procedures are followed at that courthouse for fee deferrals, you'll be able to file your first-step papers.

Put these documents aside for filing. Section B3 below will explain how and when to file these papers.

Second-Step Papers

Group together the following documents, in order:

1. Petitioner's Affidavit, Motion and Order for Default Decree (original)
2. Affidavit Supporting Decree of Dissolution Without a Hearing (original)
3. Decree (original) and 2 copies (3 if filing in Multnomah County), and any attachments with each
4. Motion and Order for Waiver of 90-Day Waiting Period (original; if used)
5. Affidavit for Waiver of 90-Day Waiting Period (original; if used)
6. Compliance With Disclosure (original).

If there are children, also include:

7. Two copies of Support Order Abstract
8. Self-addressed stamped envelope.

Put these documents aside for filing. Section B3 below will explain how and when to file these papers. You should have a copy of the original Summons and the original Affidavit of Proof of Service left over. Section B4 below will explain what to do with these forms.

3. Filing the First-Step Papers

After the completed forms have been organized according to the above instructions, you should be ready to file the first-step papers with the court.

a. You can file by mail or in person

All divorces can be filed either in person or by mail. If you file your first step in person, you may file the second step by mail, and vice versa. The differences between the two ways of filing are mostly minor and should not impact the outcome of your case. Most people base their decision on which method they find the most convenient. Note, however: If you intend to request a fee deferral and want to file your first-step papers by mail, you'll need to call the courthouse ahead of time and find out what forms are required for the fee deferral. You'll need to obtain these forms, fill them out and submit them in accordance with the procedures of your county court before filing your first-step papers by mail.

If you file in person, the court clerk will look through the papers to make sure that you have arranged everything in the right order. You pay the filing fee with cash or a money order, or a personal check if that court accepts them. For fee deferrals, call your county courthouse ahead of time to find out how to apply for one. Once you've paid the fee or obtained a fee deferral, the clerk will assign you a case number and stamp it on your forms. If you bring along your second-step forms, the clerk will stamp the case number on those forms as well.

One advantage to filing in person is that the court clerk will look over your papers and let you know immediately if something is missing or otherwise unacceptable. This can help prevent delays in your case. Also, you will get your case number right away and have it entered onto your second-step papers for you—rather than having to wait for it to be mailed to you and having to enter it onto your papers yourself. On the other hand, traveling to the courthouse, finding parking and perhaps waiting in line can all be inconvenient. You'll have to decide for yourself which method of filing you prefer.

b. Filing instructions

If you file by mail, send the first-step papers to the courthouse addressed to the Circuit Court of the county in which you're filing. Don't forget to include a money order or a personal check (call the court ahead of time to see if they accept personal checks) for the filing fee. For fee deferrals, call the court before you file to find out how to apply for one. (See note above on fee deferrals.)

If you include a self-addressed stamped envelope (SASE) with your first-step papers, the court clerk will mail you a receipt for the filing fee with your case number written on it. Otherwise, you'll have to call the court to get your case number and you won't receive a receipt for the filing fee. Put the divorce papers, the check or money order and the SASE into a large manila envelope and mail it to the courthouse. Once you know your case number, you should write it on all the remaining papers in the caption where you see "No._____" to the right of your names. Your first step of filing will then be complete.

If you file your papers in person, go to your county's Circuit Court. If the county you are filing in has a family law office you will probably be directed to file your papers in that room of the courthouse. The court clerk will look over your papers and collect the filing fee. If you want a fee deferral, it's best to call ahead so that you can fill out whatever forms are required ahead of time. If you haven't already obtained and filled out the fee deferral forms before arriving at the courthouse, ask the clerk what to do to obtain a fee deferral. See note above on fee deferrals.

Once you've paid your fee or obtained a fee deferral, the court clerk will assign you a case number. If you bring your second-step papers with you the clerk will stamp the case number on them for you. That will complete the first step of filing.

4. Serving First-Step Papers on Spouse

After you have filed your first-step papers, you must officially notify your spouse. This notification process is called service. The reason your spouse must be served is that he or she has the right to know that you have filed for divorce. In addition, your spouse has the right to file a response to your divorce Petition, answering whatever claims or statements were made in it. He or she has 30 days from being served to file a response. Service has nothing to do with getting your spouse's permission to divorce him or her, and your spouse is not required to sign anything. But they do need to be legally notified.

Serving your spouse basically goes as follows: After the first-step papers have been filed with the court and a case number has been assigned, you must arrange to have certain divorce forms (listed below) delivered to your spouse in one of the precise ways established by law. Service may be done by anyone other than yourself who is age 18 or older. If you serve the papers yourself, service is invalid and you may have to refile and start your divorce again. (See "Simplified Service" Sidebar on an exception to this rule.) You can have a friend do it, an official of the sheriff's office, or hire a professional process server. The sheriff or professionals will charge a fee. A sheriff's office can take a long time to do service (sometimes a few weeks), but is equipped to handle a violent situation. A friend or professional, on the other hand, is usually quicker. The person who actually does the service then fills out and signs—in front of a notary—a form called an Affidavit of Proof of Service stating when and where he or she served your spouse.

Simplified Service

If you are absolutely certain that your spouse will cooperate, it is possible to deliver the necessary papers to him or her without having to adhere to the formal rules of service. You can deliver the papers to your spouse yourself or through regular U.S. Mail if you include with the divorce papers an Acknowledgment of Service which your spouse must sign, notarize and return to you. An Affidavit of Proof of Service is not necessary with simplified service. You must file the notarized Acknowledgment along with the original Summons with the court within 45 days of the date of service. Service will then be complete. You will find an Acknowledgment of Service form in the Appendix.

A notarized Acknowledgment is a statement by the spouse that he or she did receive the divorce paperwork necessary to satisfy the notification requirement. If your spouse does not cooperate by notarizing and returning the Acknowledgment to you, service will be invalid and your divorce could be seriously delayed. You should not use the simplified service procedures using the Acknowledgment of Service unless you are sure that your spouse will sign, notarize and return it to you.

To fill out the Acknowlegment of Service:

- Complete the caption, filling in the county in which you are filing for divorce at the top, your name as Petitioner and your spouse's name as Respondent, and your case number. At the bottom of the caption, leave the blank after "County of" empty. Your spouse will fill this in.
- Leave the rest of this form blank for your spouse to fill in.

When your spouse fills it in:

Bottom of Caption: Spouse enters the county in which he or she is signing the form.

Section 1: Spouse fills in his or her name.

Section 2: Spouse fills in the date he or she was served with the papers, and the county in which he or she was served.

- Spouse signs in front of a notary and returns the form to you.

You have six months to have your spouse served. If your spouse is not served during the six months, the court will send you a notice giving you 28 days to complete service, or your case will be dismissed. If you are having trouble getting your spouse served in this time period, write to the court and explain why service has not been completed. If you have a good reason, such as your spouse has been hiding or otherwise avoiding service, the court may grant you some more time before they dismiss your case. Wait until you have received a 28-day notice to send the court a letter of explanation.

a. Instructions for petitioner

The instructions for having your spouse served are as follows:

1. Assemble a copy of the Summons, a copy of the Petition and any attachments, a copy of the Child Support Worksheets and the Affidavit of Compliance With U.C.C.J.A. (if you have children) and the Notice of Disclosure. (You'll keep the original Summons for filing later, along with the original Affidavit of Proof of Service.)

2. Type or write on the last page of the Petition:

"I certify this is a true and exact copy of the original." Sign your name immediately below this statement. You do not need to sign in front of a notary. Clip or rubber band the papers together to make sure none gets lost. Do not put the forms in an envelope, as the summons must be visible.

3. Give this set of papers to a friend or process server to serve (hand to) your spouse along with instructions for serving, which are printed below and in the Appendix of this book. Make a copy of the instructions from the Appendix and give it to the server. You cannot serve the papers yourself. The server must be over the age of 18.

4. The server must give the papers to your spouse. They cannot give the papers to a roommate or friend of your spouse. It must be your spouse directly. More specifics about the act of serving are provided below.

5. After service is completed, the server must fill out the Affidavit of Proof of Service. After being filled in, this form must be signed in front of a notary.

6. After filling out, signing and notarizing the Affidavit of Proof of Service the server should be sure to return it to you so you can file with the court within the deadline, which is 45 days after service was completed. Or, if the sheriff or a professional process server did service, they may file the form with the court themselves. Check with them ahead of time to find out if they will file the Affidavit of Proof of Service on their own.

7. When you file the Affidavit of Proof of Service, the original Summons should be filed along with it. If a sheriff or professional process server filed the Affidavit for you, you should file the Summons as soon as you know the Affidavit of Proof of Service has been filed.

b. Instructions for the server

To complete service, you (the server) must hand the respondent (the person being served) a copy of the Petition with a summons on top. Do not put the papers in an envelope, as the summons must be visible to the person being served. The divorce papers may contain several other documents as well, such as child support worksheets or property settlements. You should serve whatever your friend has given you to serve.

If the person you need to serve will not open his door, you cannot serve him. You could wait for him to leave the building or you could wait for him at another location where you can stand face to face with him. At that point, if he is standing in front of you but will not physically take the papers, you may drop them at his feet. As long as there is no door or other barrier between you, you can serve him by placing the papers within his reach.

Once the papers have been handed to him or placed within his reach, he has been served. If he tears up the papers or throws them away it does not matter. Service has been completed.

After completing service, you must fill out, sign and notarize the Affidavit of Proof of Service and return it to the petitioner as soon as possible. The petitioner has 45 days from the date of service to file this form with the court, so it is important that you complete it and return it quickly.

c. Filling out the Affidavit of Proof of Service

- Petitioner fills in the caption.

- Server fills in the county in which he or she is signing the form, in the blank at the end of the caption.

    Section 1: Server fills in his or her name.

    Section 2: Server fills in the state he or she lives in.

    Section 3: Server fills in the date he or she served your spouse (Respondent), the county where service took place and the server's name.

- Server must sign the form in front of a notary. The notarized form must be returned to the petitioner as soon as possible.

What If the Papers Cannot Be Served?

If your spouse is avoiding being served, you can hire a professional process server. They are experienced and know many tricks (all legal) to accomplish service. If your spouse has moved and can't be found, you will need to complete service by the procedure of posting or publication. Neither of these processes are covered in this book. An independent paralegal or attorney can help you complete the forms and get through the process to publish or post, and provide all the necessary affidavits and documentation. Then you can continue using the forms in this book to complete your divorce.

Be sure to get the Affidavit of Proof of Service back from the server in time to file it with the court. If this form is not filed with the court within 45 days of service, you may need to have the papers re-served or your divorce could be dismissed.

5. If You Use a Stipulated Decree

If, after being served with the divorce papers your spouse files an answer to your Petition, your divorce has become contested. For contested divorces we recommend consulting an attorney. If, however, you and your spouse are able to resolve your differences on your own and want to proceed with an uncontested divorce, you'll need to file a Stipulated Decree with both of your signatures. In addition you'll need to submit the Affidavit Supporting Decree of Dissolution Without a Hearing signed by both of you and notarized. Instructions for filling out both of these forms are included in Chapter 12 above.

When using a Stipulated Decree to proceed with an uncontested divorce, your second-step papers will include the following, in order:

1. Affidavit Supporting Decree of Dissolution Without a Hearing (original)

2. Stipulated Decree (original) and 2 copies (3 if filing in Multnomah County), and any attachments with each

3. Motion and Order for Waiver of 90-Day Waiting Period (original; if used)

4. Affidavit for Waiver of 90-Day Waiting Period (original; if used)

5. Compliance With Disclosure (original).

If there are children, also include:

6. Two copies of Support Order Abstract

7. Self-addressed stamped envelope for each spouse.

6. Filing Second-Step Papers

Unless a 90-day waiver is granted, you must wait 90 days from serving the papers on your spouse to file your second-step papers. If you are not requesting a 90-day waiver or if the judge did not grant you one, wait 90 days from the date of service, then file in person or mail the second-step forms. (See Section B2 above on assembling second-step papers.) If the court clerk didn't stamp the case number on your second-step forms, be sure you enter the case number on all remaining papers.

If you do want to request a waiver of the 90-day waiting period, you must wait to file your request until 30 days after your spouse has been served. The reason for this wait is to give your spouse the opportunity to respond to the Petition served upon him or her. If your spouse has not filed a response within 30 days of being served, then you can file your 90-day waiver papers (Motion and Order for Waiver of 90-day Waiting Period and Affidavit Requesting Waiver of 90-day Waiting Period), along with the rest of the second-step papers. A list of second-step papers and the order in which they should be assembled is in Section B2 above.

If the judge grants the 90-day waiver, then he or she will accept the rest of the second-step papers and proceed with your divorce. If, however, the judge does not grant you the waiver, your second-step papers will be returned to you with an explanation that your 90-day waiver request was denied. In that case, you must wait 90 days from the date of service, then you may refile the papers.

After the second-step papers have been filed, you should receive the Decree signed by the judge in about two to three weeks. The signed Decree is the document that officially establishes your divorce, but it will not become final until 30 days after the judge signed it. At that point, 30 days after the Decree was signed, you and your spouse will be officially divorced.

C. Deadlines

There are certain filing deadlines that, if not met, can result in your case being dismissed. Any time you miss a deadline, the court will send you a notice explaining the problem and giving you some time to correct it. Most often, you are given 28 days to correct a problem. Some of the common reasons that petitioners miss deadlines are:

1. Inability to serve the spouse.

2. A delay by the process server in serving the papers.

3. A reconciliation followed by a decision to go ahead with the divorce after all.

4. Failure to file the second-step papers.

5. Failure to file the Affidavit of Proof of Service

If you receive a notice of missing a deadline, act promptly to correct the problem. If you simply forgot to send in the papers, send them in to the court right away. If you are having problems with serving the papers, write a letter to the court explaining the delay and what you intend to do about it. A sample letter is included below. Be sure to include your case number on the letter.

If you do not respond to the notice of a missed deadline within the specified time period (usually 28 days) your case will be dismissed. If your case is dismissed and you still want to get divorced, you will have either to start the whole process over or to hire an attorney to reopen your case. See chapter 15 for how to hire an attorney.

```
SAMPLE LETTER

Date _____
Circuit Court _____ County
[Street Address of Circuit Court]
[City,] Oregon [Zip]
Re: Case # _____

Dear [Name of Person Who Sent the Notice]:

I received your notice stating my case would be
dismissed. I am asking you not to dismiss my
case because _____
_____
_____
_____.

Sincerely,

X _____

Name _____
Address _____
City, State, Zip _____
Phone Number _____
```

Common Reasons to Ask for More Time:

- I have been trying to locate my spouse to have him/her served and just recently found out where he/she is working.

- I hired a process server and they just located my spouse.

- My spouse and I were trying counseling but it's not working out and I want to finish my divorce.

D. Dealing With Problems With Your Papers

If there is a problem with your divorce papers, the court may return them to you. When your papers are returned, the court will usually send a letter explaining the problem. If you still do not understand why your papers were returned, call the court. When a court returns papers they will usually include a phone number for the judge who reviewed your papers. Call that number and ask to speak with the judge's clerk. If, after looking over your papers and talking with the court clerk you still don't know what is wrong, call an independent paralegal or an attorney to help you. After correcting the papers, refile them.

Papers are often returned for the following reasons:

Problem: Some papers are not signed.

Cure: Sign where needed and resubmit.

Problem: Some papers that require notarization are not notarized.

Cure: Notarize the papers that require it and resubmit.

Problem: Information is missing from a form.

Cure: Fill in the required information and resubmit.

Problem: The second-step papers were filed too early.

Cure: Wait the correct amount of time, then refile the second-step papers.

Remember, if you are not requesting a 90-day waiver, you must wait a full 90 days from the date of filing (if you are filing as co-petitioners) or 90 days from the date your spouse was served (if you are filing petitioner/respondent) to file your second-step papers. If you are requesting a 90-day waiver and you are filing petitioner/respondent, your spouse is still entitled to 30 days to respond from the date he or she was served. In this situation, you must wait 30 days to file your second-step papers.

Problem: The Petition and Decree contain conflicting information.

Cure: Re-do the Decree so that all the information in it is the same as the information in the Petition. Then refile the second-step papers.

E. Documents Issued by the Court

Besides the signed Decree, the court may send you and your spouse a number of other notices after you have filed all your papers.

1. Continuation of Health Insurance Coverage

After your papers have been filed you will receive a notice from the court explaining your rights and obligations for continuing health insurance coverage on your spouse. You will be informed that if you have been on your spouse's insurance, you are entitled to stay on that insurance and receive the same insurance coverage that you currently have. Similarly, if your spouse is on your health insurance, your spouse is entitled to continued coverage.

Continued Insurance Coverage After Divorce

An ex-spouse can continue to receive coverage under his or her former spouse's policy, but the cost will go up after the divorce. Ex-spouses must pay COBRA rates (named after a federal statute known as the Consolidated Omnibus Budget Reconciliation Act), which are higher than the rates for married dependents. From the date of your divorce, there is a deadline for filing for COBRA benefits that varies according to different circumstances. In some cases the deadline is as soon as ten days after the effective date of the divorce. If you wish to remain on a spouse's insurance policy, contact the employer providing the insurance for specifics of the policy.

Example: *Ray has insurance coverage provided by his wife Jody's employer. Even though they are getting divorced, Ray can stay on Jody's health insurance plan. He will pay for it himself according to COBRA rates which will be higher than what is currently taken out of Judy's check for his coverage.*

2. Notice of Dismissal (Multnomah County only)

If you are filing in Multnomah County you will receive a Notice of Dismissal. Residents of other counties do not receive this notice. The dismissal date is simply your deadline for filing certain forms. It is scheduled at the time of filing and is mailed to every person who files for divorce in the county. Do not be alarmed when you receive this notice. As long as you process your papers before the date appearing on the notice, your case will not be dismissed.

3. Notice of Judgment

A Notice of Judgment will be sent to you if you were granted a fee deferral judgment, a money judgment or a child support judgment. The Notice will list whatever judgments were granted to you. There are three types of judgments that may be listed on this Notice.

a. Fee deferral judgment

If you did not pay your filing fee and were granted a fee deferral, the state now has a judgment against your spouse or possibly yourself for the amount of the filing fee. The person whom the judgment is against must pay the fee, or it will be taken out of his or her next year's tax return. Call the court if you have questions about payment arrangements.

b. Debt division judgment

If you requested and were granted a judgment for debts against your spouse, this will also be listed in this notice. It will state: "Judgment Docketed and Unsatisfied," which means that the debt has not been paid. Once the debts are paid, the non-paying spouse must sign a Satisfaction of Judgment. This document allows the paying spouse to clear his or her credit record of the judgment after it's been paid off.

c. Child support judgment

If there are children and child support was ordered, the child support judgment will state: "Judgment Docketed and Unsatisfied" (unpaid). Since child support is an ongoing debt, it will be "unsatisfied" until the child is no longer a minor or until the obligation has legally ended for some other reason.

4. Signed Decree of Dissolution of Marriage and Judgment

You should receive a signed Decree from the court about two to three weeks after filing the second-step papers. If you do not receive your signed Decree, call the court. They could be dealing with a backlog of files, delaying them beyond the time it usually takes to send out a signed Decree. Or, if you did not send an SASE with your second-step papers or didn't provide enough copies of it, the court will not send you a copy of the Decree.

F. Filing Fees by County

Before filing your divorce papers, you should call the county court you are filing in to find out how they accept payment for filing fees. Some county courts do not accept personal checks, only cash or money orders.

COUNTY	ADDRESS	PHONE #	FILING FEE
BAKER	1995 3rd St. Baker, OR 97814	541-523-6305	$114.00
BENTON	120 NW 4th Corvallis, OR 97330	541-757-6826	$201.00
CLACKAMAS	807 Main Oregon City, OR 97045	503-655-8447	$251.00
CLATSOP	749 Commercial PO Box 835 Astoria, OR 97103	541-325-8583	$114.00
COLUMBIA	First Street St. Helens, OR 97051	541-397-2327	$114.00
COOS	250 N. Baxter Coquille, OR 97423	541-396-3121	$114.00
CROOK	300 E. Third Prinville, OR 97754	541-447-5116	$189.00
CURRY	450 N. Ellensburg Gold Beach, OR 97444	541-247-4511	$114.00
DESCHUTES	1164 NW Bond Bend, OR 97701	541-388-5300	$214.00
DOUGLAS	Room 201 Roseburg, OR 97470	541-957-2444	$189.00
GILLIAM	221 S. Oregon PO Box 622 Condon, OR 97823	541-384-3572	$92.00
GRANT	200 S. Canyon City PO Box 159 Canyon City, OR 97820	541-575-1438	$114.00
HARNEY	450 N. Buena Vista Burns, OR 97220	541-573-5207	$114.00
HOOD RIVER	309 State St. Hood River, OR 97031	541-386-3535	$114.00
JACKSON	100 S. Oakdale Medford, OR 97501	541-776-7171	$189.00
JEFFERSON	75 SE C St. Madras, OR 97741	541-475-3421	$189.00
JOSEPHINE	500 SW 6th Grants Pass, OR 97526	541-476-2309	$224.00
KLAMATH	317 S. 7th St. 2nd Floor Klamath Falls, OR 97601	541-883-5504	$189.00

COUNTY	ADDRESS	PHONE #	FILING FEE
LAKE	513 Center St. Lakeview, OR 97630	541-947-6051	$92.00
LANE	125 E. 8th Ave. Eugene, OR 97401	541-687-4020	$250.00
LINCOLN	225 W. Olive PO Box 100 Newport, OR 97365	503-265-4236	$114.00
LINN	4th and Broadalbin Albany, OR 97321	541-967-3845	$201.00
MALHEUR	251 B. St. W-3 Vale, OR 97918	541-473-5171	$214.00
MARION	100 High St. Salem, OR 97301	503-588-5105	$222.50
MORROW	100 N. Court PO Box 609 Hepner, OR 97836	541-676-9061	$114.00
MULTNOMAH	1021 SW 4th Portland, OR 97204	503-248-3943	$251.00
POLK	850 Main St. Dallas, OR 97338	503-623-3154	$189.00
SHERMAN	500 Court St. PO Box 402 Morow, OR 97039	541-565-3650	$114.00
TILLAMOOK	201 Laurel Tillamook, OR 97141	541-842-8014	$200.00
UMATILLA	216 SE 4th PO Box 1307 Pendleton, OR 97801	541-278-0341	$114.00
UNION	1008 K Ave. LaGrande, OR 97850	541-962-9500	$114.00
WALLOWA	101 S. River St. Enterprise, OR 97828	541-426-4991	$114.00
WASCO	511 Washington St. PO Box 821 The Dalles, OR 97058	541-296-3154	$114.00
WASHINGTON	150 N. 1st Hillsboro, OR 97124	503-648-8891	$251.50
WHEELER	P.O. Box 308 Fossil, OR 97830	541-763-2541	$92.00
YAMHILL	535 E. 5th St. McMinnville, OR 97128	503-472-9371	$189.00 ■

After the Divorce

A. Like Divorces, Modifications Can Be Contested or Uncontested	14/2
B. Arrangements That Commonly Need Modification	14/2
1. Visitation	14/2
2. Child Support	14/3

After your divorce is final, your or your spouse's circumstances may change, which may make certain terms of the divorce decree unfeasible. Couples with children are especially likely to face changes which may require them to reconsider the various arrangements established in the divorce. If either spouse changes jobs, for example, his or her change in income may necessitate a readjustment of child support payments. A change in work schedules may require a custody or visitation arrangement to be changed. Life goes on after divorce; people move, children grow and needs change.

If changed circumstances have made the terms of your divorce difficult to live by, you can have your decree modified. To do so, you must file for a Modification of the Decree and have it signed by a judge. Generally speaking, modifications are limited to cases in which a situation has changed or is presumed to have changed. This rule prevents spouses who "lost" in the divorce from going back to court to fight the same issues all over again.

Modifications are not covered in this book, though they can be simple to obtain with limited help from an attorney to draft your agreement in a format acceptable to the court. See Chapter 15 on hiring an attorney. This chapter will give a brief look at why and how to modify a divorce decree.

A. Like Divorces, Modifications Can Be Contested or Uncontested

As with the original divorce, you can file for a modification either on your own or jointly with your ex-spouse. If you and your ex-spouse are in agreement, you can outline your agreed-upon changes on your own and have an attorney help you prepare it for submission to the court. If you and your ex-spouse do not agree on modifying the decree, you can try to resolve the dispute on your own or through mediation. Otherwise, the modification will be contested and will involve going back to court to fight it out.

B. Arrangements That Commonly Need Modification

The arrangements that most commonly need modification after a divorce are visitation schedules and child support payments.

1. Visitation

If both parents are in agreement as to changing the visitation arrangements, they can file a Stipulated Decree and supporting documents with the court. The change will be effective when the Stipulated Decree is signed by the judge (ORS 107.431).

If both parents are not in agreement about changing visitation, the parent who wants the modification must show the court that there has been a change in circumstances since the divorce was final, and that the proposed modification is in the best interests of the children (ORS 107.135-107.431).

2. Child Support

In Oregon, you can request a review of child support every two years without having to prove a change in circumstances. It is presumed that in two years one or both parents' incomes will have changed.

If there is a change of circumstances, especially for the parent paying child support, it is important not to delay asking the court for a modification. Unless modified, the child support obligation ordered in the divorce decree must continue to be paid and cannot be modified retroactively. If, for instance, the paying parent loses her job and is temporarily unable to continue payments, she will be liable for the whole amount owed—sometimes including interest—unless she has obtained a modification decreasing her payment obligation. (See Chapter 9 on child support.)

Example: *Clay had been paying $750 per month for child support based on an income of $3,000 per month. Clay was laid off from his job and his income dropped to just $850 per month from unemployment benefits. Clay must file immediately for a reduction in child support payments. Until he has the decree modified, he will continue to accrue $750 per month in child support debts.*

If you wish to modify the child support obligation, see an attorney who specializes in modifying child support (see Chapter 15 for information on hiring an attorney). Due to these specialists' knowledge and efficiency in the process, their fees for this service are often quite low. ■

Beyond the Book: Attorneys, Independent Paralegals and Books

A. Attorneys 15/2
    1. Obtaining Referrals 15/2
    2. Screening Your Choices 15/3

B. Independent Paralegals 15/4

C. Books 15/4
    1. Nolo Books 15/4
    2. Divorce-Related Books by Other Publishers 15/5
    3. Legal Guides 15/5
    4. Agency Publications 15/5
    5. Books to Explain Divorce to Children 15/6

D. Legal Research 15/6
    1. Using Public Libraries 15/6
    2. Using Law Libraries 15/7
    3. Finding Background Resources 15/7
    4. Finding Oregon Statutes 15/7
    5. Finding Rules of Procedure 15/7
    6. Finding Oregon Court Cases 15/7

Throughout this book, we've alerted you to situations that may require some outside help. It is important to remember that hiring someone to help you does not necessarily mean turning your whole case over to an attorney; there are many intermediate levels of assistance you can get, not only from attorneys but from paralegals, accountants or real estate agents, for example. Often, you can do most of the work of your divorce yourself, and have a professional help you with the final details and formal presentation. Using outside resources this way will allow you not only to retain greater control of your case but can save you thousands of dollars in legal fees.

This chapter will guide you through the many different resources that may help you with your divorce. You can use any of them in conjunction with this book.

A. Attorneys

Some divorce-related issues are complex and have serious implications. When dealing with complicated issues, it may be wise to consult with an attorney, though it can be difficult to find a competent attorney whom you can trust. Your goal is to find an attorney who knows divorce law, who will communicate with you on the progress of your case, whom you can afford and who supports mediation as an alternative to court.

Issues that you should discuss with an attorney include spousal support (alimony), multiple real estate holdings, retirement funds or a power imbalance between you and your spouse. If your divorce is or will be contested, you will probably need an attorney to represent your interests and get you through the court process.

Once you've found an attorney whom you're comfortable with, you may be able to proceed mostly on your own after having the law explained to you. In some instances you might hire an attorney as a legal coach simply to review all the papers after you have completed them to make sure you haven't made any errors. Or, you could hire them merely to answer your questions as they arise throughout the divorce process. A legal coach can do as much or as little of your divorce as you hire them to do. If you are interested in hiring an attorney just for consultation purposes, you may have to shop around a bit. Not all attorneys will act as a coach.

Here we suggest several approaches to locating a good attorney. Fortunately for you, by reading this book you are in a much better position to judge an attorney's qualifications. By educating yourself about Oregon divorce law, you will be able to ask the right questions and better evaluate the attorneys you consider.

1. Obtaining Referrals

Although there is no sure-fire way to find a good lawyer, there are a few ways to get your search off on the right foot. Getting a referral can be very helpful in pointing you in the right direction.

a. References from friends, co-workers or employers

Whom did your friends or acquaintances use for their divorces? Find out whether they were satisfied with the attorneys' services, the fees and the results obtained. Often, a client will be satisfied with the results of a case but will feel the fees were too high. Another common complaint is that a lawyer failed to return phone calls and keep a client up-to-date on the progress of a case. Ask people you know how they felt about these aspects of their lawyers' services.

Your employer may also be able to refer you to a reputable attorney. Most businesses maintain relationships with attorneys to answer legal questions as they arise. Perhaps your company's attorney also does divorce cases or may be able to refer you to a colleague. Also, some employers have employee assistance programs to help employees solve various problems, including legal ones.

b. Referral agencies

If you can't find an attorney through word of mouth, you could try a referral agency. The Oregon State Bar maintains a referral system which you can reach at 503-684-3763, or toll-free at 800-452-7636. Also, check the Yellow Pages of the phone book. Besides the many advertisements for attorneys, you'll also find attorney referral companies.

c. Legal insurance

Legal insurance is sometimes provided as a benefit by employers, or may be offered through credit card accounts. If you have legal insurance you may be entitled to a free legal consultation with one of the plans' attorneys. But beware, the attorney may try to use this consultation to get into your wallet!

If You Can't Afford an Attorney

If you meet certain income requirements, you may be eligible for low-cost legal services provided by various organizations. One such service is the Oregon State Bar's Modest Means Program, which matches relatively inexperienced attorneys with clients for a lower hourly fee. You can reach the Modest Means Program at 503-684-3763, or toll-free at 800-452-7636. Another program is Legal Services (also known as Legal Aid), which you'll find in the government pages of the phone directory under Legal. Legal Services is a federally funded program that offers legal help to people with low incomes. Some law schools run legal clinics, as do some churches and community groups. These organizations may also be able to refer you to other low-income legal assistance programs.

2. Screening Your Choices

Whichever method you use to find an attorney, you will want to screen out some of your choices. When you make the initial call, ask to speak directly to the attorney so you can determine whether you are comfortable with his or her approach to clients. Ask about:

- the attorney's experience with handing divorces like yours. For example, if you are requesting a deviation from the child support guidelines, you should find out how many divorces the attorney has handled involving support deviations and how often they were successfully obtained;

- the length of time the attorney has been practicing divorce law;

- consultation fees;

- amounts of hourly fees and retainers;

- payment arrangements for fees and retainers, and whether credit cards are accepted;

- being kept up to date on the progress of the case, and whether the attorney will return your phone calls promptly;

- the use of paralegals and, if used, the hourly rate you will pay for the paralegals' work.

After the call, ask yourself whether you feel comfortable with this attorney. Did he or she answer your questions openly and directly? Can you afford the fees? If satisfied with the attorney, call back and schedule an appointment.

> **Skeletons in Your Attorney's Closet?**
>
> You can check with the Oregon State Bar Association to see if an attorney has had client complaints filed against him or her. These records are open for public inspection. To view these records, you must request the information by phone, wait a few days for the file to be located and schedule an appointment to review the file.

3. Preparing for the Initial Consultation

To save time and money you should prepare for your consultation appointment. Bring all the information and documents relevant to your divorce and a list of the issues you wish to address. Try to organize the information so you can access it quickly as you need it.

B. Independent Paralegals

If you need help in filling out your forms but do not need legal questions answered, an independent paralegal (IP) may be the answer. By law IPs are not allowed to give legal advice, but they can prepare legal documents for filing with the court. They understand court procedures and can help you through the maze of the legal system—for much less money than a lawyer.

Independent paralegals do not have law degrees, but they have education and/or experience in the mechanics of the court system. The type and amount of education and experience of IPs varies. Some IPs used to be court clerks or paralegals in law firms; others have Associate's or Bachelor's degrees; some have taken workshops specific to the services they provide; still others learned the legal system by handling their own legal problems and then decided to share their experiences with others.

When looking for an independent paralegal to help you with your divorce, try to find an IP with a good reputation who charges resonable fees. As when looking for a lawyer, ask friends, family, court clerks, co-workers, employers or community groups for recommendations.

C. Books

In certain respects, this book is like a do-it-yourself car repair guide. We give you step-by-step instructions and alert you to potential problems, but we don't provide all the tools you'll need. The books listed in this section are tools that may come in handy as you set about to do your own divorce.

Books published by Nolo Press can be ordered from the back of this book. You can also get more information about each book at Nolo's World Wide Web site (http://www.nolo.com) or at Nolo's AOL site (keyword Nolo). Most public and law libraries will also have these books. If the book is published by another publisher, look for it in your local public library, or in the law library if it is a law book written for lawyers.

1. Nolo Books

How to Mediate Your Dispute, by Peter Lovenheim (Nolo Press). This book is a comprehensive guide to the mediation process. It includes a detailed chapter on divorce mediation, both private and court-ordered.

Child Custody: Building Parenting Agreements That Work, by Mimi Lyster, 2nd Edition (Nolo Press). This book walks divorcing parents step by step through drafting an effective parenting agreement, and addresses the common custody and visitation issues that arise during divorce. Worksheets and checklists are provided.

Divorce and Money: How to Make the Best Financial Decisions During Divorce, by Violet Woodhouse and Victoria Felton-Collins, 3rd Edition (Nolo Press). The financial impact of divorce is covered in this book, which includes pension, retirement, Social Security, and tax issues. The book offers practical solutions for going through divorce without losing your life's savings, and provides financial worksheets, charts and formulas to help you with understanding how to divide your finances.

2. Divorce-Related Books by Other Publishers

Divorce Solutions, by Charles Edward Sherman (Nolo Press Occidental). This book helps you grapple with the tough economic and emotional issues that arise during divorce.

The Divorce Decisions Workbook: A Planning and Action Guide, by Margorie Louise Engel and Diana Delhi Gould (McGraw Hill). This book is oriented towards helping women make good financial choices before, during and after divorce.

Fathers Rights, by Jon Conine (Walker & Co.). This is a book for men which covers increasing and decreasing child support, visitation issues and modifying divorce decrees. The book is not current, but much of the information it contains is still relevant and helpful in assessing your choices during divorce.

Families Apart: Ten Keys to Successful Co-Parenting, by Melinda Blau (Perigee). This book offers practical ideas for creating a new model of post-divorce relationships. It encourages parents to build communication skills so that they can get along better with each other and both be more involved in their children's lives.

Legal Secretary's Complete Handbook, by Mary Ann DeVries (Prentice Hall Trade). This publication provides the forms used by legal secretaries in law offices, along with general suggestions on how to use them.

Between Love and Hate: A Guide to Civilized Divorce, by Lois Gold, M.S.W. (Plume). This book is a guide to improving communications and conflict resolution skills. It addresses the financial, emotional and legal issues in a divorce.

3. Legal Guides

Family Law Code for Oregon, by Judge Christina LaMar, updated edition available Oct. 1997 (Christopher Herron). You can order this publication directly from Judge LaMar at P.O. Box 684, Portland, OR 97207. It also can be found in the Multnomah County Law Library.

4. Agency Publications

The Extension Service of Oregon State University publishes a number of pamphlets that explain various aspects of family law. You can order them from the following address: Oregon State Extension Service, Publications Orders, Extension and Station Communications, Oregon State University, 422 Kerr, Corvallis, OR 97331-2119. Or fax your order at 541-737-0817. In addition to the title and author, be sure to include the order number for each publication. Some publications are free, while others cost a small fee. Their publications include:

Property Division and Spousal Support When Divorce Occurs, by Alice Mills Morrow (1993), order # EC 1378.

Shared Custody: Increasing Benefits and Reducing Strains, by Sue Doescher and Jan Hare (1994), order # EC 1443.

Child Support Decisions When Divorce Occurs, by Alice Mills Morrow (1995), order # EC 1379.

Modification of Child Support in Oregon, by Alice Mills Morrow (1995), order # FS 326.

Also, the Pension Rights Center offers booklets and information on pension benefits and their distribution in a divorce. Contact the Pension Rights Center at 918 16th St. NW, Suite 704, Washington, DC 20006; or phone 202-296-3776.

5. Books to Explain Divorce to Children

Divorce (Let's Talk About Series), by Angela Grunsell (Gloucester Press). This picture book provides simple, easy-to-understand answers to difficult questions.

What Kind of Family Do You Have? by Gretchen Super (Twenty-First Century Books). This picture book describes many different kinds of families, such as divorced families, step families, blended families or grandparent-led families.

How to Survive Your Parents' Divorce, by Nancy O'Keefe Bolick (Franklin Watts). For teens, this book is filled with sensible and helpful tips for dealing with the parents' breakup.

D. Legal Research

Rather than hiring an attorney to answer your legal questions, you can do your own legal research at your local law library. Tackling legal research yourself will help demystify the laws you are dealing with and will reduce your dependence on others to answer questions of law. There are many kinds of legal research. For some people, legal research will mean finding the right person to ask for the information or finding the right book that explains the law in detail. For others it will mean locating, reading and understanding the law itself—that is, a statute, regulation or court case. For still others it will mean a complete research process by which you find answers to very specific questions by:

- getting an overview of the subject in a legal treatise or encyclopedia,
- finding and reading relevant statutes,
- finding and reading cases that interpret the statutes (case law), and finally
- using certain law library tools make sure the information you've found is up-to-date.

In this section we explain how to find particular resources—legal encyclopedias, statutes, regulations and court cases. We don't, however, teach you how to conduct detailed legal research to find specific answers to specific questions. For that, we recommend that you read *Legal Research: How to Find and Understand the Law,* by Stephen Elias and Susan Levinkind (Nolo Press). Most law libraries have this book, or you can order it from the back of this book.

1. Using Public Libraries

Most regular public libraries do not maintain extensive legal research collections. However, you will usually find the collection of Oregon laws known as Oregon Revised Statutes (ORS). This is the set of laws to consult if you have a reference (citation) to a particular Oregon law. In addition to the statutes themselves, the ORS contains summaries of court cases that have interpreted the statutes. To read what the courts have said about a particular statute, look for the summaries immediately following the statute.

Updates to the statutes and to the cases interpreting them are included in the back of each volume of the ORS in a supplement called a pocket part. You should always check the pocket part for any changes to the laws. In the pocket part, turn to the statute number that you want to update. Any changes would be noted there.

(For more information on finding Oregon statutes, see Section D4 below.)

At this point your research may be done. However, you may want to go further and read the full text of the cases that have interpreted the statute. For case law, you will need to go to a law library.

2. Using Law Libraries

Every county courthouse has its own law library. Some courthouse libraries are welcoming and helpful to the general public and others are not. If there is a law school in your area you may prefer their hours and accessibility. Law school libraries are generally staffed by students who are willing to help you locate research materials. Some universities and colleges have legal information in their libraries and may even offer legal classes. If you are not a student, however, some school libraries may restrict hours of access or other use of their facilities. You should call a school library ahead of time to ask about their policies for library use by non-students.

3. Finding Background Resources

Before looking for statutes, it is often helpful to read what an expert has said about the subject in general that you are researching. One good source of general information on divorce is a series of publications for Oregon family law lawyers to keep them up to date: the Continuing Education Series of the Oregon State Bar (usually referred to as the CLE, for Continuing Legal Education), Volume 1 and 2 Family Law, 1990 with 1994 and 1996 supplements. This resource covers such topics as marriage, annulment, separation, divorce, custody and visitation, child and spousal support, retirement benefits, tax concerns, restraining orders, paternity and name changes.

4. Finding Oregon Statutes

The Oregon Revised Statutes (ORS) contains all the laws in this state except for state agency rules and regulations. If you want to find a law but don't know the statute number, look up a key word in the ORS index. For example, if you looked up "child custody" in the index, you would find the statute number that corresponds to that topic. Look up the statute number in the corresponding volume.

5. Finding Rules of Procedure

For the procedural rules that govern which papers must be filed and when, refer to the Oregon Rules of Civil Procedure 1995-96, by Lisa A. Kloppenberg.

6. Finding Oregon Court Cases

You may have learned in high school that the legislature makes laws while the courts interpret them. In family law, this is sort of true. However, it's important to understand that when a court interprets a statute, that interpretation becomes law itself. Therefore, to fully understand the meaning of a statute that has been subject to interpretation by a court, you must read the court's written opinion as well as the actual language of the statute.

Oregon court opinions are published in two different series:

Oregon Reports, Court of Appeals (Or. App.), which contains cases decided by the Oregon Court of Appeals (the court where contested divorce cases get appealed to in the first instance), and

Oregon Reports (Or.), which contains cases from the Oregon Supreme Court.

If you see a case citation that reads 284 Or. 705, the case is in volume 284 of the Oregon Reports on page 705. To find the case, first locate the series of Oregon Reports, then find volume 284, and then turn to page 705. The case will begin on that page. Likewise, if you see a citation that reads 250 Or. App. 128, find the series of Oregon Reports, Court of Appeals, then find volume 250 and turn to page 128.

If you have the name of a case but not the citation, you can use either the *Shepard's Citations for Popular Names* or the Oregon Digest. These reference books organize cases by name and by subject.

Continuing Your Research

Once you've learned how to find Oregon statutes, court cases and regulations, you may want to continue your research more in-depth. If you want to know how to proceed after finding a particular statute, case or regulation, get a copy of *Legal Research: How to Find and Understand the Law* by Elias and Levinkind (Nolo Press). ■

Legal Terms

Acknowledgment: An alternative to personal service of the divorce petition, the acknowledgement form is signed by your spouse as proof that he or she has received the court papers and that formal personal service of the papers isn't necessary.

Action: Another name for a lawsuit.

Affidavit: A sworn statement in support of other documents.

Alimony: The old term for spousal support. Alimony is paid to an ex-spouse who is temporarily or permanently unable to be self-supporting due to factors such as lack of job skills, age or illness.

Amend: To change parts of documents filed with the court.

Amendment: The form used to amend papers.

Annulment: Termination of a marriage as though it had never occurred.

Answer: A form used by the person who has been served in a divorce (respondent) to let the court know they are contesting some aspect of what the person filing the divorce (petitioner) is asking for in the divorce petition.

Appeal: To request a higher court to review a lower court's decision and overturn some or all of it. In Oregon, an appeal from a divorce decree is first filed in the Oregon Court of Appeals. If one of the parties doesn't like the decision of that court, the case can then be appealed to the Oregon Supreme Court.

Appearance: The act of the spouse who is sued for divorce formally entering the case, usually by filing an answer contesting some or all of what is asked for in the petition. If a spouse who is sued for divorce fails to respond—as happens in a default divorce—then he or she does not make an "appearance," and is not entitled to receive any notification from the court as to subsequent events.

Assets: Tangible or intangible property owned by a person, such as bank accounts, cars, furniture or real estate.

Case number: The number given by the court to your case. It will appear on all documents in your case file.

Certified: Proved authentic by the court clerk. Certified documents are stamped by the clerk.

Clerk: An employee of the court who keeps the records of the court and with whom papers are filed.

Conservator: Someone appointed by the court to oversee someone else's finances.

Contempt of court: A violation of a court order. Contempt of court can be punished by fine or jail.

Contest: To fight some or all of what is being asked for in the divorce petition. Contested divorces are usually based on disagreements over child custody or support, or property division.

Court: The legal entity that will issue orders regarding your divorce, including the final decree. Sometimes, an individual judge's ruling is described as a ruling of the court. In addition to the trial court, there is also the Court of Appeal and the Oregon Supreme Court.

Custody: A legal term that defines the overall power relationship between parents and children. If a parent has sole custody, then that parent alone raises the child. If there is shared custody, then both parents have some measure of control over the child and a voice in how the child is raised.

Decree: The final court order signed by the judge that officially establishes the divorce.

Deed: Document showing ownership of real estate.

Default: Failure to file an answer to the divorce petition. When a respondent does not file an answer, the divorce is granted by default.

Deferral: A court-approved delay in payment.

Discharge: In bankruptcy, for debts to be erased.

Dismiss: To throw a case out of court, thus ending the case; done by a judge. Cases are often dismissed when papers are not filed on time.

Dissolution: Another word for divorce, as in dissolution of marriage.

Equitable: Fair under all the circumstances. Equitable does not necessarily mean equal.

Equity: The difference between what a house or other property is worth minus the debt owed on it.

Ex parte: Attended by only one party, usually a hearing. Some hearings are ex parte due to the nature of the matter being heard, such as a hearing on obtaining a restraining order against a violent spouse. Ex parte hearings are also sometimes used for temporary orders involving custody, support and asset freezes.

Guardian: A person appointed by the court to take care of another person, usually a child. Guardianships commonly are created when a grandparent, stepparent or someone other than the child's parents need legal control over the child because the parents are unable to do the job. Guardianships are seldom part of divorce actions, since one or both of the natural parents generally get custody of children on the basis that they are the child's natural parents.

Guardian ad litem: A person appointed by the court to represent a minor for a specific purpose such as a name change or a guardianship hearing.

Legal description: For real property, a specific type of description required by the county recorder's office for real estate transactions. Modern description example: Lot 3, Block 45, Woodville subdivision, County of Washington, State of Oregon. Older legal descriptions actually outline the survey lines (Beginning at an iron bar...).

Legal notice: A statement published in a newspaper giving someone notice of a court case against him or her.

Mediation: A dispute resolution method involving a neutral third party called a mediator. A mediator helps the disputants reach an agreement, and does not (like a judge or an arbitrator) make a decision for them.

Mediator: A professional who helps resolve disputes between people.

Modify: To change a court order. Orders such as custody, visitation, child support or spousal support may be modified in certain circumstances and according to specific procedures.

Money judgment: A court order for one party to pay a specified amount on a specified schedule to another party.

Motion: A request that the court make some specific order.

Obligee: Person to receive payments, such as child support.

Obligor: Person to make payments, such as child support.

Order: A document signed by a judge that has the force of law.

Parties: The people involved in a legal action such as a divorce.

Personal property: Assets other than real estate, such as furniture, cars, bank accounts, businesses, retirement plans, investments, art, jewelry, clothing, etc.

Petition: The document filed with the court to start the divorce process.

Petitioner: The person (or persons, if co-petitioners) who files the petition.

Pleadings: The papers filed in the court outlining the reasons for the petitioner's case and the respondent's answer.

Process: The act of serving someone with legal papers. When served, the person has received process.

Process server: The person who serves legal papers on a respondent.

Real property: Land or assets that are attached to land, like houses or other buildings.

Rebuttal: The form that a spouse who disagrees with the amount of child support set by the state formula must file to have a different amount of child support awarded in the divorce decree.

Reconcile: To solve your differences and not wish to divorce.

Residence: The place a person lives.

Respondent: The person who files a response.

Response: Another term for answer, which is filed by a respondent who wants to contest a divorce.

Restraining order: Papers signed by a judge that require a person to stay away from another person.

Serve: To personally deliver papers to a spouse notifying the spouse that a divorce petition has been filed against him or her (called personal service), or to mail papers to a spouse notifying the spouse that an answer has been filed or that other papers have been filed or hearings scheduled (called service by mail).

Server: The person who serves papers on another person.

Service: The process of properly serving legal papers.

Spousal support: The modern term for alimony. Spousal support is paid to an ex-spouse who is temporarily or permanently unable to be self-supporting due to factors such as lack of job skills, age or illness.

Spouse: The person to whom you are married.

Status quo: The state of affairs at the time something is filed with the court.

Statutes: Laws written by the legislature.

Vacate: To end or terminate a court order or decree.

Waive: To give up or be exempted from. In some divorces you may have the 90-day waiting period waived, which means that you will not have to wait for 90 days for the judge to sign your divorce decree.

Writ of assistance: A court-issued document that orders a sheriff or other police department to help a person obtain property. Used if someone ignores an order for property division. ∎

APPENDIX A

Co-Petitioner Forms

Certificate of Residency
Certificate of Document Preparation
Petition for Dissolution of Marriage
Affidavit of Compliance With U.C.C.J.A.
Decree of Dissolution of Marriage and Judgment
Support Order Abstract
Property Settlement (A)
Property Settlement (B)
Motion and Order for Waiver of Ninety-Day Waiting Period
Affidavit Requesting Waiver of Ninety-Day Waiting Period
Affidavit Application for Decree
Waiver of Disclosure

APPENDIX B

Petitioner/Respondent Forms

Certificate of Residency
Certificate of Document Preparation
Petition for Dissolution of Marriage
Affidavit of Compliance With U.C.C.J.A.
Decree of Dissolution of Marriage and Judgment
Support Order Abstract
Property Settlement (A)
Property Settlement (B)
Motion and Order for Waiver of Ninety-Day Waiting Period
Affidavit Requesting Waiver of Ninety-Day Waiting Period
Summons for Dissolution of Marriage
Affidavit of Proof of Service
Acknowledgement of Service
Petitioner's Affidavit, Motion and Order for Default Decree
Affidavit Supporting Decree of Dissolution Without a Hearing
Compliance With Disclosure
Stipulated Decree of Dissolution of Marriage and Judgment

IN THE CIRCUIT COURT OF THE STATE OF OREGON

FOR THE COUNTY OF _____

In the Matter of the Marriage of)
)
_____) No. _____
Petitioner)
and) CERTIFICATE OF RESIDENCY
)
)
_____)
Respondent)

1.

I, _____, the Petitioner, certify that one or both the Petitioner or Respondent currently reside in the County in which the Petition for Dissolution of Marriage is being filed.

DATED: _____, 19____.

X _____
   Petitioner

Submitted by:

Name _____

Address _____

_____

Phone _____

Page 1- CERTIFICATE OF RESIDENCY

IN THE CIRCUIT COURT OF THE STATE OF OREGON

FOR THE COUNTY OF _____

In the Matter of the Marriage of)
)
_____) No. _____
Petitioner,)
and)
) CERTIFICATE OF
) DOCUMENT PREPARATION
_____)
Respondent.)

1.

You are required to truthfully complete this certificate regarding the document you are filing with the court.

    a. ☐ I selected this document for myself, and I completed it without paid assistance.

    b. ☐ I paid or will pay money to _____ for assistance in preparing this form/document.

X_____
  Petitioner

SUBSCRIBED AND SWORN to before me this _____ day of _____, 19 _____.

_____
  Notary Public for Oregon

My Commission expires _____, 19 _____.

IN THE CIRCUIT COURT OF THE STATE OF OREGON

FOR THE COUNTY OF _____

In the Matter of the Marriage of)
)
_____) No. _____
Petitioner)
and)
) PETITION FOR DISSOLUTION
_____) OF MARRIAGE
Respondent)

1.

I request a dissolution of the marriage because irreconcilable differences between the husband and wife have caused the irremediable breakdown of the marriage.

2.

No domestic relations suit or support petition involving this marriage is pending in this state or any other state.

3.

a. ☐ I am a resident of Oregon and have been continuously for the past six months before filing this petition.

b. ☐ My spouse is a resident of Oregon and has been continuously for the past six months before filing this petition.

4.

a. There have been _____ child(ren) born to Petitioners (before or during the marriage), or adopted by them.

NAME	ADDRESS	SOCIAL SECURITY #	BIRTHDATE

b. The wife is not ☐ is ☐ currently pregnant. The expected due date is _____.

5.

a. ☐ There are no minor children of the marriage.

b. ☐ Attached is a copy of the parenting plan/mediation agreement which includes provisions for child custody, visitation or parenting time, holiday schedules, and medical insurance.

c. The custody of the minor child(ren) shall be awarded as follows:

_____

_____

_____

d. Visitation or parenting time with the child(ren) shall be as follows:

_____

_____

_____

6.

Health insurance for the child(ren) shall be maintained by _____.

Uninsured medical expenses for the children shall be paid by _____.

Page 2 - PETITION FOR DISSOLUTION OF MARRIAGE

7.

_____ shall have the right to claim the child(ren) as dependents for state and federal income tax purposes.

8.

_____ shall pay to _____ the sum of $_____ beginning _____, 19_____, and on or before the first day of the month thereafter by immediate income withholding making payment through the Department of Human Resources. The child support worksheets which comply with the child support guidelines are attached as Exhibit 1. Collection, accounting, distribution, and enforcement services shall be provided by the Department of Human Resources. Interest shall be collected on any arrearage. Said child support shall continue until each child is eighteen years of age emancipated, or otherwise self-supporting except that support should continue so long as the child is unmarried, is under twenty-one years of age and is a student as defined by Oregon law.

9.

a. ☐ There is no personal property of the marriage.

b. ☐ The personal property of the marriage shall be divided as follows:

c. The husband shall be awarded the following personal property:

_____

_____

_____

_____

d. The wife shall be awarded the following personal property:

   _____
   _____
   _____
   _____

10.

   a. ☐ There is no real property of the marriage.

   b. ☐ The parties own the real property on attached real property settlement agreement.

11.

My spouse and I shall sign any documents necessary to remove his or her name as owner of personal or real property awarded to the other party.

12.

   a. ☐ There are no debts of the marriage.

   b. ☐ The debts of the marriage shall be divided as follows:

   c. The husband shall pay the debts listed below and hold the wife harmless:

   _____
   _____
   _____
   _____

   d. The wife shall pay the debts listed below and hold the husband harmless:

   _____
   _____
   _____
   _____

13.

The name of _____ is restored to

_____.

14.

Other provisions: _____

_____

_____

_____

_____

15.

If the court defers payment of court costs and service fees, I request that when the court grants the decree the court enter judgment for these costs and fees in favor of the state against:

☐ Me   ☐ My spouse

16.

The following relevant data pertains to this marriage:

Husband's Name: _____

Husband's Address: _____

Husband's Social Security Number: _____

Husband's Age: _____ Husband's Birth Date: _____

Wife's Name: _____

Wife's Address: _____

Wife's Social Security Number: _____

Wife's Age: _____ Wife's Birth Date: _____

Wife's Former Names: _____ (Maiden): _____

Date of Marriage: _____ Place of Marriage: _____

DATED: _____, 19 _____.

X_____
  Petitioner

SUBSCRIBED AND SWORN to before me this _____ day of _____, 19 _____.

_____
  Notary Public for Oregon

My Commission expires _____, 19 _____.

IN THE CIRCUIT COURT OF THE STATE OF OREGON

FOR THE COUNTY OF _____

In the Matter of the Marriage of)
)
_____) No. _____
Petitioner,)
and) AFFIDAVIT OF
) COMPLIANCE WITH
_____) U.C.C.J.A.
Respondent.)
)
)
STATE OF OREGON) ss.
)
County of _____)

1.

I, _____, swear and affirm under oath that:

2.

With respect to each minor child subject to this proceeding the children's present address, the places where the children have lived for the last five years (includes dates), and the names and present addresses of the persons with whom the children have lived during this period are as follows:

Children's Present Address: _____

Children's Addresses in the Past 5 Years: _____

_____

_____

Page 1 - AFFIDAVIT OF COMPLIANCE WITH U.C.C.J.A.

Names/Present Addresses of Persons Who Lived with Children in Past 5 Years:

_____

_____

X_____
    Petitioner

SUBSCRIBED AND SWORN to before me this _____ day of _____, 19 _____.

_____
    Notary Public for Oregon

My Commission expires _____, 19 _____.

Page 2 - AFFIDAVIT OF COMPLIANCE WITH U.C.C.J.A.

IN THE CIRCUIT COURT OF THE STATE OF OREGON

FOR THE COUNTY OF _____

In the Matter of the Marriage of)
)
_____) No. _____
Petitioner)
and)
) DECREE OF DISSOLUTION
_____) OF MARRIAGE AND
Respondent) JUDGMENT

1.

This matter is before the Court on the default of the respondent. The Petitioner appeared by affidavit.

IT APPEARING that no other domestic relations suits or support petitions are pending between the parties;

IT IS HEREBY ORDERED, ADJUDGED AND DECREED THAT:

2.

This marriage is dissolved and shall terminate on _____, 19_____.

3.

Any Will previously executed by either spouse, with provisions in favor of the other spouse, is revoked with respect to those provisions, unless the Will expresses a different intent.

Page 1- DECREE OF DISSOLUTION OF MARRIAGE AND JUDGMENT

4.

a. There have been _____ child(ren) born to Petitioners (before or during the marriage), or adopted by them.

NAME	ADDRESS	SOCIAL SECURITY #	BIRTHDATE

b. The wife is not ☐ is ☐ currently pregnant. The expected due date is_____.

5.

a. ☐ There are no minor children of the marriage.

b. ☐ Attached is a copy of the parenting plan/mediation agreement which includes provisions for child custody, visitation or parenting time, holiday schedules, and medical insurance.

c. The custody of the minor child(ren) shall be awarded as follows:

_____

_____

_____

d. Visitation or parenting time with the child(ren) shall be as follows:

_____

_____

_____

6.

Health insurance for the child(ren) shall be maintained by _____.

Uninsured medical expenses for the children shall be paid by _____.

7.

_____ shall have the right to claim the child(ren) as dependents for state and federal income tax purposes.

8.

_____ shall pay to _____ the sum of $_____ beginning _____, 19_____, and on or before the first day of the month thereafter by immediate income withholding making payment through the Department of Human Resources. The child support worksheets which comply with the child support guidelines are attached as Exhibit 1. Collection, accounting, distribution, and enforcement services shall be provided by the Department of Human Resources. Interest shall be collected on any arrearage. Said child support shall continue until each child is eighteen years of age emancipated, or otherwise self-supporting except that support should continue so long as the child is unmarried, is under twenty-one years of age and is a student as defined by Oregon law.

9.

a. ☐ There is no personal property of the marriage.

b. ☐ The personal property of the marriage shall be divided as follows:

c. The husband shall be awarded the following personal property:

_____
_____
_____
_____

d. The wife shall be awarded the following personal property:

_____

_____

_____

_____

10.

a. ☐ There is no real property of the marriage.

b. ☐ The parties own the real property on the attached real property settlement agreement.

11.

My spouse and I shall sign any documents necessary to remove his or her name as owner of personal or real property awarded to the other party.

12.

a. ☐ There are no debts of the marriage.

b. ☐ The debts of the marriage shall be divided as follows:

c. The husband shall pay the debts listed below and hold the wife harmless:

_____

_____

_____

_____

d. The wife shall pay the debts listed below and hold the husband harmless:

_____

_____

_____

_____

13.

The name of _____ is restored to _____.

14.

Other provisions: _____
_____
_____
_____
_____

15.

☐ Filing fees were not deferred.

☐ Filing fees were deferred. Petitioner requests that a judgement be entered against _____, Petitioner, or_____, Respondent, in favor of the state in the amount of $_____.

16.

CHILD SUPPORT JUDGMENT

a. JUDGMENT CREDITOR: _____

b. JUDGMENT DEBTOR: _____

c. PRINCIPAL AMOUNT OF JUDGMENT: Child Support: _____, per month;

d. INTEREST: Nine percent (9%) per annum on any unpaid monthly installment of child support.

17.

MONEY JUDGMENT

a. JUDGMENT CREDITOR: _____

b. JUDGMENT DEBTOR: _____

c. PRINCIPAL AMOUNT OF JUDGMENT: _____;

d. INTEREST OWED TO DATE OF JUDGMENT: Nine percent (9%) per annum.

18.

FEE DEFERRAL JUDGMENT

a. JUDGMENT CREDITOR: State of Oregon

b. JUDGMENT DEBTOR: _____

c. PRINCIPAL AMOUNT OF JUDGMENT: _____ ;

d. INTEREST OWED TO DATE OF JUDGMENT: Nine percent (9%) per annum.

DATED: _____, 19_____.

_____
  JUDGE

19.

NOTICE OF INCOME WITHHOLDING

THE SUPPORT ORDER IS ENFORCEABLE BY INCOME WITHHOLDING UNDER ORS 25.311-25.318, 25.351-25.367, AND 25.722. WITHHOLDING SHALL OCCUR IMMEDIATELY, WHENEVER THERE ARE ARREARAGES AT LEAST EQUAL TO THE SUPPORT PAYMENT FOR ONE MONTH, WHENEVER THE OBLIGATED PARENT REQUESTS SUCH WITHHOLDING OR WHENEVER THE OBLIGEE REQUESTS WITHHOLDING FOR GOOD CAUSE. THE DISTRICT ATTORNEY OR, AS APPROPRIATE, THE SUPPORT ENFORCEMENT DIVISION OF THE DEPARTMENT OF JUSTICE WILL ASSIST IN SECURING SUCH WITHHOLDING. EXCEPTIONS MAY APPLY IN SOME CIRCUMSTANCES.

20.

RELEVANT DATA

The following relevant data pertains to this marriage

Husband's Name: _____

Husband's Address: _____

Husband's Social Security Number: _____

Husband's Age: _____ Husband's Birth Date: _____

Wife's Name: _____

Wife's Address: _____

Wife's Social Security Number: _____

Wife's Age: _____ Wife's Birth Date: _____

Wife's Former Names: _____ (Maiden): _____

Date of Marriage: _____ Place of Marriage: _____

IN THE CIRCUIT COURT OF THE STATE OF OREGON

FOR THE COUNTY OF _____

SUPPORT ORDER ABSTRACT

PETITIONER _____)	SUPPORT ORDER ABSTRACT
Address: _____)	This is a new order
SS# _____ D.O.B. _____ Sex _____)	Case No. _____
RESPONDENT _____)	Date of Order: _____
Address: _____)	Type of Proceedings: Dissolution
SS# _____ D.O.B. _____ Sex _____)	

Date/Place of Marriage: _____, 19_____, _____

Date/Place of Separation: _____, 19_____, _____

Obligor (person to pay support): _____

Obligor's Employer's Name/Address: _____

Pmt $ _____ Freq. MONTHLY Next Due Date _____ Arrearage $ _____

BENEFICIARY(IES)	BIRTHDATE	RELATIONSHIP	SS#	AMOUNT	LIMIT
_____	_____	_____	___	_____	Statutory
_____	_____	_____	___	_____	Statutory
_____	_____	_____	___	_____	Statutory

Proceedings Disposition: <u>Dissolution</u>

DATED:_____, 19____.

_____
Judge

IN THE CIRCUIT COURT OF THE STATE OF OREGON

FOR THE COUNTY OF _____

In the Matter of the Marriage of)
)
_____) No. _____
Petitioner,)
and) PROPERTY SETTLEMENT (A)
)
)
)
_____)
Respondent.)

1.

Petitioner states:

    For the purpose of resolving all issues regarding real property of the marriage the Petitioner agrees as follows:

    The parties shall continue to jointly own the real property described below and shall actively market the property for sale. The net proceeds from the sale of the property, after all costs of sale and provision for income taxes, shall be divided as follows:

_____

2.

    The property is commonly described as:

_____

_____

Page 1 - PROPERTY SETTLEMENT (A)

And legally described as:

_____

_____

_____

_____

3.

If a dispute arises under this agreement that cannot be resolved the parties shall mediate the dispute with a mutually agreed-upon mediator. The cost of mediation shall be shared equally.

4.

I am the Petitioner in the above entitled suit for the Dissolution of our Marriage. I have prepared the Property Settlement, know its contents, and believe it to be true.

DATED: _____, 19_____.

X_____
  Petitioner

SUBSCRIBED AND SWORN to before me this _____ day of _____, 19____.

_____
  Notary Public for Oregon

My Commission expires _____, 19_____.

Page 2 - PROPERTY SETTLEMENT (A)

IN THE CIRCUIT COURT OF THE STATE OF OREGON

FOR THE COUNTY OF _____

In the Matter of the Marriage of)
)
_____) No. _____
Petitioner,)
and) PROPERTY SETTLEMENT (B)
)
_____)
Respondent.

1.

Petitioner states:

    For the purpose of resolving all issues regarding real property of the marriage the Petitioner agrees as follows:

_____ shall be awarded as his/her sole and separate property, free and clear of any interest on the part of _____, all of the parties' right, title, and interest in the real property described below.

2.

    The property is commonly described as:

_____

_____

And legally described as:

_____

_____

3.

_____ shall take this real property subject to all encumbrances and taxes and shall indemnify and hold _____ harmless therefrom.

4.

If a dispute arises under this agreement that cannot be resolved the parties shall mediate the dispute with a mutually agreed-upon mediator. The cost of mediation shall be shared equally.

5.

I am the Petitioner in the above entitled suit for the Dissolution of our Marriage. I have prepared the Property Settlement, know its contents, and believe it to be true.

DATED: _____, 19_____.

X_____
  Petitioner

SUBSCRIBED AND SWORN to before me this _____ day of _____, 19_____.

_____
  Notary Public for Oregon

My Commission expires _____, 19_____.

Page 2 - PROPERTY SETTLEMENT (B)

IN THE CIRCUIT COURT OF THE STATE OF OREGON

FOR THE COUNTY OF _____

In the Matter of the Marriage of)
)
_____) No. _____
Petitioner)
and)
) MOTION AND ORDER FOR
_____) WAIVER OF NINETY-DAY
Respondent) WAITING PERIOD

BASED UPON the Petitioner's affidavit filed herein, the Petitioner moves the Court for its Order waiving the remainder of the ninety-day waiting period for the dissolution of their marriage.

X_____
Petitioner

ORDER

IT IS SO ORDERED.

DATED: _____, 19_____.

_____
JUDGE

Page 1- MOTION AND ORDER FOR WAIVER OF NINETY-DAY WAITING PERIOD

IN THE CIRCUIT COURT OF THE STATE OF OREGON

FOR THE COUNTY OF _____

In the Matter of the Marriage of)
)
_____) No. _____
Petitioner,)
and)
)
_____) AFFIDAVIT REQUESTING
Respondent.) WAIVER OF NINETY-DAY
) WAITING PERIOD
)
STATE OF OREGON) ss.
)
County of _____)

1.

I, _____, swear and affirm on oath that:

2.

I am the Petitioner. I believe that there is no hope of reconciliation between Respondent and myself because:

_____

_____

_____

Page 1- AFFIDAVIT REQUESTING WAIVER OF NINETY-DAY WAITING PERIOD

3.

Furthermore, the following emergency justifies the waiver of the remaining ninety-day waiting period:

_____
_____
_____
_____

4.

I make this affidavit in support of my motion that the remaining ninety days be waived, and that a Decree of Dissolution be granted immediately.

X_____
   Petitioner

SUBSCRIBED AND SWORN to before me this _____ day of _____, 19 _____.

_____
Notary Public for Oregon

My Commission expires _____, 19 _____.

IN THE CIRCUIT COURT OF THE STATE OF OREGON

FOR THE COUNTY OF _____

In the Matter of the Marriage of)
)
_____) No. _____
Petitioner,)
and) SUMMONS FOR
) DISSOLUTION OF
_____) MARRIAGE
Respondent.)
)

TO: _____ Address: _____

YOU HAVE BEEN SUED. The court may decide against you without your being heard unless you respond within 30 days of the day you received these papers. Read the information below.

NOTICE TO RESPONDENT: READ THESE PAPERS CAREFULLY

Your spouse has filed a petition with the court to end your marriage and asking to divide your property and debts, and settle issues related to children including custody, visitation, child support, and health insurance, if any. You must "appear" in this case or the court will grant your spouse's requests. To "appear" you must file with the court a legal paper called a "motion" or "answer." The "motion" or "answer" must be given to the court clerk or administrator at: _____ within 30 days of the day you received these papers, along with the required filing fee. It must be in proper form and you must show that your spouse has been served with a copy of it.

X _____
    Petitioner

    Address: _____

_____

Identifying Information About the Respondent

Height: _____ Weight: _____

Description: _____

Date of Birth: _____

Automobile license number: _____

Auto description: _____

Best time and place to locate: _____

IN THE CIRCUIT COURT OF THE STATE OF OREGON

FOR THE COUNTY OF _____

In the Matter of the Marriage of)
)
_____) No. _____
Petitioner,)
and) AFFIDAVIT OF PROOF
) OF SERVICE
_____)
Respondent.)
)
)
STATE OF OREGON) ss.
)
County of _____)

1.

I, _____, swear and affirm under oath that:

2.

I am a resident of the State of _____. I am a competent person over the age of 18 years of age. I am not an attorney for or a party to this case, or an officer, director or employee of any party to this case.

On _____, 19_____, I served the Summons and Petition for Dissolution of Marriage, and a copy of ORS 107.089 in this case personally upon the above named Respondent in _____ County by delivering to the Respondent a copy of those papers, each of which was certified to be a true copy of each original. Name of Server _____

X_____

SUBSCRIBED AND SWORN to before me this __ day of _____, 19__.

Notary Public for Oregon

My Commission expires _____, 19 _____.

IN THE CIRCUIT COURT OF THE STATE OF OREGON

FOR THE COUNTY OF _____

In the Matter of the Marriage of)
)
_____)   No. _____
Petitioner,)
and)
) ACKNOWLEDGEMENT
_____) OF SERVICE
Respondent.)

STATE OF OREGON) ss.
)
County of _____)

1.

I, _____, swear/affirm under oath that:

2.

I received a copy of the Summons and Petition for Dissolution of Marriage in the above entitled cause

on the _____ day of _____, 19_____ , in _____ County.

X_____

SUBSCRIBED AND SWORN to before me this _____ day of _____, 19_____.

_____
Notary Public for Oregon

My Commission expires _____, 19 _____.

Page 1- ACKNOWLEDGEMENT OF SERVICE

IN THE CIRCUIT COURT OF THE STATE OF OREGON

FOR THE COUNTY OF _____

In the Matter of the Marriage of)
)
_____) No. _____
Petitioner,)
and) PETITIONER'S AFFIDAVIT
) MOTION AND ORDER FOR
_____) DEFAULT DECREE
Respondent.)
)
)
STATE OF OREGON) ss.
)
County of _____)

1.

I, _____, swear and affirm under oath that:

I am the Petitioner. The Respondent is not now, nor was, at the time of the beginning of this suit, in the military service of the United States; nor is the Respondent a legally mentally incapacitated person; nor is the Respondent under 18 years of age.

2.

The Respondent was served with the Summons and Petition for Dissolution of Marriage on

_____, 19_____, in _____ County and has failed to answer or appear.

X_____
    Petitioner

SUBSCRIBED AND SWORN to before me this _____ day of _____, 19_____.

_____
Notary Public for Oregon

My Commission expires _____, 19_____.

MOTION

Petitioner asks the Court for an order entering the default of the Respondent.

Address:_____

_____

ORDER

IT IS SO ORDERED.

DATED: _____, 19_____.

_____
JUDGE

IN THE CIRCUIT COURT OF THE STATE OF OREGON

FOR THE COUNTY OF _____

In the Matter of the Marriage of)
)
_____) No. _____
Petitioner,)
and) AFFIDAVIT SUPPORTING
) DECREE OF DISSOLUTION
_____) WITHOUT A HEARING
Respondent.)
)
STATE OF OREGON) ss.
)
County of _____)

1.

I, _____, swear and affirm under oath that:

2.

I am the Petitioner herein. The Respondent and I were married on _____ 19_____, in _____, and have since been and are now husband and wife.

3.

Respondent and I have been living separate and apart since _____.

4.

Irreconcilable differences between us have caused the irremediable breakdown of our marriage.

5.

I have been a resident of the state of Oregon for more than six months prior to filing this action.

Page 1 - AFFIDAVIT SUPPORTING DECREE OF DISSOLUTION WITHOUT A HEARING

6.

No domestic relations suit or support petition involving this marriage is pending in this state or any other state.

7.

With respect to each minor child subject to this proceeding, the children's present address, the places where the children have lived for the last five years, and the names and present addresses of the persons with whom the children have lived during this period are as follows:

_____

_____

_____

_____

8.

I have not participated, as party, witness, or in any other capacity, in any other litigation concerning a child subject to this proceeding.

I have no information of any custody proceeding pending in a court of this or any other state concerning a child subject to this proceeding.

I do not know of any person nor a party to this proceeding who has physical custody or claims to have custody or visitation rights with respect to any child subject to this proceeding.

I am aware that I have a continuing duty to inform the court of any information that I may obtain of any custody proceeding, in this or any other state, concerning any child subject to this proceeding.

9.

It is reasonable that custody, visitation and support of the child(ren) be awarded as requested in the Petition. To the best of my knowledge, the Respondent's gross monthly income is _____, and the source of that income is _____. My gross monthly income is _____, and the source of that income is _____.

Page 2 - AFFIDAVIT SUPPORTING DECREE OF DISSOLUTION WITHOUT A HEARING

10.

It is reasonable that the properties, real and personal, that are described in the Petition should, be awarded as requested in the Petition.

11.

It is reasonable that the debts and obligations included in the Petition should be awarded and assumed as requested in the Petition.

12.

Respondent was served with the Petition for Dissolution on _____, 19_____.

13.

☐ Respondent has not filed an answer to the Petition for dissolution.

☐ Respondent filed answer to the Petition for Dissolution on _____, 19_____. Since that date, Respondent and Petitioner have reached an agreement reflected in the Stipulated Decree of Dissolution and request the court to sign the Decree without a hearing.

14.

The allegations of my Petition are true. I make this Affidavit in support of a Decree of Dissolution Without a Hearing.

X_____
  Petitioner

SUBSCRIBED AND SWORN to before me this _____ day of _____, 19_____.

_____
  Notary Public for Oregon

My Commission expires _____, 19 _____.

IN THE CIRCUIT COURT OF THE STATE OF OREGON

FOR THE COUNTY OF _____

In the Matter of the Marriage of)
)
_____) No. _____
Petitioner,)
and)
) COMPLIANCE WITH DISCLOSURE
)
_____)
Respondent.)

1.

I certify compliance with providing a copy of ORS 107.089 which requires each party to furnish to the other copies of certain documents.

X_____
  Petitioner

SUBSCRIBED AND SWORN to before me this _____ day of _____, 19_____.

_____
  Notary Public for Oregon

My Commission expires _____, 19_____.

IN THE CIRCUIT COURT OF THE STATE OF OREGON

FOR THE COUNTY OF _____

In the Matter of the Marriage of)
)
_____) No. _____
Petitioner,)
and) STIPULATED
) DECREE OF DISSOLUTION
_____) OF MARRIAGE AND JUDGMENT
Respondent.)

1.

This matter is before the Court on affidavit of Petitioner and Respondent. IT APPEARING that no other domestic relations suit or support petitions are pending between the parties;

IT IS HEREBY ORDERED, ADJUDGED AND DECREED THAT:

2.

This marriage is dissolved and shall terminate on _____, 19_____.

3.

Any Will previously executed by either spouse, with provisions in favor of the other spouse, is revoked with respect to those provisions, unless the Will expresses a different intent.

4.

a. There have been _____ child(ren) born to Petitioners (before or during the marriage), or adopted by them.

NAME	ADDRESS	SOCIAL SECURITY #	BIRTHDATE
_____	_____	_____	_____
_____	_____	_____	_____
_____	_____	_____	_____
_____	_____	_____	_____

b. The wife is not ☐ is ☐ currently pregnant. The expected due date is _____.

5.

a. ☐ There are no minor children of the marriage.

b. ☐ Attached is a copy of the parenting plan/mediation agreement which includes provisions for child custody, visitation or parenting time, holiday schedules, and medical insurance.

c. The custody of the minor child(ren) shall be awarded as follows:

_____

_____

_____

d. Visitation or parenting time with the child(ren) shall be as follows:

_____

_____

_____

6.

Health insurance for the child(ren) shall be maintained by _____.

Uninsured medical expenses for the children shall be paid by _____.

7.

_____ shall have the right to claim the child(ren) as dependents for state and federal income tax purposes.

8.

_____ shall pay to _____ the sum of $_____ beginning _____, 19_____, and on or before the first day of the month thereafter by immediate income withholding making payment through the Department of Human Resources. The child support worksheets which comply with the child support guidelines are attached as Exhibit 1. Collection, accounting, distribution, and enforcement services shall be provided by the Department of Human Resources. Interest shall be collected on any arrearage. Said child support shall continue until each child is eighteen years of age emancipated, or otherwise self-supporting except that support should continue so long as the child is unmarried, is under twenty-one years of age and is a student as defined by Oregon law.

9.

a. ☐ There is no personal property of the marriage.

b. ☐ The personal property of the marriage shall be divided as follows:

c. The husband shall be awarded the following personal property:

_____
_____
_____
_____

d. The wife shall be awarded the following personal property:

_____

_____

_____

_____

10.

a. ☐ There is no real property of the marriage.

b. ☐ The parties own the real property on attached real property settlement agreement.

11.

My spouse and I shall sign any documents necessary to remove his or her name as owner of personal or real property awarded to the other party.

12.

a. ☐ There are no debts of the marriage.

b. ☐ The debts of the marriage shall be divided as follows:

c. The husband shall pay the debts listed below and hold the wife harmless:

_____

_____

_____

_____

d. The wife shall pay the debts listed below and hold the husband harmless:

_____

_____

_____

_____

13.

The name of _____ is restored to

_____.

14.

Other provisions: _____

_____

_____

_____

_____

15.

☐ Filing fees were not deferred

☐ Filing fees were deferred. Petitioner requests that a judgement be entered against

_____, Petitioner, or _____, Respondent, in favor of

the state in the amount of $_____.

16.

CHILD SUPPORT JUDGMENT

a. JUDGMENT CREDITOR: _____

b. JUDGMENT DEBTOR: _____

c. PRINCIPAL AMOUNT OF JUDGMENT: Child Support: _____, per month;

d. INTEREST: Nine percent (9%) per annum on any unpaid monthly installment of child support.

17.

MONEY JUDGMENT

a. JUDGMENT CREDITOR: _____

b. JUDGMENT DEBTOR: _____

c. PRINCIPAL AMOUNT OF JUDGMENT: _____;

d. INTEREST OWED TO DATE OF JUDGMENT: Nine percent (9%) per annum.

18.

FEE DEFERRAL JUDGMENT

a. JUDGMENT CREDITOR: State of Oregon

b. JUDGMENT DEBTOR: _____

c. PRINCIPAL AMOUNT OF JUDGMENT: _____ ;

d. INTEREST OWED TO DATE OF JUDGMENT: Nine percent (9%) per annum.

DATED: _____, 19_____.

_____
  JUDGE

19.

NOTICE OF INCOME WITHHOLDING

THE SUPPORT ORDER IS ENFORCEABLE BY INCOME WITHHOLDING UNDER ORS 25.311-25.318, 25.351-25.367, AND 25.722. WITHHOLDING SHALL OCCUR IMMEDIATELY, WHENEVER THERE ARE ARREARAGES AT LEAST EQUAL TO THE SUPPORT PAYMENT FOR ONE MONTH, WHENEVER THE OBLIGATED PARENT REQUESTS SUCH WITHHOLDING OR WHENEVER THE OBLIGEE REQUESTS WITHHOLDING FOR GOOD CAUSE. THE DISTRICT ATTORNEY OR, AS APPROPRIATE, THE SUPPORT ENFORCEMENT DIVISION OF THE DEPARTMENT OF JUSTICE WILL ASSIST IN SECURING SUCH WITHHOLDING. EXCEPTIONS MAY APPLY IN SOME CIRCUMSTANCES.

20.

RELEVANT DATA

The following relevant data pertains to this marriage:

Husband's Name: _____

Husband's Address: _____

Husband's Social Security Number: _____

Husband's Age: _____ Husband's Birth Date: _____

Wife's Name: _____

Wife's Address: _____

Wife's Social Security Number: _____

Wife's Age: _____ Wife's Birth Date: _____

Wife's Former Names: _____ (Maiden): _____

Date of Marriage: _____ Place of Marriage: _____

X _____ DATE: _____, 19____.
   Petitioner

X _____ DATE: _____, 19____.
   Petitioner

PAGE 7 - STIPULATED DECREE OF DISSOLUTION OF MARRIAGE AND JUDGMENT

APPENDIX C

Child Support

Child Support Computation Worksheet A
Child Support Computation Worksheet B
Child Support Computation Worksheet C
Child Support Computation Worksheet D
Child Support Computation Worksheet E
Oregon Scale of Basic Child Support Obligations

Support Case No. _____

Worksheet A
Nonjoint Child Credit Computation

FOR: ☐ PARENT 1   ☐ PARENT 2

1. PARENT'S GROSS MONTHLY INCOME $_____

2. Add or subtract spousal support paid or received $_____

3. ADJUSTED GROSS INCOME $_____

4. TOTAL NUMBER OF NONJOINT CHILDREN _____
   (including children to whom parent has been ordered to pay
   support by prior order) (Do not include stepchildren)

   Name(s) and date(s) of birth:

   _____
   _____
   _____
   _____
   _____
   _____
   _____
   _____
   _____
   _____

5. SUPPORT OBLIGATION FOR NONJOINT CHILDREN $_____
   (using only this parent's adjusted gross monthly income
   from line 3; from scale in OAR 137-50-490)

SED 109A (Rev. 5/96)

Support Case No. _____

Worksheet B
Support Calculation—Regular Custody

	Custodial	Non-custodial	Combined
1. Gross monthly income	_____ p/m	_____ p/m	
2. Add or subtract spousal support paid or received	_____	_____	
3. Subtract credit for nonjoint child(ren) from worksheet A, line 3	_____	_____	
4. Adjusted gross monthly income	_____	_____	_____ p/m
5. Percentage share of income (each parent's line 4 income divided by combined income)	_____ %	_____ %	
6. Basic child support obligation (combined income @ # of children) (see scale)			_____
A. Child care costs			_____
B. Medical expenses (OAR 137-50-430) NOTE: DO NOT INCLUDE INSURANCE COSTS– SEE 11 BELOW			_____
7. Total child support obligation (line 6 + 6A + 6B)	_____	_____	_____
8. Each parent's child support obligation (line 5 x line 7 for each parent) ($50 minimum order)	_____	_____	
9. Monthly child support obligation (line 8 non-custodial)		_____	
10. Cost of insurance (for joint child(ren) only) in column for parent who will provide. If non-custodial providing, and line 10 is more than line 9, fill in ZERO	_____	_____	
11. Each parent's pro rata share of insurance cost (line 5 times line 10 for each parent)	_____	_____	
12. TOTAL PRESUMED CHILD SUPPORT If non-custodial provides insurance, line 9 MINUS line 11 custodial. If custodial provides insurance, line PLUS line 11 non-custodial.		_____	

Other comments or rebuttal to calculations:

SED 109B (Rev. 5/96)

Support Case No. _____

Worksheet C
Support Calculation—Split Custody

Total joint children: _____   # children w/parent 1: _____   # children w/parent 2: _____

	Parent 1	Parent 2	Combined
1. Gross monthly income	_____ p/m	_____ p/m	
2. Add or subtract spousal support paid or received	_____	_____	
3. Subtract credit for nonjoint child(ren) from worksheet A, line 3	_____	_____	
4. Adjusted gross monthly income	_____	_____	_____ p/m
5. Basic child support obligation (apply line 4 combined income on scale for ALL joint children & list total support in each column)	_____	_____	
6. Prorated percentage (children w/each parent divided by total joint children)	_____ %	_____ %	
7. Prorated basic support for children with each parent (line 6 times line 5 for each parent)	_____	_____	

8. ADDITIONAL COSTS/EXPENSES

	Parent 1	Parent 2
A. Health insurance (place amount paid by each parent in column for that parent)	_____	_____
B. Child care as defined in OAR 137-50-420 (place amount paid by each parent in column for that parent)	_____	_____
C. Recurring medical costs as defined in OAR 137-50430 (place amount paid by each parent in column for that parent)	_____	_____

9. TOTAL SUPPORT COSTS

   A. Line 7 parent 1 plus lines 8A, 8B and 8C for parent 1   _____

   B. Line 7 parent 2 plus lines 8A, 8B and 8C for parent 2   _____

10. ALLOCATION TO PARTIES

    A. Percentage share of income (each parent's line 4 income divided by combined income)   _____ %   _____ %

    B. Parent 1 owes to parent 2 (line 10A parent 1 times line 9B)   _____

    C. Parent 2 owes to parent 1 (line 10A parent 2 times line 9A)   _____

11. NET OBLIGATION (if applicable)
    Subtract the smaller from the larger amounts in lines 10B and 10C and place the result in the parent's column with the larger amount in line 10B or 10C.   _____   _____

Other comments and rebuttals to calculations:

SED 109C (Rev. 5/96)

Support Case No. _____

Worksheet D
Support Calculation—Shared Custody

	Parent 1	Parent 2	Combined
1. Gross monthly income	_____ p/m	_____ p/m	
2. Add or subtract spousal support paid or received	_____	_____	
3. Subtract credit for nonjoint child(ren) from worksheet A, line 3	_____	_____	
4. Adjusted gross monthly income	_____	_____	_____ p/m
5. Basic child support obligation (apply line 4 combined income on scale for all joint children and list total support in each column)	_____	_____	
6. Basic support (line 5) times 1.5	_____	_____	
7. Percentage of time child(ren) will be in custody of each parent IF ONE PARENT'S PERCENT = LESS THAN 35, DO NOT USE THIS WORKSHEET. INSTEAD USE THE REGULAR CUSTODY WORKSHEET (WORKSHEET B)	_____ %	_____ %	
8. Prorated basic support for children (line 7 times line 6 for each parent)	_____	_____	
9. ADDITIONAL COSTS/EXPENSES			
A. Health insurance (place amount paid by each parent in column for that parent)	_____	_____	
B. Child care as defined in OAR 137-50-420 (place amount paid by each parent in column for that parent)	_____	_____	
C. Recurring medical costs as defined in OAR 137-50-430 (place amount paid by each parent in column for that parent)	_____	_____	
10. TOTAL SUPPORT/COSTS			
A. Line 8 for parent 1 plus lines 9A, 9B and 9C for parent 1	_____		
B. Line 8 for parent 2 plus lines 9A, 9B and 9C for parent 2		_____	
11. ALLOCATION TO PARTIES			
A. Percentage share of income (each parent's line 4 income divided by combined income)	_____ %	_____ %	
B. Parent 1 owes to parent 2 (line 11A parent 1 times line 10B)	_____		
C. Parent 2 owes to parent 1 (line 11A parent 2 times line 10A)		_____	
12. NET OBLIGATION (if applicable) Subtract the smaller from the larger amounts in lines 11B and 11C and place the result in the parent's column with the larger amount in line 11B or 11C	_____	_____	

Other comments and rebuttals to calculations:

SED 109D (Rev. 5/96)

Support Case No. _____

Worksheet E
Child Care Credit

When calculating the basic child support obligation, credit is given for actual, reasonable costs incurred on behalf of any *joint* child(ren) under OAR 137-50-420. The amount of the credit is the gross child care expense minus the federal and state income tax credit. Use the formula below.

A. Does the custodial parent pay child care for a joint child to enable the parent to work or seek employment?
   If yes, proceed. If no, stop here.

B. Is the child 12 years old or less, or if older, is the child disabled and not able to care for itself?
   If yes, proceed. If no, stop here.

C. What is the monthly cost of child care? $_____ [C]

D. If there is only one joint child, enter the lesser of C or $200.
   If there are two or more children, enter the lesser of C or $400. $_____ [D]

E. Find the custodial parent's income below on the Federal Tax Credit Table.
   Using the percentage of tax credit corresponding with the parent's
   income, multiply the percentage by D above. This amount
   is the federal monthly child care credit. Enter on line at right. $_____ [E]

F. Find the custodial parent's income on Oregon's tax credit table
   below. Using the percentage of tax credit corresponding with the
   parent's income, multiply the percentage by D above. This amount
   is the Oregon monthly child care credit. Enter on line at right. $_____ [F]

G. Add together E and F. Enter on the line at right. $_____ [G]

H. Subtract line G from C to arrive at net child care cost.
   Enter result on line at right. $_____ [H]

Federal Tax Credit Table

Gross Monthly Income			Tax Credit %
$ 0	to	833	.30
834	to	1,000	.29
1,001	to	1,166	.28
1,167	to	1,333	.27
1,334	to	1,500	.26
1,501	to	1,666	.25
1,667	to	1,833	.24
1,834	to	2,000	.23
2,001	to	2,166	.22
2,167	to	2,333	.21
2,334	to	9,999	.20

Oregon Tax Credit Table

Gross Monthly Income			Credit %
$ 0	to	416	.30
417	to	833	.15
834	to	1,250	.08
1,251	to	2,083	.06
2,084	to	2,916	.05
2,917	to	3,750	.04

SED 109E (Rev. 12/92)

Oregon Scale of Basic Child Support Obligations

Gross Income	\multicolumn{6}{c}{Number of Children}	Gross Income	\multicolumn{6}{c}{Number of Children}
	1	2	3	4	5	6		1	2	3	4	5	6
750	50	50	50	50	50	50	2200	286	443	555	626	680	731
800	78	79	80	81	82	83	2250	292	453	566	639	695	746
850	85	86	87	88	89	90	2300	299	463	580	655	712	763
900	90	104	105	106	107	108	2350	305	473	590	668	726	779
950	95	122	123	125	126	127	2400	312	484	605	683	742	802
1000	105	146	148	150	152	153	2450	318	493	617	696	757	825
1050	113	156	172	174	176	177	2500	325	504	631	712	774	848
1100	121	187	196	198	200	202	2550	331	513	642	725	788	871
1150	126	195	216	218	220	222	2600	338	524	656	740	804	894
1200	134	209	242	245	247	250	2650	344	533	667	753	819	917
1250	143	222	269	272	275	278	2700	351	544	681	769	835	940
1300	156	242	303	309	312	315	2750	357	553	693	782	850	963
1350	162	251	315	331	335	339	2800	364	564	706	797	866	986
1400	168	261	327	355	359	362	2850	370	574	718	810	881	1009
1450	174	270	337	378	382	386	2900	377	584	731	826	897	1032
1500	180	279	349	394	405	410	2950	383	594	743	839	912	1055
1550	186	288	361	407	429	434	3000	398	616	771	870	939	1078
1600	192	298	372	420	457	458	3050	412	639	799	902	966	1100
1650	198	307	384	434	471	482	3100	418	648	811	915	993	1113
1700	204	316	396	447	486	508	3150	425	659	825	931	1020	1126
1750	210	326	407	460	500	535	3200	432	670	838	946	1047	1140
1800	216	334	419	473	514	552	3250	438	679	850	959	1074	1153
1850	222	344	431	486	528	566	3300	454	703	880	993	1090	1167
1900	228	353	442	499	543	582	3350	469	727	910	1017	1103	1180
1950	234	363	454	512	557	597	3400	478	743	929	1026	1112	1190
2000	245	380	475	536	583	625	3450	488	759	936	1034	1121	1199
2050	256	397	497	561	609	653	3500	494	768	943	1042	1129	1208
2100	267	414	519	586	636	682	3550	499	776	950	1050	1138	1217
2150	279	432	541	611	664	711	3600	505	785	957	1057	1146	1226

Gross Income	Number of Children						Gross Income	Number of Children					
	1	2	3	4	5	6		1	2	3	4	5	6
3650	510	793	964	1065	1155	1236	5250	689	970	1138	1258	1363	1459
3700	516	802	971	1073	1163	1245	5300	694	975	1144	1264	1370	1466
3750	521	811	978	1081	1172	1254	5350	699	980	1149	1270	1376	1473
3800	527	819	985	1089	1180	1263	5400	704	984	1155	1276	1383	1480
3850	532	828	992	1097	1189	1272	5450	709	989	1160	1282	1390	1487
3900	538	837	999	1104	1197	1281	5500	714	994	1166	1288	1396	1494
3950	543	845	1006	1112	1206	1290	5550	719	998	1171	1294	1403	1501
4000	549	854	1014	1120	1214	1299	5600	725	1003	1177	1300	1409	1508
4050	555	864	1021	1128	1223	1308	5650	730	1008	1183	1307	1416	1516
4100	561	873	1028	1136	1231	1317	5700	735	1015	1190	1315	1426	1525
4150	568	878	1034	1142	1238	1325	5750	740	1021	1198	1324	1435	1535
4200	574	882	1038	1147	1243	1331	5800	745	1028	1205	1332	1444	1545
4250	579	886	1043	1152	1249	1336	5850	750	1035	1213	1340	1453	1555
4300	585	890	1047	1157	1255	1342	5900	755	1041	1221	1349	1462	1564
4350	591	894	1052	1162	1260	1348	5950	760	1048	1228	1357	1471	1574
4400	597	899	1057	1168	1266	1354	6000	765	1054	1236	1366	1480	1584
4450	602	903	1061	1173	1271	1360	6050	770	1061	1243	1374	1489	1594
4500	608	907	1066	1178	1277	1366	6100	775	1068	1251	1382	1499	1603
4550	614	911	1071	1183	1282	1372	6150	780	1074	1259	1391	1508	1613
4600	619	915	1075	1188	1288	1378	6200	785	1081	1266	1399	1517	1623
4650	625	919	1080	1193	1293	1384	6250	790	1087	1274	1408	1526	1633
4700	631	923	1084	1198	1298	1389	6300	796	1094	1281	1416	1535	1642
4750	637	927	1088	1203	1304	1395	6350	801	1100	1289	1424	1544	1652
4800	642	931	1093	1207	1309	1400	6400	806	1107	1296	1432	1553	1661
4850	648	935	1097	1212	1314	1406	6450	811	1113	1303	1440	1561	1671
4900	653	939	1101	1217	1319	1412	6500	816	1119	1311	1448	1570	1680
4950	659	943	1106	1222	1325	1418	6550	821	1125	1318	1456	1579	1689
5000	664	947	1111	1228	1331	1424	6600	826	1131	1325	1464	1587	1698
5050	669	951	1116	1233	1337	1430	6650	831	1137	1332	1472	1596	1707
5100	674	956	1122	1239	1343	1438	6700	836	1144	1339	1480	1604	1717
5150	679	961	1127	1245	1350	1445	6750	839	1150	1346	1488	1613	1726
5200	684	965	1133	1252	1357	1452	6800	843	1156	1354	1496	1621	1735

Gross Income	\multicolumn{6}{c}{Number of Children}	Gross Income	\multicolumn{6}{c}{Number of Children}
	1	2	3	4	5	6		1	2	3	4	5	6
6850	847	1162	1361	1504	1630	1744	8450	956	1351	1581	1747	1894	2027
6900	851	1168	1368	1512	1639	1753	8500	959	1357	1588	1755	1902	2035
6950	854	1174	1375	1520	1647	1763	8550	962	1363	1595	1762	1910	2044
7000	858	1181	1382	1528	1656	1772	8600	965	1369	1601	1770	1918	2053
7050	862	1187	1390	1535	1664	1781	8650	968	1374	1608	1777	1926	2061
7100	865	1193	1397	1543	1673	1790	8700	970	1380	1615	1785	1934	2070
7150	869	1199	1404	1551	1682	1799	8750	973	1386	1622	1792	1942	2078
7200	873	1205	1411	1559	1690	1808	8800	976	1392	1628	1799	1951	2087
7250	877	1211	1418	1567	1699	1818	8850	979	1397	1635	1807	1959	2096
7300	880	1218	1425	1575	1707	1827	8900	982	1403	1642	1815	1967	2105
7350	884	1224	1433	1583	1716	1836	8950	985	1410	1650	1823	1976	2114
7400	888	1230	1440	1591	1725	1845	9000	987	1416	1657	1831	1985	2124
7450	891	1236	1447	1599	1733	1854	9050	990	1422	1665	1839	1994	2134
7500	895	1242	1453	1606	1741	1863	9100	993	1428	1672	1848	2003	2143
7550	899	1247	1460	1614	1749	1871	9150	996	1434	1680	1856	2012	2153
7600	903	1253	1467	1621	1757	1880	9200	999	1440	1687	1864	2021	2162
7650	906	1259	1474	1628	1765	1889	9250	1002	1446	1695	1873	2030	2172
7700	910	1265	1480	1636	1773	1897	9300	1004	1453	1702	1881	2039	2181
7750	914	1271	1487	1643	1781	1906	9350	1007	1459	1710	1889	2048	2191
7800	917	1276	1494	1651	1789	1915	9400	1009	1465	1717	1897	2057	2201
7850	921	1282	1501	1658	1797	1923	9450	1012	1471	1724	1906	2066	2210
7900	925	1288	1507	1666	1805	1932	9500	1014	1477	1732	1914	2075	2220
7950	928	1294	1514	1673	1814	1940	9550	1016	1483	1739	1922	2084	2229
8000	931	1299	1521	1680	1822	1949	9600	1019	1490	1747	1930	2092	2239
8050	934	1305	1527	1688	1830	1958	9650	1021	1496	1754	1939	2101	2249
8100	937	1311	1534	1695	1838	1966	9700	1024	1502	1762	1947	2110	2258
8150	939	1317	1541	1703	1846	1975	9750	1026	1508	1769	1955	2119	2268
8200	942	1322	1548	1710	1854	1984	9800	1029	1514	1777	1963	2128	2277
8250	945	1328	1554	1718	1862	1992	9850	1031	1520	1784	1972	2137	2287
8300	948	1334	1561	1725	1870	2001	9900	1034	1526	1792	1980	2146	2296
8350	951	1340	1568	1732	1878	2009	9950	1036	1533	1799	1988	2155	2306
8400	954	1346	1575	1740	1886	2018	10000	1039	1539	1807	1996	2164	2316

APPENDIX D

Miscellaneous Forms

Letter to Creditors
Notary Form
Mediated Settlement Agreement
Notice of Asset Disclosure
Standard Visitation

Date: _____

Creditor Name: _____

Creditor Address: _____

_____

Re: Account # _____

To whom it may concern:

Please close the account effective immediately.
Thank you for your time.

Sincerely,

Your Name: _____

Your address: _____

_____

X_____

SUBSCRIBED AND SWORN to before me this _____ day of _____, 19 _____.

_____
Notary Public for Oregon

My Commission expires: _____, 19 _____.

Mediated Settlement Agreement
David and Susan Jones
May 1, 1996

We, ~~David Scott Jones~~ [Tony Lee Hernandez] and ~~Susan Smith Jones~~ [Carrie Sawyer H.], herein referred to as Father and Mother, are husband and wife. We have two children, ~~John William Jones~~ [Shaun Anthony Hernandez], born April 21, 1985; and ~~Allison Fay Jones, born May 31, 1988~~. We have decided to divorce due to irreconcilable differences and wish to resolve all issues related to this divorce while keeping the children's best interests our highest concern.

We voluntarily agreed to use the process of mediation as provided by ~~mediation specialist, Laura L. Taylor.~~ [Paralegal Jackie Brown] We understand that she does not represent either or both of us in any legal matter, and that we may have sought a larger or different settlement through attorney-assisted negotiation or litigation. We have been encouraged to consult with private attorneys to understand our legal rights and obligations, and to do any necessary processing for this divorce. We understand that this is an informal document unless or until submitted to and ratified by the court.

We further agree that we have disclosed to each other and the mediator all assets and obligations of joint or individual responsibility, and we have not unreasonably overstated or understated the value of any asset or the amount of any obligation. We further agree that we have not transferred or placed in the hands of any other person, under express or implied agreement, any assets of the parties without full disclosure to the other.

We hereby agree between us as follows:

I. Joint and Shared Responsibilities

1. Both parents feel that it is in the best interest of their son and daughter that they both continue to have a full, active and constructive role in their children's lives in order to advance their emotional and physical well-being, and to give them a sense of security as well as the benefit of a good relationship with each parent. Father and Mother have therefore agreed to joint legal custody of their son and daughter.

2. Mother and Father agree to share the rights and responsibilities for major decisions concerning the children, including all major matters of religious upbringing, educational programs, discipline, counseling, social environment, non-emergency health and dental care of the children, and financial decisions regarding the children's trust accounts.

3. The children's primary residence will be with their mother. If son and daughter go to public school, they will attend the school that services their mother's residence.

II. Parenting and Living Arrangements

1. Both Mother and Father agree to cooperate with one another in establishing mutually acceptable guidelines and standards for development, education and health. Both parents recognize that, in order for this arrangement to succeed, whenever possible they must act in the children's best interests. Father and Mother agree to discuss all major issues jointly and that day-to-day decisions and obligations for the children will be the responsibility of the parent in residence. Both Father and Mother recognize that it is important to help the other parent in addressing the children's needs.

2. Son and daughter will, at the minimum, be with their father every other weekend from Friday after school through Sunday at 4:00 p.m., as well as every Wednesday evening from 5:00 to 9:00 p.m. Mother will bring the children to Father's residence after school on Friday on the weekends the children will be with their father. Father will bring the children to Mother's residence on Sunday at 4:00 p.m.

3. Both Father and Mother agree to work flexibly with each other's schedule to maximize the time son and daughter share with both parents, keeping the children's well-being the highest priority in all decisions. Each agrees to give the other reasonable notice of any changes to the current schedule. Each agrees to give the other parent the right of first refusal should the parent scheduled to have the children not be available to care for them during their scheduled time.

4. Mother and Father will work together to share birthday and holiday times with their children, in general alternating three-day weekends and other holidays. Sharing of specific holidays will be as follows:

   a) Spring vacation will be equally divided each year.

   b) In 1996 and every even numbered year thereafter, the children will spend Easter, Labor Day weekend, Halloween, and the first day of Christmas vacation until approximately 9:00 a.m. Christmas morning with Mother. In 1996 and every even numbered year thereafter the children will spend the Thanksgiving holiday weekend, Memorial Day weekend, the Fourth of July and from 9:00 a.m. Christmas morning through New Years Day at 5:00 p.m. with Father.

   c) In 1997 and every odd numbered year thereafter the children will spend the Thanksgiving holiday weekend, Memorial Day weekend, the Fourth of July and 9:00 a.m. Christmas morning through New Years Day at 5:00 p.m. with Mother. In 1997 and every odd numbered year thereafter, the children will spend Easter, Labor Day weekend, Halloween, and the first day of Christmas vacation until approximately 9:00 a.m. Christmas morning with Father.

   d) Every year the children will share Father's Day with Father, and Mother's Day with Mother.

   e) In 1996, and every even numbered year thereafter, the son will spend his birthday with his father, and the daughter will have her birthday with her mother. In 1997, and every odd numbered year thereafter, the son will spend his birthday with his mother, and the daughter will have her birthday with her father.

   f) Both Father and Mother will have the option to have son and daughter with them for two weeks during the year, in addition to visits specified elsewhere in this agreement Each will give the other parent information on their vacation plans before the end of May of the year in question. The division of that two week period will be in keeping with the children's ages and current child development recommendations on the separation periods best tolerated at each age of the children.

III. Communication

1. Father and Mother will communicate directly with each other as much as possible and will not fall into the habit of using son or daughter as a messenger between them. In accepting the special responsibilities imposed by this joint and shared agreement, each parent specifically agrees that this agreement shall not be exercised for the purpose of frustrating or controlling the social development of the other parent. They shall work to share information and make joint decisions concerning their children as efficiently as possible to reduce the number of interactions needed between them.

2. Each parent shall advise the other at once of any change in his or her street address or telephone number.

3. Father and Mother shall exert every effort to maintain free access and unhampered contact between son and daughter and the other parent, and to foster affection and respect between the children and the other parent. Neither parent shall do anything that would estrange the children from the other parent, that would injure the opinion of the children of the other parent, or that would impair the natural development of the children's love and respect for each parent. Both parents also agree to encourage son and daughter to discuss their grievances with the parent in question. It is their intent to encourage a direct child-parent bond.

4. Both Father and Mother shall ensure that the other has full access to all information available from the children's schools, as well as medical, dental and religious information.

5. Each parent shall have the unlimited right to correspond with son and daughter and to telephone them during reasonable hours without interference or monitoring by the other parent or anyone else in any way.

IV. Other Parenting Issues

1. Neither parent shall keep son or daughter from regularly scheduled school attendance without the consent of the other parent except in the event of the child's illness.

2. Neither Mother nor Father shall move their residence more than sixty (60) miles from the other parent unless sixty (60) days prior written notice has been given to the other parent, and both parents have met to determine how son and daughter will be transported between Mother and Father under these living arrangements.

3. Both Father and Mother recognize the importance of grandparents in their children's lives. Both parents will allow and encourage reasonable and flexible contact between son and daughter and their grandparents.

V. Review

1. A review of the parenting agreement set forth above shall be made jointly by Father and Mother on an annual basis. This parenting agreement will also be reviewed and renegotiated if necessary if either of the following takes place:

    a) A major or substantial change in the lifestyle of one of the parents;

    b) Mental or physical disability or impairment of one of the parents.

2. Father and Mother will make every effort to cooperatively resolve any disagreements they may have concerning son and daughter. If they alone cannot resolve a conflict they shall seek mediation from a mutually agreed-upon mediator to decide how the disagreement will be resolved. Both parents shall share in the costs. The mediation shall be followed to its conclusion, or until one or both parties give written notice to the other party and the mediator that they are terminating the mediation, before either party shall seek relief from the court. While the dispute is being resolved, neither parent shall take substantial action in the area of the disagreement which would prejudice the interests of the other parent. Both parents commit to actively work to resolve the disagreement in as speedy a manner as possible.

VI. Child Support

1. Both parents agree to be responsible for the financial support of their children. Father will provide Mother $526.00/month as child support for the children's care, beginning on the first day of the month after the divorce is final. These figures are in basic compliance with the Oregon Child Support Guidelines in effect as of October 15, 1994, and are based on the incomes of both Mother and Father as of May 1, 1996. See attached Support Computation Worksheet B.

2. As further child support, Father will pay Mother 15% of the gross of any bonuses received during the course of his employment

3. This will continue for support and maintenance for each child until that child reaches 18 years of age or is otherwise emancipated by marriage or voluntary entry into the military. Said support shall continue until age 21 for each child who is a student attending school full-time as defined by Oregon law. It will in any event cease on the date of any child's death, should any die before age 21.

4. Both Mother and Father will contribute to the cost of child care. Each will pay a portion of the cost of child care according to the same income percentages used to determine child support.

5. Parents both agree to provide the other with copies of their Federal and State income tax returns by April 30th of the year following the one for which the returns were filed. Should the tax returns reflect a plus or minus change of income of 25% or more for either parent, the child support may be modified according to the State of Oregon Child Support Guidelines.

6. Both Mother and Father agree that Father will pay his child support by check directly to Mother on the fifteenth day of every month, beginning with the first month after the divorce is final. (*ALTERNATE: Both parents agree that Father will pay his child support through the Department of Human Resources, Support Enforcement Division. For the first three months, after the divorce is final, Father will write a check directly to Mother. Every month thereafter he will mail the check to the Department of Human Resources.*)

VII. Other Financial Issues

1. Both parents recognize the benefits of formal education beyond the high school level and agree to work to plan for the expense of such education. (*ALTERNATE: Both parents recognize the benefits of formal education beyond the high school level and agree to work to plan for the expense of such education. They will serve as joint trustees. for the children's college fund, currently valued at $_____ and held at Acme Bank, account no._____ . Parents will meet once each year, in May, to review the children's education fund, and assess additional investments and/or contributions to this fund. Signatures of both Mother and Father will be required to make withdrawals from current and future investment accounts for the children's college fund.*)

2. Father will carry a life insurance policy on himself for $_____ , which is sufficient to cover his child support commitment until his youngest child reaches 18 years of age, or 21 years of age if the child is a full-time student. The children will be the sole beneficiaries of this policy and this cannot be changed at any time. In the event of the children's deaths before age 21, the policy will be cancelled. Father will pay the premiums on this policy and the insurance carrier will be ordered to give Mother notice of expiration of policy or change of beneficiary.

3. Mother will carry a life insurance policy on herself for $_____, which is sufficient to cover her child support commitment until her youngest child reaches 18 years of age, or 21 years of age if the child is a full-time student. The children will be the sole beneficiaries of this policy and this cannot be changed at any time. In the event of the children's deaths before age 21, the policy will be cancelled. Mother will pay the premiums on this policy and the insurance carrier will be ordered to give Father notice of expiration of policy or change of beneficiary.

4. Father will carry the children on his medical and dental insurance policies as long as they are available through his employment. This coverage will be equal to the standard coverage available from Father's employer. Parents agree to evenly divide any medical or dental costs not covered by insurance. Each will keep complete records of these expenses to better facilitate dividing the costs. They will reimburse one another as necessary to balance their accounts.

VIII. Spousal Support (Parties are hereafter referred to as "Husband" and "Wife".)

1. Husband will pay Wife $_____ by personal check or automatic transfer on the first day of every month. These payments will begin the first day of the month after the divorce is final and end _____ months later.

2. Wife has available to her 18 months of medical insurance from Husband's employer through the COBRA plan. Wife would pay the premiums for this insurance. Should Wife want this coverage, she understands that she must enroll in the plan within thirty (30) days after the divorce is final.

IX. Taxes

1. If their divorce is final by December 31, 1996, Husband and Wife will file separate state and federal income tax returns for the year 1996 and each year thereafter.

2. Husband will claim the dependency exemptions for the children on his income returns beginning in 1996, and each year thereafter. Wife will claim Head of Household status on her income tax returns beginning in 1996, and each year thereafter. Should Wife's income increase to more than $_____ per year, both agree that each will have one dependency exemption.

X. Division of Personal Property

1. Wife and Husband will divide the majority of the furniture, appliances, and miscellaneous household items and tools in a manner deemed fair to both of them, and do not wish to place a monetary value on these items.

2. Husband agrees that Wife shall own as her separate property, free and clear of any interest of Husband, the jointly owned automobile, a 1991 Honda Accord, license number XXX 123. Husband agrees to sign the appropriate DMV documents to have his name removed from the title no later than ten days after the divorce is final.

3. All other personal property assets are divided as listed on the attached "Assets and Liabilities" document

XI. Division of Real Property

1. Wife will retain sole ownership of the family home, 5555 Main Street, Hometown, OR 97000. Wife will be awarded all right, title and interest in the property and she shall not hold Husband responsible for the property taxes, insurance, and mortgage indebtedness of approximately $_____ still owing to _____ (Account # _____) and shall assume and pay the indebtedness and hold Husband harmless thereon.

2. The necessary conveyances to affect the transfer of title will be completed within ninety days after the divorce is final. Husband will sign a Quitclaim deed within sixty days after the divorce is final.

3. Wife will pay Husband $20,000.00 as his share of the equity in the home. $10,000.00 will he paid to Husband within _____ days after the divorce is final. The remaining $10,000.00 will be paid to Husband within five years of the date of the divorce or at the time the house is sold, whichever comes first.

XII. Debt Distribution

1. All debts will be viewed as joint debt up through June 1, 1996. Any new debt incurred after that date will be the responsibility of the individual incurring the expense.

2. The division of joint debt will be as listed on the attached "Assets and Liabilities" document.

3. Each party will be entirely responsible for repayment of their debt as assigned on the "Assets and Liabilities" sheet and shall hold the other entirely harmless thereon.

XIII. Retirement Assets

Husband and Wife agree that each is entitled to one half of the present value of Husband's retirement account, as established at the time of the final degree. Wife will receive disbursement of funds when Husband is entitled to receive benefits, either after Husband leaves his employment at Acme Company, or at the time of retirement, whichever comes first.

Wife and Husband have paid equally for the cost of mediation, and it is their intention to file a copy of this mediated plan (in revised format acceptable to the court), along with other forms that they or their attorneys may choose, so that it may be made a part of the divorce decree and have the full force and effect of the court. They will contribute equally to necessary process and costs and filing fees, but will pay separately for any legal costs to determine their separate interests.

Since both Husband and Wife have had ample opportunity to review and modify this document and seek legal counsel prior to signing, and since all agreements were voluntary, they agree to hold the mediator harmless against any errors or omissions.

I UNDERSTAND AND AGREE TO ABIDE BY THE TERMS OF THE ABOVE MEDIATED AGREEMENT:

_____   _____
David Scott Jones   Susan Smith Jones

SUBSCRIBED AND SWORN to before me this _____ day of _____, 1996.

_____
Notary Public for Oregon

My commission expires: _____, 19____.

(SEAL)

Mediator:

Laura L. Taylor
315 Russell St.
Beaverton, OR 97005

503-555-1234

Notice of Asset Disclosure Pursuant to ORS 107.089

NOTE: Petitioner: a copy of ORS 107.089 must be served on the Respondent. You must provide proof of service to the Court.

107.089 Documents parties in suit must furnish to each other; effect of failure to furnish.

1. Each party in a suit for legal separation or for dissolution shall provide to the other party copies of the following documents in their possession or control:

    a. All federal and state income tax returns filed by either party for the last three calendar years;

    b. If income tax returns for the last calendar year have not been filed, all W-2 statements, year-end payroll statements, interest and dividend statements and all other records of income earned or received by either party during the last calendar year;

    c. All records showing any income earned or received by either party for the current calendar year;

    d. All financial statements, statements of net worth and credit card and loan applications prepared by or for either party during the last two calendar years;

    e. All documents such as deeds, real estate contracts, appraisals and most recent statements of assessed value relating to real property in which either party has any interest;

    f. All documents showing debts of either party, including the most recent statement of any loan, credit line or charge card balance due;

    g. Certificates of title or registrations of all automobiles, motor vehicles, boats or other personal property registered in either party's name or in which either party has any interest;

    h. Documents showing stocks, bonds, secured notes, mutual funds and other investments in which either party has any interest;

    i. The most recent statement describing any retirement plan, IRA pension plan, profit-sharing plan, stock option plan or deferred compensation plan in which either party has any interest; and

    j. All bank, credit union or brokerage account records on any account in which either party has had any interest or signing privileges in the past year, whether or not the account is currently open or closed.

2. a. Except as otherwise provided in paragraph (b) of this subsection, the party shall provide the information listed in subsection (1) of this section to the other party no later than 30 days after service of the Petition.

    b. If a support hearing is pending fewer than 30 days after service of the Petition, the party shall provide the information listed in subsection (1)(a) to (d) of this section no later than three judicial days before the hearing.

3. a. If a party does not provide information as required by subsections (1) and (2) of this section, the other party may apply for a Motion to Compel as provided in ORCP 46.

b. Notwithstanding ORCP 46 A(4), if the Motion is granted and the Court finds that there was willful noncompliance with the requirements of subsections (1) and (2) of this section, the Court shall require the party whose conduct necessitated the Motion or the party or attorney advising the action, or both, to pay to the moving party the reasonable expenses incurred in obtaining the Order, including attorney fees.

4. If a date for a support hearing has been set and the information listed in subsection (1)(a) to (d) of this section has not been provided as required by subsection (2) of this section:

   a. By the obligor, the judge shall postpone the hearing, if requested to do so by the obligee, and provide in any future Order for support that the support obligation is retroactive to the date of the original hearing; or

   b. By the obligee, the judge shall postpone the hearing, if requested to do so by the obligor, and provide that any support ordered in a future hearing may be prospective only.

5. The provisions of this section do not limit in any way the discovery provisions of the Oregon Rules of Civil Procedure or any other discovery provision of Oregon law.

Standard Visitation

The non-custodial parent will have visitation with the minor children on alternating weekends from 6 p.m. on Friday to 6 p.m. Sunday.

In the absence of a showing that such would not permit the maintenance of a significant preexisting parent-child attachment, visitation with children less than three years of age shall be:

Birth to 18 months: Two times per week for two hours per visit.

18 to 30 months: Once per week for six hours.

30 to 36 Months: Friday 6 p.m.–Saturday 6 p.m. on alternate weekends.

The non-custodial parent shall also have visitation for fourteen uninterrupted days during the summer with children six and over. The non-custodial parent shall notify the custodial parent in writing before May 1 of each year which days the non-custodial parent has selected for visitation. The custodial parent shall likewise have the right to a two-week vacation each summer during which the non-custodial parent's visitation need not be honored if the vacation is out of town. The custodial parent shall advise the non-custodial parent of such vacation plans by June 1 of each year. Once designated, changes in the summer visitation schedule shall not be allowed except by agreement of both parties. Failure of either parent to make a timely designation of summer visitation will not result in forfeiture of visitation rights, but will result in the custodial parent having the right to designate the summer visitation time, or, in the case of the custodial parent failing to give notice, the visitation lost by the non-custodial parent shall be subject to make-up visitation.

The children shall be ready for visitation and be picked up from the front steps of the custodial parent's residence no earlier than fifteen minutes early or fifteen minutes late. Return of the children to the front steps of the custodial parent's residence is also subject to the fifteen-minute rule. The non-custodial parent shall feed the children the evening meal prior to returning them.

Except as to children under three, whenever the weekend or other visitation provided herein falls adjacent to a school holiday or legal holiday, including Labor Day, each weekend or other visitation shall include the adjacent holiday, either Friday or Monday.

Only substantial medical problems are a sufficient basis for postponement of visitation. A make-up visitation will be allowed to the non-custodial parent on the next succeeding available weekend. However, if the non-custodial parent fails for any reason to exercise his or her visitation, there will be *no* make-up visitation period.

Both parties will provide addresses and contact telephone numbers to the other party and will immediately notify the other party of any emergency circumstances or substantial changes in the health of the children. However, both parties shall refrain from release of the other party's telephone number to third parties.

The non-custodial parent shall also have the unlimited right to correspond with the children and may telephone the children no more than once per week for fifteen minutes or less during reasonable hours without interference or monitoring by the custodial parent or anyone else in any way. Each parent shall allow the children to telephone the other parent at reasonable hours and with reasonable frequency if the child wishes.

Both parties are restrained and enjoined from making derogatory comments about the other party or in any other way diminishing the love, respect and affection that the children have for either party.

In addition to the visitation specified above, the non-custodial parent shall have visitation as follows:

Christmas: For children 30 months–six years of age:

In even-numbered years, on Christmas Eve from noon to 10 a.m. Christmas Day.

In odd-numbered years, from 10 a.m. to 8 p.m. Christmas Day.

For children six years of age and over:

The time from commencement of the school holiday through 10 a.m. Christmas Day in even-numbered years. In odd years, from 10 a.m. Christmas Day until January 1 at noon.

Thanksgiving:

Thanksgiving Day in years ending in odd numbers from 10 a.m. to 7 p.m.

Father's Day & Mother's Day: Father's Day/Mother's Day each year from 10 a.m. to 7 p.m.

Children are not permitted to determine whether they wish to visit with the non-custodial parent. Personal plans of the custodial parents or children, school activities, church activities and other considerations are not reasons for failing to adhere to the visitation schedule set forth in this order. Visitation, however, between teenagers and parents shall take into consideration the child's employment and age-appropriate activities.

No modification of these specific visitation conditions will be allowed *unless* such modification is in the form of a stipulated order signed by the Court, or unless the attorneys for the parties, through written correspondence, agree to temporary modifications.

INDEX

A

Acknowledgment of Service form, 13/9, Appendix B
Adopted children, 8/4
Affidavit Application for Decree
   co-petitioner, 11/14-15, Appendix A
Affidavit of Compliance with U.C.C.J.A.
   co-petitioner, 11/8, Appendix A
   petitioner/respondent, 12/8, Appendix B
Affidavit of Proof of Service
   petitioner/respondent, 12/15, 13/8, 13/10-11, Appendix B
Affidavit Requesting Waiver of 90-Day Waiting Period
   co-petitioner, 11/14, Appendix A
   petitioner/respondent, 12/14-15, 13/11, Appendix B
Affidavit Supporting Decree of Dissolution Without a Hearing
   petitioner/respondent, 4/6, 12/16, 12/17, 13/11, Appendix B
Agreements
   child custody, 8/8
   marital debt repayment, 7/9
   mediation, 6/7
   parenting plan, 8/7-8
   visitation, 8/7-8
Alimony. *See* Spousal support
Annulments, 4/8
Answer, to divorce petition, 3/3
Arrearage, 9/2
Asset disclosure
   notice, Appendix D
   waiver
      co-petitioner, 11/15, Appendix A
      petitioner/respondent, 7/4, 12/16, Appendix B

Assets, freezing, 5/4
Attachments, to divorce papers, 6/7, 10/4-5
Attorneys. *See* Lawyers

B

Bank accounts, 5/2
   listed in divorce papers, 11/6, 12/6
Bankruptcy, 7/6, 7/9
Bigamy, 4/8
Book resources, 2/3, 15/4-6

C

Case number, 13/4, 13/7, 13/8
Certificate of Document Preparation
   co-petitioner, 11/2, Appendix A
   petitioner/respondent, 12/2, Appendix B
Certificate of Residency
   co-petitioner, 11/2, Appendix A
   petitioner/respondent, 12/2, Appendix B
"Child attending school," defined, 8/2
Child Care Credit Worksheet E, 9/21-23, Appendix C
Child care expenses, and child support, 9/4
Child custody, 8/2-7, 8/8
   agreements, 8/8
   temporary, 4/6-7, 5/3-4
   types, 8/5-7
Child support, 9/2-23
   calculating, 9/6
   duration, 9/2
   enforcement, 9/5-6
   expenses, 9/3-4

judgments, 13/14
listing in divorce papers, 11/2-4, 11/9, 11/10, 12/2-4, 12/9, 12/10-11
modifications, 9/5, 14/3
nonpayment, 9/4-6
requesting, 9/2
statutory guidelines, 9/3, 9/6, 9/15, Appendix C
    deviation from, 9/3
temporary, 4/6-7, 5/4
who will pay, 9/2-3
worksheets, 9/6-21, Appendix C

Child Support Enforcement Division, 9/6

Children
adopted, 8/4
books to explain divorce to, 15/6
marital, 8/4-5
nonjoint, 9/10-12
non-marital, 8/4-5, 9/10
See also Child custody; Child support; Visitation; *etc.*

COBRA (Consolidated Omnibus Budget Reconciliation Act), 13/13-14

College expenses, and child support, 9/4

Compliance With Disclosure form
petitioner/respondent, 7/4, 12/16, Appendix B

Contested divorces, 2/2, 3/3
turning into uncontested, 3/3, 4/6, 6/7, 8/2

Co-petitioner divorces
defined, 3/2
forms, 10/3, 11/2-16, Appendix A
    attachments, 10/4-5
    completing, 10/4-5
    copies, 13/2-3
    deadlines, 13/12
    filing, 13/2-5
    filing fees, 4/4, 13/7, 13/14-16
    instructions, 11/2-16
    problems, 13/13
length of process, 4/4
overview, 3/2-3

Counties, Oregon
Child Support Enforcement Divisions, 9/5-6
filing fees, chart, 13/15-16
mediation chart, 6/8
parenting classes, chart, 6/8

Courts, Oregon
addresses, 13/15-16
appropriate, for filing divorce papers, 4/3-4
filing fees, 4/4, 13/7, 13/14-16

hearing, 4/6
judgments
    child support, 13/14
    debt collection, 7/9, 11/7, 11/9, 12/7, 12/9, 12/10, 13/14
    fee deferral, 13/14
and mediation, 6/3, 6/7-8

Credit accounts, 5/2
Credit card debts, 7/8
Creditors
letter to, 5/2, Appendix D
rights, 7/7
Credit record, 5/2, 7/9
Custody of children. *See* Child custody

D

Daycare. *See* Child care
Debt division judgments, 7/9, 11/7, 11/9, 12/7, 12/9, 12/10, 13/14
Debts of marriage. *See* Marital debts
Decree of Dissolution of Marriage
co-petitioner, 11/8-10, Appendix A
Decree of Dissolution of Marriage and Judgment, 13/14
petitioner/respondent, 12/8-10, Appendix B
Dismissal, of divorce case, 4/7
Divorce
book resources, 2/3, 15/4-6
contested, 2/2, 3/3
forms, 10/2-6, 11/2-16, 12/2-18, 13/2-16, Appendixes A, B, D
    filing, 4/3-4, 13/2-16
length of process, 4/4
questions and answers, 4/3-9
types, 3/2-3
uncontested, overview, 3/2-3, 4/4
See also specific forms, or other aspects of topic
Divorce mediators, 6/2-3. *See also* Mediation and mediators
DMV transfer, from information in divorce papers, 11/6, 12/6
Domestic violence, 5/3
Driver's licenses, and child support obligations, 9/5-6

E

Education expenses, and child support, 9/4
Equitable distribution of property, 7/2
Equity in home, 7/5-6
Expenses, and child support, 9/3-4. *See also* Child support

F

Family businesses, 4/9
Family home. *See* Real estate
Family medical debts, 7/8
Family purchases, 7/8
Filing fees, 4/4, 13/7, 13/14-16
    deferred, 4/4, 12/7-8, 13/7
        judgment, 13/14
Financial accounts, 5/2
Forms, 10/2-6, 11/2-16, 12/2-18, 13/2-16, Appendixes A, B, D
    co-petitioner, 10/3, 11/2-16, Appendix A
    filing, 4/3-4, 13/2-16
    petitioner/respondent, 10/3, 12/2-18, Appendix B
    See also names of specific forms
Fraud, 4/8

G

Gross monthly income, calculating, 9/7-9

H

Health insurance, 9/3-4, 13/13
Hearing, in court, 4/6
Home equity, 7/5-6
Home of family. *See* Real estate

I

Icons, used in book, vi
Illness, severe, and child support obligations, 9/5
Income, gross monthly, calculating, 9/7-9
Independent paralegals, 15/4
Injury, and child support obligations, 9/5
Insurance
    health, 9/3-4, 13/13
    life, 7/3
Internet, and mediation Web sites, 6/4
Investments, 5/2
    listed in divorce papers, 11/6, 12/6

J

Job loss, and child support obligations, 9/5
Joint custody, 8/5-6
    child support, 9/2, 9/7
        worksheets, 9/18-21, Appendix C
Joint legal custody of child. *See* Joint custody
Joint physical custody of child. *See* Joint custody
Judgments. *See* Courts, judgments

L

Law libraries, 15/7
Lawyers, 15/2-4
    and divorce process, 1/2, 2/2, 2/3, 2/4, 4/5, 6/7, 7/5
    and mediation, 6/2
Legal research, 15/6
Legal separation, 4/3, 4/8
Libraries, 15/6-7
Licenses, and child support obligations, 9/5-6
Liens, 7/6
Life insurance policies, 7/3

M

Marital children, 8/4-5. *See also* Child custody; Child support; *etc.*
Marital debts, 7/7-9
    agreements for repayment, 7/9
    division, 7/8-9
    listing in divorce papers, 11/6-7, 12/6-7
    refinancing, 7/8
    separately owned, 7/8
Marital property, 7/2, 7/3-7
    division, 7/4-7
    listing on divorce papers, 11/5-6, 11/10-12, 12/4-6, 12/11-12
    See also Property
Mediation and mediators, 4/5, 6/2-8, 8/3
    agreements, 6/7
        example, Appendix C
    court-ordered, 6/3, 6/7-8
    and lawyers, 6/2
    locating, 6/4-5
    private, 6/3, 6/7-8
    process, 6/5-7
    types, 6/3
    and visitation agreements, 8/8
    Web site, 6/4
Mediation services, compared to solo mediators, 6/3-4
Minor, defined, 8/2
Modifications, contested and uncontested, 14/2-3
Money judgments. *See* Debt division judgments
Monthly income, calculating, 9/7-9
Mothers, preference in custody decisions, 8/5

Motion and Order for Waiver of 90-Day Waiting Period
    co-petitioner, 11/14, Appendix A
    petitioner/respondent, 12/14, 13/11, Appendix B
Moving, before divorce is final, 4/7
Multnomah Bar Association, address, 6/4

N

Names
    changes after divorce, 4/9
    on forms, 10/4
National Academy of Family Mediators, 6/4
National Domestic Violence Hotline, 5/3
90-day waivers, of waiting period, 3/2-3, 4/4
    co-petitioner, 11/14, 13/5, 13/13, Appendix A
    petitioner/respondent, 12/14-15, 13/11, 13/13, Appendix B
    See also Affidavit Requesting Waiver; Motion and Order for Waiver
No-fault divorce, 4/6
Non-custodial parents, 8/3-4
Nonjoint Child Credit Computation Worksheet A, 9/11, Appendix C
Nonjoint children, 9/10
    child support worksheets, 9/10-12, Appendix C
Non-marital children, 8/4-5
    child support worksheets, 9/10-12, Appendix C
Notarization, of divorce forms, 10/5-6
    form, 10/5, Appendix D
Notice of Asset Disclosure form, Appendix D
Notice of Dismissal (Multnomah County), 13/14
Notice of Judgment, 13/14

O

Oregon counties. *See* Counties, Oregon
Oregon courts. *See* Courts, Oregon
Oregon Department of Motor Vehicles
    and driver's licenses, 9/5-6
    and vehicle transfer from information in divorce papers, 11/6, 12/6
Oregon Lawyers Alternative Dispute Resolution Directory, 6/4
Oregon Mediation Association (OMA), 6/4
Oregon Revised Statutes, 15/7
Oregon Rules of Civil Procedure, 15/7
Oregon Scale of Basic Child Support Obligations, chart, Appendix C
Oregon State Bar legal services, 15/3

P

Paralegals, 15/4
Parenting plan agreements, regarding visitation, 8/7-8
Parents, rights, 8/3-4. *See also* Mothers
Pensions, 4/8
Personal property, 7/4-5
Petition for Dissolution of Marriage
    co-petitioner, 11/2-8, Appendix A
    petitioner/respondent, 12/2-8, Appendix B
Petitioner's Affidavit, Motion, and Order for Default Decree
    petitioner/respondent, 12/15-16, Appendix B
Petitioner/respondent divorces
    defined, 3/3
    forms, 10/3, 12/2-18, Appendix B
        attachments, 10/4-5
        completing, 10/4-5
        copies, 13/5-6
        deadlines, 13/12
        filing, 13/5-11
        filing fees, 4/4, 13/7, 13/14
        instructions, 12/2-18
        problems, 13/13
    length of process, 4/4
    overview, 3/3
Power imbalance, in relationships, 4/5
Private caucuses, in mediation, 6/6
Private school expenses, and child support, 9/4
Professional licenses, and child support obligations, 9/5-6
Property
    disclosure, 7/3-4, 12/16
        waiver, 7/3, 11/15
    division, 7/2, 7/4-7
    marital, 7/2, 7/3-7
    personal, 7/4-5
    separate, 7/2-3
Property Settlement form
    co-petitioner, 11/10-12, Appendix A
    petitioner/respondent, 12/11-12, Appendix B
Public libraries, 15/6-7

R

Real estate
    division, 7/5-7
    legal description, 11/12, 12/12
    listing in divorce papers, 11/10-12, 12/11-12
    multiple holdings, 7/7
    tax liabilities, 7/6

INDEX

"Rebutting the presumption of support," defined, 9/3
Refinancing debts, 7/8
Repayment agreement, for debts, 7/9
Residency requirement, 4/3
Restraining orders, 4/7, 5/3
Retirement funds, 4/8

S

Safe deposit boxes, 5/2
School expenses, and child support, 9/4
Separate property, 7/2-3. *See also* Property
Separately owned debts, 7/8
Separation, legal, 4/3, 4/8
Service of papers, 3/3, 13/6, 13/8-11
    simplified, 13/9
Shared custody. *See* Joint custody
Signatures, on divorce forms, 10/5
Simplified service of papers, 13/9
Sole custody, 8/5
    child support, 9/2
        worksheets, 9/12-15, Appendix C
Sole petitioner. *See* Petitioner/respondent divorces
Split custody, 8/6-7
    child support, 9/2
        worksheets, 9/15-18, Appendix C
Spousal support (alimony), 4/7
    temporary, 5/4
Spouse
    absent or missing, 2/3
    out-of-state, 4/3
Standard visitation
    defined, 8/7
    example, Appendix D
Status quo orders, 5/4
Stipulated Decree of Dissolution of Marriage and Judgment
    petitioner/respondent, 2/2, 4/6, 6/7, 12/16-17, 13/11, Appendix B
Stocks, 5/2
Summons for Dissolution of Marriage
    petitioner/respondent, 12/15, Appendix B
Support Calculation—Child Care Credit Worksheet E, 9/22, Appendix C
Support Calculation—Regular Custody Worksheet B, 9/14, Appendix C
Support Calculation—Shared Custody Worksheet D, 9/20, Appendix C
Support Calculation—Split Custody Worksheet C, 9/17, Appendix C

Support of children. *See* Child support
Support Order Abstract
    co-petitioner, 11/10, Appendix A
    petitioner/respondent, 12/10-11, Appendix B

T

Tax liabilities, and house sale, 7/6
Temporary custody. *See* Child custody, temporary
Temporary support. *See* Child support, temporary; Spousal support, temporary
30-day post-decree waiting period, 4/4
Travel costs, and visitation, 8/7
Trust deeds, 7/6

U

Uncontested divorces. *See* Co-petitioner divorces; Petitioner/respondent divorces

V

Vacating, of divorce case, 4/7
Visitation, 8/2-4, 8/5, 9/7-8
    agreements, 8/7-8
        modification, 14/2
    standard
        defined, 8/7
        example, Appendix D
Vital Records form
    co-petitioner, 11/12-13
    examples, 11/13, 12/13
    petitioner/respondent, 12/12-14

W

Waiting periods
    90-day pre-decree period, 3/2-3, 4/4
    30-day post-decree period, 4/4
    waiver, 3/2-3, 4/4
Waiver of Disclosure form, 7/3
    co-petitioner, 11/15, Appendix A
Web sites, mediation, 6/4
Wills, 11/8, 12/8
Women's Crisis Line, 5/3
Worksheets
    child care, 9/21-23, Appendix C
    child support, 9/6-21, Appendix C
    errors noted, 9/10, 9/12, 9/16, 9/19 ∎

CATALOG
...more from Nolo Press

	EDITION	PRICE	CODE

BUSINESS

	The Employer's Legal Handbook	2nd	$29.95	EMPL
	Form Your Own Limited Liability Company	1st	$24.95	LIAB
▣	Hiring Independent Contractors: The Employer's Legal Guide, (Book w/Disk—PC)	2nd	$29.95	HICI
▣	How to Form a Nonprofit Corp., Book w/Disk (PC)—National Edition	3rd	$39.95	NNP
▣	How to Form Your Own Calif. Corp.—w/Corp. Records Binder & Disk—PC	1st	$39.95	CACI
	How to Handle Your Workers' Compensation Claim (California Edition)	1st	$29.95	WORK
	How to Mediate Your Dispute	1st	$18.95	MEDI
	How to Write a Business Plan	4th	$21.95	SBS
	The Independent Paralegal's Handbook	4th	$29.95	PARA
	Legal Guide for Starting & Running a Small Business, Vol. 1	3rd	$24.95	RUNS
	Marketing Without Advertising	2nd	$19.00	MWAD
▣	The Partnership Book: How to Write a Partnership Agreement, (Book w/Disk—PC)	5th	$34.95	PART
	Sexual Harassment on the Job	2nd	$18.95	HARS
	Starting and Running a Successful Newsletter or Magazine	1st	$24.95	MAG
▣	Taking Care of Your Corporation, Vol. 1, (Book w/Disk—PC)	1st	$29.95	CORK
▣	Taking Care of Your Corporation, Vol. 2, (Book w/Disk—PC)	1st	$39.95	CORK2
	Tax Savvy for Small Business	2nd	$26.95	SAVVY
	Trademark: How to Name Your Business & Product	2nd	$29.95	TRD
	Your Rights in the Workplace	3rd	$19.95	YRW

CONSUMER

How to Win Your Personal Injury Claim	2nd	$24.95	PICL
Nolo's Everyday Law Book	1st	$21.95	EVL
Trouble-Free Travel...And What to Do When Things Go Wrong	1st	$14.95	TRAV

ESTATE PLANNING & PROBATE

	8 Ways to Avoid Probate (Quick & Legal Series)	1st	$15.95	PRO8
	Make Your Own Living Trust	2nd	$21.95	LITR
▣	Nolo's Will Book, (Book w/Disk—PC)	3rd	$29.95	SWIL
	Plan Your Estate	3rd	$24.95	NEST
	The Quick and Legal Will Book	1st	$15.95	QUIC

FAMILY MATTERS

A Legal Guide for Lesbian and Gay Couples	9th	$24.95	LG
Child Custody: Building Parenting Agreements that Work	2nd	$24.95	CUST
Divorce & Money: How to Make the Best Financial Decisions During Divorce	3rd	$26.95	DIMO
Get A Life: You Don't Need a Million to Retire Well	1st	$18.95	LIFE
How to Adopt Your Stepchild in California	4th	$22.95	ADOP
How to Do Your Own Divorce in California	21st	$24.95	CDIV
How to Do Your Own Divorce in Texas	6th	$19.95	TDIV
How to Raise or Lower Child Support in California	3rd	$18.95	CHLD
The Living Together Kit	8th	$24.95	LTK
Nolo's Law Form Kit: Hiring Childcare & Household Help	1st	$14.95	KCHLO
Nolo's Pocket Guide to Family Law	4th	$14.95	FLD
Practical Divorce Solutions	1st	$14.95	PDS
Smart Ways to Save Money During and After Divorce	1st	$14.95	SAVMO

GOING TO COURT

How to Sue For Up to 25,000...and Win!	2nd	$29.95	MUNI
Everybody's Guide to Small Claims Court (National Edition)	6th	$18.95	NSCC
Mad at Your Lawyer	1st	$21.95	MAD
Represent Yourself in Court: How to Prepare & Try a Winning Case	1st	$29.95	RYC

▣ Book with disk

CALL 800-992-6656 OR USE THE ORDER FORM IN THE BACK OF THE BOOK

	EDITION	PRICE	CODE

HOMEOWNERS, LANDLORDS & TENANTS

Title	Edition	Price	Code
Dog Law	3rd	$14.95	DOG
▫ Every Landlord's Legal Guide (National Edition)	1st	$34.95	ELLI
How to Buy a House in California	4th	$24.95	BHCA
Leases & Rental Agreements (Quick & Legal Series)	1st	$18.95	LEAR
Neighbor Law: Fences, Trees, Boundaries & Noise	2nd	$16.95	NEI
Safe Homes, Safe Neighborhoods: Stopping Crime Where You Live	1st	$14.95	SAFE

HUMOR

Title	Edition	Price	Code
29 Reasons Not to Go to Law School	4th	$9.95	29R
Poetic Justice	1st	$9.95	PJ

IMMIGRATION

Title	Edition	Price	Code
How to Become a United States Citizen	5th	$14.95	CIT
How to Get a Green Card: Legal Ways to Stay in the U.S.A.	2nd	$24.95	GRN
U.S. Immigration Made Easy	5th	$39.95	IMEZ

MONEY MATTERS

Title	Edition	Price	Code
Chapter 13 Bankruptcy: Repay Your Debts	2nd	$29.95	CH13
Credit Repair (Quick & Legal Series)	1st	$15.95	CREP
How to File for Bankruptcy	6th	$26.95	HFB
Money Troubles: Legal Strategies to Cope With Your Debts	4th	$19.95	MT
Nolo's Law Form Kit: Personal Bankruptcy	1st	$14.95	KBNK
Stand Up to the IRS	3rd	$24.95	SIRS

PATENTS AND COPYRIGHTS

Title	Edition	Price	Code
The Copyright Handbook: How to Protect and Use Written Works	4th	$29.95	COHA
Copyright Your Software	1st	$39.95	CYS
The Patent Drawing Book	1st	$29.95	DRAW
Patent, Copyright & Trademark: A Desk Reference to Intellectual Property Law	1st	$24.95	PCTM
Patent It Yourself	6th	$44.95	PAT
▫ Software Development: A Legal Guide (Book with disk—PC)	1st	$44.95	SFT

RESEARCH & REFERENCE

Title	Edition	Price	Code
● Law on the Net, (Book w/CD-ROM—Windows/Macintosh)	2nd	$39.95	LAWN
Legal Research: How to Find & Understand the Law	4th	$19.95	LRES

SENIORS

Title	Edition	Price	Code
Beat the Nursing Home Trap	2nd	$18.95	ELD
Social Security, Medicare & Pensions	6th	$19.95	SOA

SOFTWARE
Call for special direct discounts on Software

Title	Edition	Price	Code
Living Trust Maker 2.0—Macintosh	2.0	$79.95	LTM2
Living Trust Maker 2.0—Windows	2.0	$79.95	LTWI2
Small Business Legal Pro Deluxe CD—Windows/Macintosh CD-ROM	2.0	$79.95	SBCD
Nolo's Partnership Maker 1.0—DOS	1.0	$79.95	PAGI1
Personal RecordKeeper 4.0—Macintosh	4.0	$49.95	RKM4
Personal RecordKeeper 4.0—Windows	4.0	$49.95	RKP4
Patent It Yourself 1.0—Windows	1.0	$229.95	PYP12
WillMaker 6.0—Macintosh	6.0	$49.95	WM6B
WillMaker 6.0—Windows	6.0	$49.95	WIW6B

Special Upgrade Offer
Get 25% off the latest edition off your Nolo book

It's important to have the most current legal information. Because laws and legal procedures change often, we update our books regularly. To help keep you up-to-date we are extending this special upgrade offer. Cut out and mail the title portion of the cover of your old Nolo book and we'll give you 25% off the retail price of the NEW EDITION of that book when you purchase directly from us. For more information call us at 1-800-992-6656. This offer is to individuals only.

▫ Book with disk
● Book with CD-ROM

CALL 800-992-6656 OR USE THE ORDER FORM IN THE BACK OF THE BOOK

ORDER FORM

Code	Quantity	Title		Unit price	Total
			Subtotal		
		California residents add Sales Tax			
		Basic Shipping ($6.00 for 1 item; $7.00 for 2 or more)			
		UPS RUSH delivery $7.50—any size order*			
			TOTAL		

Name

Address

(UPS to street address, Priority Mail to P.O. boxes)   * Delivered in 3 business days from receipt of order. S.F. Bay Area use regular shipping.

FOR FASTER SERVICE, USE YOUR CREDIT CARD AND OUR TOLL-FREE NUMBERS

Order 24 hours a day	1-800-992-6656
Fax your order	1-800-645-0895
e-mail	cs@nolo.com
General Information	1-510-549-1976
Customer Service	1-800-728-3555, Mon.-Fri. 9am-5pm, PST

METHOD OF PAYMENT

☐ Check enclosed
☐ VISA ☐ MasterCard ☐ Discover Card ☐ American Express

Account #   Expiration Date

Authorizing Signature

Daytime Phone

PRICES SUBJECT TO CHANGE.

VISIT OUR OUTLET STORES!

You'll find our complete line of books and software, all at a discount.

BERKELEY
950 Parker Street
Berkeley, CA 94710
1-510-704-2248

SAN JOSE
111 N. Market Street, #115
San Jose, CA 95113
1-408-271-7240

VISIT US ONLINE!

on the Internet
www.nolo.com

NOLO PRESS 950 PARKER ST., BERKELEY, CA 94710

Take 1 minute & Get a 1-year Nolo *News* subscription free!*

CALL
1-800-992-6656

FAX
1-800-645-0895

E-MAIL
NOLOSUB@NOLOPRESS.com

OR MAIL US THIS POSTAGE-PAID REGISTRATION CARD

*U.S. ADDRESSES ONLY.
ONE YEAR INTERNATIONAL SUBSCRIPTIONS:
CANADA & MEXICO $10.00;
ALL OTHER FOREIGN ADDRESSES $20.00.

With our quarterly magazine, the **NOLO** *News*, you'll

- **Learn** about important legal changes that affect you
- **Find out first** about new Nolo products
- **Keep current** with practical articles on everyday law
- **Get answers** to your legal questions in *Ask Auntie Nolo's* advice column
- **Save money** with special Subscriber Only discounts
- **Tickle your funny bone** with our famous *Lawyer Joke* column.

It only takes 1 minute to reserve your free 1-year subscription or to extend your **NOLO** *News* subscription.

REGISTRATION CARD

NAME   DATE

ADDRESS

                                                    PHONE NUMBER

CITY   STATE   ZIP

WHERE DID YOU HEAR ABOUT THIS BOOK?

WHERE DID YOU PURCHASE THIS PRODUCT?

DID YOU CONSULT A LAWYER? (PLEASE CIRCLE ONE)   YES   NO   NOT APPLICABLE

DID YOU FIND THIS BOOK HELPFUL?   (VERY)   5   4   3   2   1   (NOT AT ALL)

SUGGESTIONS FOR IMPROVING THIS PRODUCT

WAS IT EASY TO USE?   (VERY EASY)   5   4   3   2   1   (VERY DIFFICULT)

DO YOU OWN A COMPUTER? IF SO, WHICH FORMAT? (PLEASE CIRCLE ONE)   WINDOWS   DOS   MAC

We occasionally make our mailing list available to carefully selected companies whose products may be of interest to you. If you do not wish to receive mailings from these companies, please check this box ❑

ODIV 1.0

NOLO IN THE NEWS

"Nolo helps lay people perform legal tasks without the aid—or fees—of lawyers."
—**USA TODAY**

Nolo books are ..."written in plain language, free of legal mumbo jumbo, and spiced with witty personal observations."
—**ASSOCIATED PRESS**

"...Nolo publications...guide people simply through the how, when, where and why of law."
—**WASHINGTON POST**

"Increasingly, people who are not lawyers are performing tasks usually regarded as legal work... And consumers, using books like Nolo's, do routine legal work themselves."
—**NEW YORK TIMES**

"...All of [Nolo's] books are easy-to-understand, are updated regularly, provide pull-out forms...and are often quite moving in their sense of compassion for the struggles of the lay reader."
—**SAN FRANCISCO CHRONICLE**

BUSINESS REPLY MAIL
FIRST-CLASS MAIL PERMIT NO 3283 BERKELEY CA

POSTAGE WILL BE PAID BY ADDRESSEE

NO POSTAGE
NECESSARY
IF MAILED
IN THE
UNITED STATES

NOLO PRESS
950 Parker Street
Berkeley, CA 94710-9867